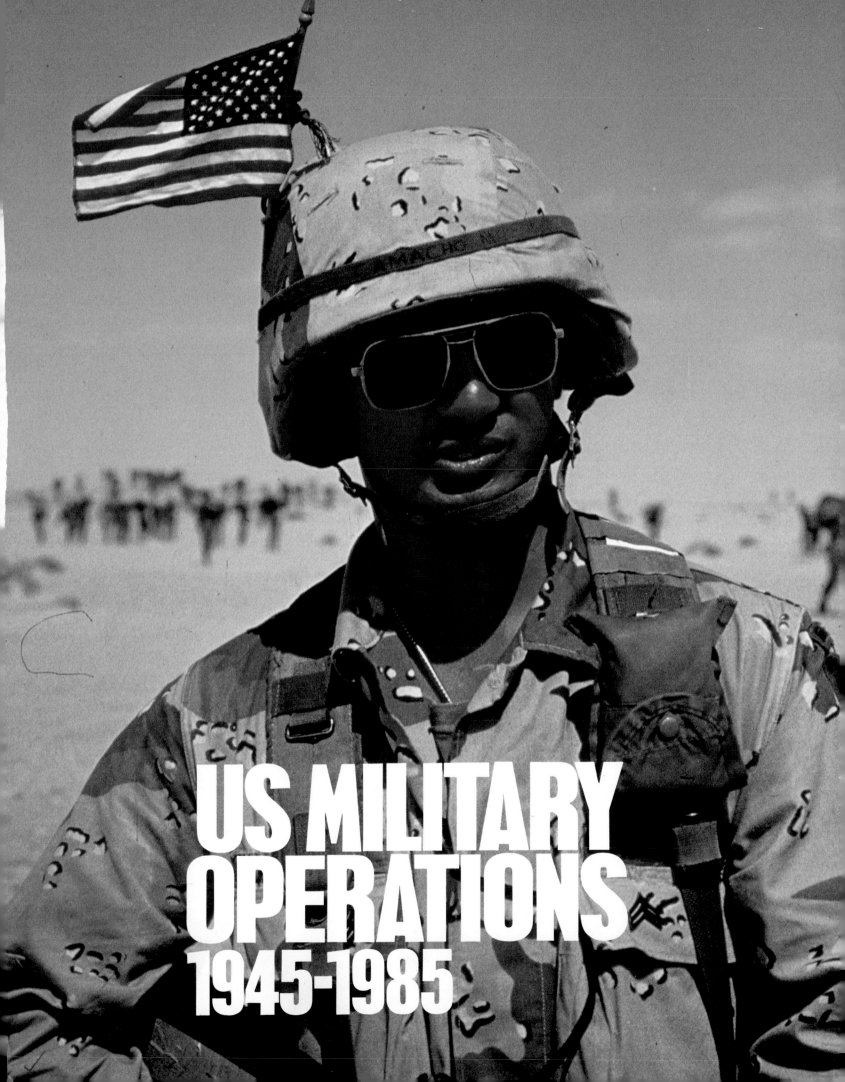

US MILITARY OPERATIONS
1945-1985

US MILITARY OPERATIONS
1945-1985

Kenneth Anderson

THE MILITARY PRESS
Distributed by Crown Publishers Inc.
New York

 A Bison Book

This edition is published by
The Military Press, distributed by
Crown Publishers Inc.

Produced by
Bison Books Corp.
17 Sherwood Place
Greenwich, CT 06830
USA

Printed in Hong Kong

ISBN 0-517-439212

h g f e d c b a

Library of Congress Catalog Card Number 84-60741

Page 1: A US soldier armed with an M-16 automatic rifle
during Operation Bright Star.
Page 2-3: An impressive bow-on view of the carrier USS
John F Kennedy. On deck are A-7, S-3 and F-14 aircraft of
carrier Air Wing 1.
This page: The standard US flight-refuelling tanker KC-135
refuels a prototype Rockwell B-1B prototype, the new US
strategic bomber.

CONTENTS

BRUSH FIRES
OF THE COLD WAR

One of the last documented battles of World War II occurred on 18 August 1945 —four days after the unconditional surrender of Japan was announced by President Harry Truman—when 14 Japanese Navy A6M2 and Army Ki-44 fighters jumped a pair of newly introduced US B-32 bombers on a photo-reconnaissance mission over Tokyo. The incident foreshadowed the way in which the results of World War II would reverberate, creating new tensions and leading to conflict throughout the world. The official Japanese surrender, however, had followed quickly after the first use of atomic bombs, which in 1945 were relatively crude metal cylinders that carried the destructive force of more than 20,000 tons of TNT. By one official count, 71,379 persons died in the explosion at Hiroshima, where the force of the blast drove concrete columns into the ground like giant spikes.

As General MacArthur and the advance contingent of his occupation forces moved onshore to establish headquarters in Yokohama on 30 August 1945—three days before the actual signing of the surrender document aboard the USS *Missouri* anchored in Tokyo Bay—the United States began to evolve a new military doctrine that would influence the nation's military and diplomatic orientation for the next 40 years. It was a concept based on the notion that a military power with possession of nuclear weapons would have little further need of a large standing army and navy. The US military doctrine would eventually influence the political and military policies of nations around the world.

The years between 1939 and 1945 had brought the world beyond the threshold of total combat, marshaling technological resources and manpower to an unprecedented degree. The war had put some 95 million men and women under arms, including 14 million Americans. The US cost alone was officially calculated to be $341 billion. World War II had started with soldiers on horseback resisting tanks, piston-engined

Previous page: The slow process of clearing up and rebuilding gets under way in Tokyo. Providing stable government for the defeated Axis powers was one of America's first aims in the postwar world.

Right: Colonel Paul Tibbets, the pilot of the Hiroshima mission, poses in front of his B-29 bomber *Enola Gay.*

Opposite: The characteristic mushroom cloud of an atomic explosion rises above Hiroshima.

Below: General MacArthur signs the Japanese surrender aboard the USS *Missouri* in Tokyo Bay on 2 September 1945. Looking on are Generals Wainwright (left) and Percival.

aircraft, and chemical explosives. It ended with antitank rockets, jet-powered aircraft, and atomic bombs, and with the United States emerging as the greatest military power on earth. Within four years, America had come from a great economic depression into an industrial boom, mustering millions of civilians into a fighting force equal in manpower to the USSR's Red Army of 1945, with the world's largest navy, the world's largest strategic air force, and the world's first atomic bomb.

Even in the months following the devastation of Hiroshima and Nagasaki by atomic weapons, the world did not share America's concept of nuclear deterrence. Joseph Stalin commented publicly that atomic bombs were 'only feared by weaklings.' Mao Tse-tung said that 'bourgeois influence' had made some individuals 'look on the atom bomb as something miraculous.' Lord Louis Mountbatten, Supreme Allied Commander of Southeast Asia, remarked that it was 'the worst possible mistake to think the atom bomb can decide a war.'

The notion that the US could depend upon its nuclear monopoly to prevent future aggression in the world would soon prove to be as false as the early postwar myth that Russia wanted only *peredyshka*, or a period of golden peace in which to recover from the wounds of war. And if President Truman believed the Russians were not already developing their own atomic bombs when he met with Churchill and Stalin at Potsdam on 24 July 1945, he soon found that he had sadly misjudged Soviet intelligence expertise. Russia had been monitoring US atomic research almost since the day in 1939 when Albert Einstein urged President Franklin D. Roosevelt to begin development of the atomic bomb.

Keeping the Peace: Demobilization and Deterrence

Soon after the death of President Roosevelt in 1945 the US returned to a policy of anti-Communism, a policy that went hand in hand with the desire to establish democratic and capitalistic governments throughout the world. Russia, for its part, saw an opportunity to surround itself with a barrier of satellite nations built from Germany's former domain— the defenseless and chaotic Eastern European states. President Roosevelt had promised that all US troops would be removed from Europe within two years after the end of hostilities. Demobilization was a pressing domestic issue in the US, even though jobs and homes for returning servicemen were lacking. New York City held its biggest parade in 25 years as four million citizens lined the streets to welcome the return of the 82nd Airborne Division. And overseas there were mass 'get-us-home' demonstrations in the streets of London, Paris,

Manila and other cities until General Dwight Eisenhower issued an order banning such agitation.

Still, demobilization of American forces was remarkably swift. More than seven million officers and men of World War II had been discharged within 12 months after the end of fighting in Europe. In approximately one year, the US moved from a condition of tough fighting strength to having a largely untrained peacetime military. The transition from one extreme to another would soon become a problem, as when Navy officers on the newly commissioned USS *Midway* complained the ship might not be able to leave port because there were not enough qualified engine-room personnel to operate the ship. The *Midway* finally put to sea with a skeleton crew of demobilization replacements, most of whom had never been on a warship before.

Despite the rapid rate of demobilization at the end of hostilities in Europe, the US planned to retain the largest peacetime military force

Right: Returning GIs crowd the hangar deck of the carrier *Enterprise* on their way back from the Pacific War Zone, November 1945.

Below: GIs return from Europe aboard the former German luxury liner *Europa.* The ship is shown entering New York harbor with some 4300 troops aboard.

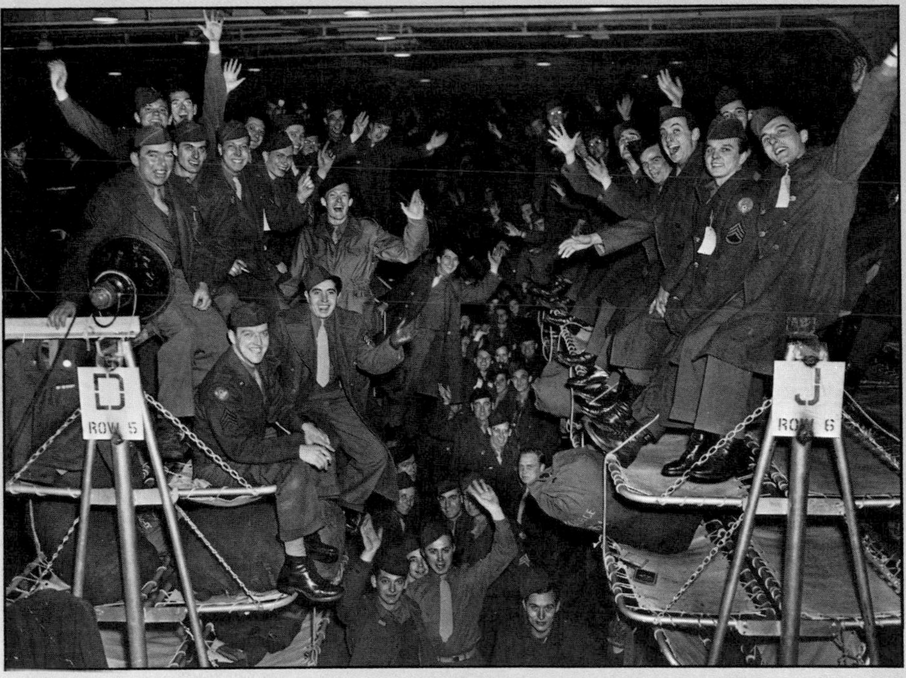
D
ROW 5
J
ROW 6

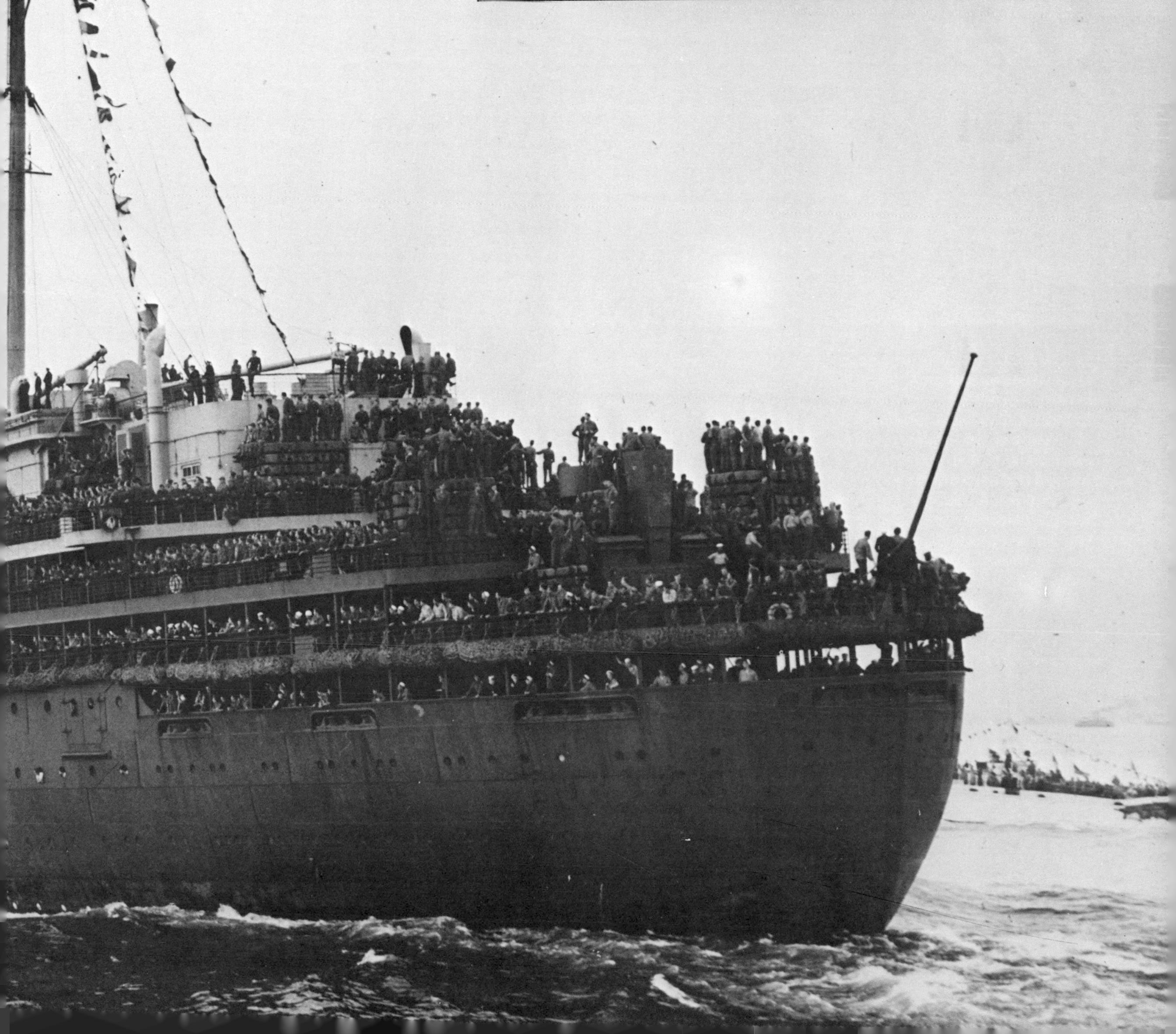

in its history. This included several hundred thousand members of army and air national guard units, and organized reserves that had armored divisions for the first time. World War II resulted in some changes in names and emphasis. Coast artillery units were no longer necessary because fixed coastal guns had been discontinued, but helicopter ambulance units were created in the new MASH tradition. And the horse cavalry had metamorphosed through mechanized cavalry and into sky cavalry battalions for the next war.

Because the US had the atomic bomb, Washington's political and military experts were not concerned about the sudden loss of conventional military strength. The US sincerely believed that minor international disputes could be settled by the newly created United Nations Organization and that any serious political aggression by conventional warfare was no longer thinkable by any rational nation. America's atomic monopoly would be the perfect barrier to any foreign threat. The term 'nuclear deterrence' became a national motto. And all future military planning would be based on a combination of strategic air superiority and atomic weapons possessed by no other nation.

Five months after the end of World War II, the United Nations Organization held its first

session in London during January and February 1946. An attempt was made to see if member nations might be able to get along with each other better than before the war, but the agenda foreshadowed diplomatic problems that would persist through future decades. Russia exercised the first use of a veto in the UN Security Council on the matter of French and British troops in Syria and Lebanon. Russia also demanded that British troops be removed from Greece and Indonesia. Iran, meanwhile, demanded the removal of Russian troops from its oil fields.

For its part, the US made a gesture toward keeping the peace with massive demobilization. At the end of the war the US had abandoned or destroyed mountains of weapons and equipment, including millions of captured guns, despite a plea by Prime Minister Churchill to store at least two million German rifles in England for possible future use. Nearly 30,000 US warplanes were sent to the scrap heap, many of them rendered obsolete by the wartime development of 500 mph jet fighters that already were practicing landings on aircraft carriers. Russia had only one effective aircraft in quantity, the Stormovick, but no real navy. The US and its allies divided the surviving ships of the German fleet. The US had so many surplus warships at the end of the war that scores were sold for scrap metal—including the cruiser *Concord*, which fired the navy's final shot of the war. A small fleet of vessels was donated to the Nationalist Chinese Government. Some ships were used to store grain or destroyed as target practice. In a single atom bomb test at Bikini atoll in 1946, 73 surplus warships were used as a target.

Military manpower, too, was being rapidly reduced. By October 1946 it was reported that US military strength had been reduced to 1,100,000, of which 550,000 were still stationed overseas. The US had handed back to British authorities its wartime bases in England. Of the millions of men and women sent to Europe from the US, only 220,000 remained there a year after the end of the war. Great Britain, by comparison, still had one and a half million in uniform and Russia three million.

But at the same time the US was moving a fleet of warships into the Mediterranean, sending flights of B-29s on nonstop jaunts between Florida and Germany, and putting on other well-publicized deployment exercises, such as Task Force Frigid, staged on Russia's Arctic doorstep. And when Russian newspapers denounced the visit of a US Navy task force to Greece as 'pressure tactics,' Admiral William F. 'Bull' Halsey retorted: 'We'll go anywhere we damned please.' Until the American atomic monopoly was broken, the US established itself as the custodian of world peace. The *London Daily Mail* parodied the new US foreign policy in a cartoon showing the American eagle with an olive branch in one claw, an atomic bomb in the other, while its beak held a banner reading: 'Peace Or Else!'

But military reorganization and unification was also the order of the day, as events before and after the war hastened completion of plans to reorganize the US military structure. The Spanish-American War at the turn of the century had been a starting point for the realization that America could not successfully support army combat units overseas without the cooperation of the Navy. Difficulties encountered during World War I led to preparation in 1921 of the Frank Willoughby Report recommending unification of the various armed services into a single military force. The US Army opposed the Willoughby Report, contending it was a plot to weaken army influence under the guise of reducing federal expenditure for the military.

The 1941 disaster at Pearl Harbor greatly magnified the hazards of an uncoordinated military establishment. During congressional hearings at the end of World War II, testimony revealed a gross lack of cooperation between the army and navy during the months before December 1941 when decoded messages revealed plans for a Japanese attack on the United States.

Of the many proposals for unification that emerged in 1945 and 1946 was one originated by the Navy and supported by the new Navy Secretary James Forrestal. It provided for a joint-command arrangement with each of the services represented by a chief of staff. As finally adopted under the National Security Act of 1947, the chiefs of staff for each of the three services and a chief of staff to the president would function as the Joint Chiefs of Staff. A department of the Federal government was created, the National Military Establishment, which later became the Department of Defense in 1949. At the same time the Secretaries of Army, Navy, and Air Force were made subordinate to a Secretary of Defense. Later, the Joint Chiefs of Staff became a five-person team that included the Commandant of the Marine Corps and a Chairman of the Joint Chiefs of Staff.

Universal Military Training had also been considered during the early postwar years. A proposal was submitted to Congress on 23 October 1945 by President Truman, calling for one year of active service for all males between the ages of 18 and 20, followed by six years in the General Reserve. But Congress merely extended the Selective Service Act to 31 March 1947 instead, theorizing that with atomic bombs mass armies were no longer necessary. But later the Korean War revived interest in Universal Military Training and the act was passed in 1951. The US would recognize its error when postwar idealism and overconfidence suffered a rude awakening.

The Iron Curtain Descends

As early as 1943 the question of zones of occupation in postwar Germany had been discussed among the Big Three—the US, Great Britain and Russia. A European Advisory Commission was created, composed of representatives from the three nations and which met in London under the chairmanship of the British deputy prime-minister, Clement Attlee.

Left: Former prisoners of war are among those lining the decks of one of the first convoys of transports to return to the US after VE-Day. The convoy is shown entering New York on 19 May 1945.

Below: The carrier *Midway* passing Portsmouth, Virginia, in 1947. The *Midway* was a much enlarged version of the successful *Essex* design but was completed too late to see service in World War II. Her large size, however, made her particularly well suited to operate the larger and heavier jet aircraft which were coming into service immediately after the war.

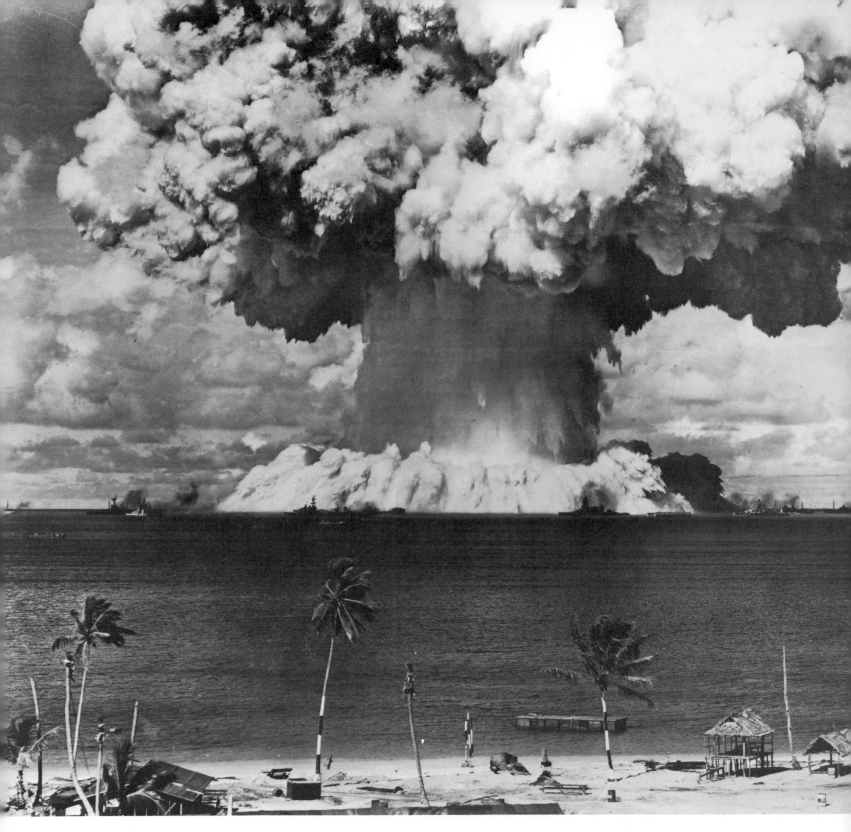

At that time a plan was devised to partition postwar Germany into three zones. But when Roosevelt, Stalin and Churchill met at Yalta in the Crimea in February 1945, an agreement was made that the US and Britain would give part of their share to France. Thus Germany came to be divided into four zones, with a further subdivision of Berlin, which was 115 miles inside the Russian-occupied zone. Administration of Berlin was entrusted to an agreed military quadrapartite organization. This zonal division appeared necessary to achieve harmony among the allied nations. The Yalta Declaration pledged the 'common determination to maintain and strengthen in the peace to come that unity of purpose and of action which has made victory possible and certain for the United Nations in this war.' However the unity of purpose was soon in shambles and the line separating the Russian zone and those of the western Allies would be seen as part of an 'iron curtain.'

Among many generous concessions made by the Allies to enhance the spirit of Allied-Soviet cooperation, Russia also had been promised control of Outer Mongolia, the southern half of Sakhalin and the Kurile Islands near Japan, an occupation zone in Korea, privileged rights in Manchuria, the Chinese cities of Port Arthur and Darien, a base in Turkey, and access to a warm water port through Iran. Russia saw the postwar future as a communist world. But the reality would be quite different from the Russian dream, and one which would

soon be recognized as the Cold War, with brush fires throughout the world.

There were geopolitical clues to future events in the early postwar months. Russia had learned that oil was essential for the survival of an industrial economy. In fact, the USSR had nearly lost its war with Germany when oil supplies were almost depleted. Russia was able to increase her petroleum reserves by acquiring control of Poland, Rumania, Hungary and Austria, which had been the sources of Nazi oil. But more important were the oil fields in Iran, on Russia's southern border.

During 1945 both the British and the US had stationed small garrisons in southern Iran while the Red Army stationed troops in the Azerbaijan region of Iran, between Turkey and the Caspian Sea. In the autumn of 1945, a Communist 'revolution' developed in Iran's Azerbaijan Province. Russian troops prevented Iranian military units from entering their own territory to put down the rebellion. The US contingent of 4000 men was no match for the Red Army and Moscow seemed quite confident that Washington would not use its atomic weapon, or even threaten its use, in a direct confrontation with the USSR. Russia won the test in its bloodless confrontation with US troops in Iran but nevertheless withdrew its troops in 1946 after a year of diplomatic maneuvering through the United Nations during which the Soviets offered to settle for joint USSR-Iranian control of the oil fields in Azerbaijan.

In March 1946 Winston Churchill and President Truman traveled together to Westminster College in Fulton, Missouri. There Churchill called for closer Anglo-American military cooperation in meeting the challenge of Soviet expansionism. 'From Stettin in the Baltic to Trieste in the Adriatic an iron curtain has descended across the Continent. Behind that line lie all the capitals of the ancient states of central and eastern Europe, and the populations around them lie in what I might call the Soviet sphere . . . subject to control from Moscow. Police governments are pervading from Moscow.' US Secretary of State James Byrnes later responded to the Churchill plea by stating that his country would enter into no alliance but would instead seek its security in the United Nations.

Winston Churchill had warned his US ally before the invasion of Normandy in 1944 that Russia should not be permitted to fill the political and economic vacuum being created by the withdrawal of Nazi dominance of Greece, Yugoslavia, Czechoslovakia and other countries in the Balkans region. Churchill had urged that a part of the Allies' invasion force be sent into Europe through the Balkans. But US military advisers rejected the plan as a waste of manpower and materiel which they felt could be used more effectively in one big smash at the European continent through Normandy.

In October that same year, Churchill had met with Stalin at Moscow. According to Churchill's memoirs, they had reached an agreement on the division of responsibility to be made among the Allies in the Balkans when the war ended. Russia would retain 90 percent control of Rumania, while the Western allies would retain 10 percent. Russia would keep 75 percent control of Bulgaria, while the rest of that country, again, would remain in the hands

Above: An underwater atomic bomb test at Bikini Atoll in July 1946. Tests were conducted with obsolete or war-damaged ships moored at varying distances from the explosion to investigate its power.

Right: US Navy personnel help train men of the Philippine Navy early in 1947.

of the western Allies. Britain and Russia were to share control of Yugoslavia and Hungary on a 50-50 basis.

In accord with the US, Great Britain would have 90 percent postwar control of Greece. Churchill felt that Britain had a particular interest in Greece because 30,000 British troops had been lost in fighting a German-Italian invasion of Greece earlier in the war. But in spite of this agreement made between Churchill and Stalin, when the war ended, there were Communist guerrillas in Greece, functioning as a separate Communist state, fighting the British.

On 1 February 1946, the Soviets announced their own successful nuclear reaction. (And within three years, on 23 September 1949, President Truman would announce that the US no longer had a monopoly on atomic bombs. The USSR exploded one of its own.) An attempt was then made on 14 June 1946 to deter nuclear proliferation. At the first meeting of the UN Atomic Energy Commission, Bernard Baruch, the US representative, declared the US was willing to destroy its atomic bombs and release its atomic secrets for peaceful purposes to an international atomic development authority.

But at the end of the year, when international control of atomic energy was put before the UN General Assembly, Russia and Poland refused to vote.

Meanwhile, events were building around the world which, unforeseen then, would draw the US into further military action. In March, France announced its recognition of the Vietnam Republic as a 'free state within the Indochinese Federation and French Union.' Great Britain made a move to pull back from east of Suez by offering India the 'right to full independence' and announced its withdrawal of troops from Egypt. In Palestine, some 50,000 Jews called a strike against British government services and an Anglo-American Committee of Inquiry recommended relocating 100,000 Jews from Europe to Palestine, causing an uprising by Palestinian Arabs.

The US and Britain also discovered in 1946 that while Russia did not openly renege on its agreement to share postwar control of Yugoslavia on a 50-50 basis, the USSR did nothing to stop the attacks by the partisan Communist leader Josip (Tito) Broz on allied troops stationed in Trieste. Both Italy and Yugoslavia claimed Trieste. In July 1946, American

troops killed two Yugoslavian soldiers in a clash near the Yugoslav-Trieste border. On 9 August 1946 and again on 19 August, Yugoslavian fighter planes attacked US Army transport aircraft. Several passengers on the downed American aircraft were killed and the survivors were taken prisoner. The captive passengers were released only after the US delivered an ultimatum to Tito's government. American and British soldiers were also the targets of several Yugoslavian demonstrations in Trieste. In one incident, five American soldiers were wounded when a grenade exploded near them as they watched a bicycle race. Trieste came under the protection of the UN in 1947, when Italy gave up its claims to the city. Formed into the Free Territory of Trieste, which included the Istrian Peninsula of Yugoslavia, it was divided into two military zones. One, which included the city, was administered by Anglo-American troops and the other was put under Yugoslav military jurisdiction.

Meanwhile, Tito threatened Greece, recalling the Yugoslavian ambassador from Athens on charges that Greek newspapers had published articles critical of the communist influence in Yugoslavia. Greece was the West's key to the Dardanelles and the only Balkan country outside the Iron Curtain. Bulgaria and Rumania fell easily into the Soviet domain as the Red Army withdrew. Tens of thousands of Russians had been relocated to Black Sea coastal communities of Bulgaria and Rumania. Typical of the Soviet maneuver was the relocation of 50,000 Russian citizens to Constanta, a Rumanian city on the Black Sea, within easy striking distance of the Dardanelles.

The guerrilla armies fighting the British troops in Greece had infiltrated from the neighboring Soviet-bloc countries. The British claimed their role was merely one of maintaining order while the Greek political leaders

established a government of moderation. But during 1946 the Greek Civil War flared up and in December the UN Security Council began an investigation into Greek charges that the guerrilla forces were being supported by Yugoslavia, Bulgaria and Albania. By the spring of 1947, Britain, economically depleted, had to suspend its assistance to Greece. With that, President Truman came forward with what is called the Truman Doctrine. He announced that the US 'would support free peoples who are resisting subjugation by armed minorities or by outside pressure.' It was a reversal of the Monroe Doctrine, which was a policy of hands-off the Western hemisphere. The Truman Doctrine thus brought about a determined US policy of assistance to Greece and Turkey. Extensive aid was then given Greece, including military equipment and training of the Greek Army by an American military advisory group —the first test of the Truman Doctrine of resisting Communist coercion anywhere in the world. The US government contributed $250 million in credit to the anti-Communist Greek government, plus $245 million in aid. During the years of civil war in Greece, the UN Security Council and the General Assembly had investigated and condemned the influence of Yugoslavia, Bulgaria and Albania in Greece, but without the aid of Britain and the US, a free Greece might not have come about. The Communist resistance was finally quelled in the autumn of 1949, and the Greek Civil War came to an end.

During the same period of time, Russia also claimed that among the many promises made at Potsdam, Yalta, Moscow and other wartime meetings with the Allies, the USSR had been granted postwar military bases in Turkey. The US did not agree that the Soviets had been granted authority to fortify the Dardanelles or to include Turkey in the USSR orbit of satellite states. The Truman Doctrine, therefore, was directed originally toward keeping Greece and Turkey, and the eastern Mediterranean, free from Communist control. Finding itself in the role of an anti-communist imperialist power, the US accepted its international role as the only postwar nation with the capability of

Left: President Truman in conversation with Israeli leaders Ben Gurion (front right) and Aba Eban (behind). In a rare case of unanimity both the United States and the Soviet Union recognized the infant state of Israel as soon as its existence was proclaimed in May 1948.

Bottom left: A Boeing B-50 heavy bomber. A development of the wartime B-29, the B-50 served with the newly-formed US Air Force's Strategic Air Command in its early years.

Below: President Truman. In a speech in March 1947 Truman declared that it would by US policy 'to support free peoples who are resisting attempted subjugation by armed minorities or outside pressures.' This so-called Truman doctrine governed US foreign policy throughout the remainder of his presidency as the Cold War developed.

opposing the Communist powers. There was also a gradual realization in Washington that despite dependence upon the United Nations and nuclear superiority, the US would have to show a strong hand or lose the world by default.

Although most of the world was still at peace in 1947, the various nations supported a total of 19 million men under arms at an annual cost of nearly $25.5 billion. Even though the Axis partners were no longer included, the armies of the world were larger than in 1938, the last year before the start of World War II. And despite its global military obligations in 1947, the US maintained one of the smaller ground forces, with only 675,000, compared to the Soviet Union's ground forces of 3,800,000.

What were beginning to be known as the Communist Bloc Nations would become testing grounds for Soviet intentions. In January 1947, Poland held its first free elections as agreed by the United States, Great Britain and Russia at the 1945 meetings. However, western observers charged the elections were rigged to ensure that Communist bloc candidates, headed by Provisional Premier Boleslaw Beirut, would win an 'overwhelming victory.' Hungary had similar treatment. In May 1947, USSR-backed Communists took over the government. The party of Premier Ferenc Nagy, which had won 59 percent of the votes in a 1946 free election, against 17 percent for the Communist party, gradually lost power through a series of arrests of the party leaders by Communist-controlled police. When Nagy and his family went to Switzerland for a vacation, he was informed by a telephone call that he would face a 'people's court' when he returned. Nagy resigned without returning to Hungary and the postwar Communist 'club' had gained one more country.

The United States, which had extended $30 million in credit to Hungary, reacted only by suspending the remaining funds, about half the original amount. At the same time, the US announced it would release Italian assets frozen by Washington during the war because Premier Alcide de Gasperi had finally established a Communist-free cabinet. Altogether, by 1947 Russia had won Poland, Rumania, Bulgaria, Albania, Yugoslavia and Hungary on the European Front, while the US had managed to salvage Greece, Turkey and Italy. Among the cards still to be played were Czechoslovakia and Germany.

France, which had a strong Communist party, was burdened with its own problems beyond its borders. Although it faced the loss of Algeria, the French in early 1947 transferred a division of paratroopers from Algiers to Vietnam where France was reported making slow headway in a struggle with a political party that called itself the 'League of Independence for Viet Nam.' The League became better known by its abbreviated Vietnamese name of 'Viet Minh.' The party was headed by a 55-year-old Communist, Ho Chi-minh, who had once served in a Soviet consulate in the United States.

France had agreed to recognize a 'free state of Vietnam' as part of the 'French Union,' but Ho Chi-minh had insisted on greater autonomy. Although France maintained a force of 80,000—including Foreign Legionaires—in Indochina, the Viet Minh built a guerrilla army of 100,000, equipped with mortars and other weapons taken from the former Japanese occupation forces. It was reported that fighting between the Viet Minh and the French forces had become so fierce that even the tough veterans of the Foreign Legion were deserting. As the French cruiser *Duquesne* sailed eastward with reinforcements, Washington had no inkling that some years in the future it would have to extend the Truman Doctrine to still another part of the world.

The Berlin Blockade

Lessons learned in Hungary helped the Communist world to add Czechoslovakia to the list of USSR allies in February 1948. Both US and Soviet forces had withdrawn from Czechoslovakia in December 1945, leaving prewar President Eduard Benes as the nation's political leader again. In a free election held 26 May 1946, the Czechoslovak Communist Party received 38 percent of the votes cast. A coalition government was arranged with Communist Klement Gottwald. By slowly infiltrating vari-

Above: US personnel at Rhein Main Air Base receive the news that the Berlin Blockade is over. Rhein Main (Frankfurt) remains an important US base in Germany to the present day.

Left: German laborers working under American supervision work to complete the airfield at Tegel in the French sector of Berlin during the Blockade.

Right: The routes employed during the Berlin Blockade. Soviet aircraft often harassed the transports flying into the surrounded city.

ous branches of the government, the Communists penetrated key areas of the state apparatus, and friction developed over control of the police. When new elections were held, only Communist party leaders were allowed to run. Non-Communist party leaders gradually disappeared through purges and show trials held through 1954.

One important objective of Russia that remained in Europe was control of Germany, occupied by British, French, and US forces in the West and by Soviet forces in the East. The former capital city, Berlin, also was divided into Communist and non-Communist zones. The Allied Control Council established by the four powers—the United States, Great Britain, France, and Russia—to coordinate administration of occupied Germany was beginning to break down. The United States had initiated the Marshall Plan, named for former General and later US Secretary of State George Marshall, to provide economic relief to the war-devastated countries of Europe. But the USSR, feeling that the US plan included too many stipulations, refused to participate in the European Recovery Program and directed its satellite countries to boycott the plan. Moscow announced that the USSR would create its own economic recovery program for the Communist countries. Problems with transportation of supplies between the Anglo-American and Russian zones of Berlin increased during the early months of 1948 and incidents were reported almost daily. Harassment by the Russians included confiscation of newspapers, magazines and books published in the West.

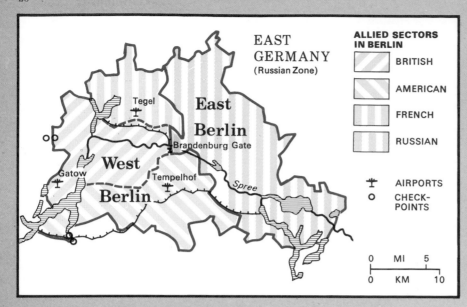

EAST
GERMANY
(Russian Zone)

**ALLIED SECTORS
IN BERLIN**

BRITISH

AMERICAN

FRENCH

RUSSIAN

✈ AIRPORTS
○ CHECK-
POINTS

0   MI   5

0   KM   10

Above: The Allied sectors in Berlin.

On 31 March 1948, the Soviet Military Administration issued an order preventing the movement of US military trains from West Germany to Berlin unless Soviet personnel checked both passengers and baggage. The order was challenged by the US as a violation of the agreement with the USSR exempting American personnel from customs, border controls, or seizure by Soviet authorities. On 1 April 1948, Soviet representatives issued another order forbidding freight trains to leave Berlin without Russian permission. As the US and USSR traded messages rejecting each others claims, General Clay sent a 'test train' with armed guards into the Soviet zone to see whether it would be stopped by force. The Russians shunted the train onto a siding where it remained for several days as negotiations continued. The USSR next ordered a halt to passenger trains leaving Berlin.

Some British and French dependents were evacuated from Berlin as the threat of a possible war between the US and Russia increased. General Clay announced that while he would honor any request for the evacuation of an American, the request would apply to the entire family. General Clay said that he wanted 'no one with me in Berlin who had sent his family home,' adding that it was 'unbecoming

US military trains were boarded by Russian troops who claimed the right to check the identity of each passenger on a train. When the US placed guards on its trains to prevent Soviet 'inspectors' from boarding, the trains were held on sidings for hours. The American military, anticipating some Soviet action in Germany, began preparing for action.

to an American to show signs of nervousness.' Clay also advised Washington that in his opinion, 'When Berlin falls, western Germany will be next. If we mean to hold Europe against Communism, we must not budge.' When General Clay started a small airlift, the Russians increased pressure by expelling US Army Signal Corps units responsible for maintaining telephone and teletype lines between Berlin and West Germany, intercepting mail, and eventually closing down all railroad, highway, and canal barge traffic because of various 'technical difficulties.'

Rail traffic out of Berlin had been reduced by June 1948 almost entirely to the removal of empty cars. Only passenger transportation was still allowed for those who were willing to subject themselves to Soviet inspections. A serious confrontation then occurred on 10 June 1948 when the US had to send armed guards to prevent a Soviet attempt to remove switching locomotives and railroad cars from the US sector of Berlin. The blockade did not become complete until 24 June 1948, the day on which the West Deutschemark became the legal currency for the non-Communist sectors of Berlin. At 6 am on that date, the British, French, and US sectors of Berlin had on hand a 45-day supply of coal and a 36-day supply of

food for a West Berlin population of 2,500,000. Electricity was limited because it was controlled from the Soviet zone, the Russians having removed electricity generating plants from the western sectors when they invaded the city three years earlier.

In Washington, General Hoyt Vandenberg recommended that the US batter open a corridor to Berlin with troops and tanks. President Truman chose an alternative response: increase the airlift started by General Clay at the beginning of the showdown. The choice was not an easy one for the US forces in Europe to implement. General Clay estimated that the French, British, and US occupation forces in Berlin required 500 tons of food and fuel every day. The German population required at least 4000 tons of food and fuel to prevent starvation and to maintain normal daily activity. The Americans could muster about 100 C-47 transports, most of which were war-worn but could hold 5000 pounds of cargo. The French had no transport planes at all, and the British could contribute only a few.

Lieutenant General Curtis LeMay was asked to divert all available C-47s to the Berlin Airlift. The first planeloads of food began arriving at Berlin airports the following morning, 25 June 1948. Within 24 hours the airlift

Below: Gatow airfield during the Blockade with US transport planes in the background. The buses in the foreground are being pressed into service as offices for personnel supporting the airlift.

was fully organized and was dubbed 'Operation Vittles' by American pilots, some of whom had been transferred from bases as far away as Alaska, Hawaii, and Panama.

The C-47 'Gooney Birds' were diverted to air bases at Wiesbaden and Rhein-Main in the US zone of West Germany. The British joined in the effort by sending 40 four-engine York transports and a number of two-engine Dakotas to an air base at Fassberg in the British zone. British planes were able to deliver about 1000 tons of supplies daily from Fassberg to the Gatow airfield in the British sector of Berlin. The US planes initially flew a route between Wiesbaden and Rhein-Main and the Templehof Airfield in West Berlin. But as the pace of the airlift increased and the first of 225 four-engine C-54 transports began arriving at the end of June 1948, some of the American runs were shifted to the Fassberg site, which had the advantages of flat landscape and a much shorter geographical distance to Berlin. The C-54s were requested by General Clay early in the airlift because they had the capacity of 10 tons per flight, or approximately four times the cargo ability of the C-47s, which were gradually phased out of the operation.

While the French had no aircraft to contribute to the effort, their military forces did try one or two experimental flights from Paris to Berlin. It was decided that France could participate by providing a third airfield in the French sector of Berlin. The site chosen was at Tegel, a former Nazi drill area that was free of buildings and had only one obstacle, a 900-foot radio antenna used by an East German station. Thousands of Berlin residents were recruited to help build the Tegel airfield, using rubble from bombed out Berlin buildings as foundation material for runways. Heavy construction equipment was cut into pieces with acetylene torches in West Germany, flown to Berlin, and welded together again for work on the project. When the field was ready to help relieve the congestion of flights into Gatow and Templehof airfields, only the radio antenna remained as a problem. Wary of causing a further incident between East and West Berlin, an American crew was reluctant to remove the tower. A group of French soldiers dealt with the situation by seizing the crew and locking them in a nearby office. The French troops then planted charges at the base of the antenna and destroyed it without consulting the Soviet officials.

With C-54 transports able to move along three 20-mile wide corridors to three Berlin airports, daily cargo averages passed the 4500 tons per day mark in December 1948. By February 1949, the average was 5500 tons per day, and on one record day of good flying weather the total reached 13,000 tons. The British gave further assistance to the operation by offering the US forces a former Luftwaffe fighter base at Celle, near Hanover, which could be refurbished for transport flights to Berlin. England also supplied seaplanes that could land on waterways in West Berlin, where fuel and other supplies could be ferried to docks. During the spring of 1949, with the help of British pilots who called their part of the airlift 'Operation Planefare,' the average daily cargo amount reached 8000 tons, which was equivalent to the size of rail and water shipments into Berlin before the blockade.

After the airlift began, the military governors of the three western zones were asked to meet again with Marshal Sokolovsky to attempt to find a solution to the blockade. Sokolovsky informed the West German representatives that the 'technical difficulties' causing interruption of travel between Berlin and the western zones would continue until the allies abandoned their plans for a West German government. The US Government moved flights of B-29 bombers to British bases, within striking distance of targets in the Soviet sphere. And US soldiers in the American sector of Berlin were instructed to set up road blocks on roads used by Soviet officers traveling through West Berlin. Speeders were stopped and questioned. In one dangerous incident, a car carrying Marshal Sokolovsky was stopped by US soldiers. When armed Russian bodyguards leaped out of a following car with guns drawn, a US soldier jammed a gun into the pit of Sokolovsky's stomach and held it there until the Soviet soldiers backed off. Sokolovsky was held for an hour until an American officer was able to identify and release the Soviet General. General Clay apologized the next day but explained the US soldier was only doing his assigned duty.

Plans for a possible long-term airlift also had become somewhat more serious: an airbase in Montana became a training center for Berlin Airlift pilots with approach paths, navigation aids, and flight corridors duplicating those used in Germany. In good weather, transport aircraft were landing and taking off at a rate of one every three minutes at Templehof and two minutes at Gatow and Tegel. Professional air controllers were called back into military service to help handle the flow of traffic. A newly developed radar system was installed along with high-intensity approach lights. Each flight carried a code that designated it as inbound or outbound, the base of origin and its destination, and sometimes its type of cargo. When the plane arrived, ground crews were ready to unload and service it quickly for the return flight.

The Berlin Blockade was lifted after midnight 11 May 1949, as trains and trucks passed through East Germany to West Berlin without incident. Many attempts had been made to end the blockade, but the deadlock was not broken until a conference of the foreign ministers of the US, Great Britain, France and Russia was agreed upon after an adjournment of two years. The Berlin Airlift continued until 30 September 1949 after ferrying more than 2,300,000 tons of cargo into West Berlin. The airlift was continued for an additional 20 weeks to build stockpiles of food and other supplies to last West Berlin through another winter, if needed. During the 19 months of blockade, with as many as 900 flights a day, only 75 lives were lost in accidents—31 Americans, 39 British, and five Germans. They were honored by dedication on 11 July 1951 of the huge Airlift Memorial in West Berlin.

Above: Seventh Fleet sailors ashore in Shanghai on leave soon after World War II are mobbed as they pass out chewing gum to eager Chinese.

Right: (L to R) Chou En-lai, Mao Tse-tung and General Chu Teh wait to meet General Marshall.

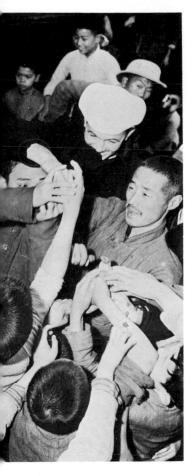

Despite the expressed worries that a miscalculation could result in World War III, the Berlin Blockade and Airlift proved to be a somewhat gentlemanly encounter. The Soviets did not retaliate for the blowing up of their radio transmitter at Tegel. Electricity for the West Berlin airfield at Gatow was supplied by generators in the Russian sector, and electricity for a Soviet fighter airbase came from generators in the British sector. West Berlin residents were still allowed to register for food rations in the Russian sector and were not prohibited from doing so by authorities in the West Berlin sector.

Meantime, the walkout of the Russians from the Allied Control Council and the Berlin Kommandatura in 1948 had helped bring about a legal partition of Germany. And on 8 April 1949, France agreed to a merger of its western zone with those of the US and Great Britain, creating the German Federal Republic with a capital city of Bonn. Also, a week earlier, on 2 April 1949, the North Atlantic Treaty Organization was created, linking US military interests in Europe with those of wartime allies England, Canada, Belgium, and the Netherlands plus Denmark, Iceland, Norway, Italy, Portugal, and Luxembourg. The alliance later expanded to include West Germany and the first beneficiaries of the Truman Doctrine, Greece and Turkey.

Although the US still held its atomic bomb monopoly, Washington found—somewhat to the surprise of many of its own leaders—that the strategies and psychology required for conventional warfare still worked in a superpower showdown. With the loss of only 75 lives in accidents, the western Allies had held an important objective against a potential enemy whose main resource was an enormous land army.

The blockade and airlift response was, as General Clay had anticipated, more of a political struggle than a military encounter. The US forces, however, did gain a great deal of experience in military operations. The airlift was the first real test of the newly created US Air Force to meet an emergency. The event also was the first test of the Air Force's Military Airlift Command, which had just been formed on 1 June 1948 from a planned merger of the old US Military Air Transport Service and the air transport services of the old Army Air Corps. The airlift proved that the US military services could work together smoothly and in concert with military forces of other nations.

The US military also gained valuable cost-accounting experience in delivering various types of cargo by air transport. It was determined, for example, that it was less expensive to transport flour and fuel for baking bread than to carry baked loaves of bread which were 30 percent water. But it was cheaper to fly real coffee than the fuel and ingredients for manufacturing synthetic coffee. And the experience showed that dehydrated vegetables, such as potatoes, required only 20 percent as much cargo space as fresh vegetables.

Confrontation In China

The USSR had entered the war against Japan on 8 August 1945—two days after the US atom bomb attack on Hiroshima—and overran Manchuria and Korea. The Red Army troops disarmed the Japanese and occupied the industrial cities of the north Asian areas. During World War II a smoldering civil war had been going on between the Koumintang forces of Nationalist China (KMT) and the Chinese Communist Party (CCP). The two groups had been feuding and fighting since Chiang Kai-shek's KMT squads began executing CCP members in 1927. Chinese Communist troops in North China also began to disarm Japanese soldiers, leading to a new confrontation between the Koumingtang (KMT) and the Chinese Communist Party (CCP).

As the war between the US and Japan was being concluded in August 1945, there were some Chinese troops fighting each other in China, and others united in a common goal, fighting the Japanese. The latter group was called the 'Against Japan' army. On 14 August 1945 General MacArthur issued an order—in violation of the Potsdam agreement—that only Chiang's troops were authorized to accept Japanese surrenders in China. Thus Chiang ordered Communist commanders of the 'Against Japan' armies not to accept Japanese sur-

Left: US Marines in the unfamiliar role of protecting Japanese civilians—from angry Chinese in Tientsin immediately after World War II. The US forces were ordered to ensure the safe evacuation of the Japanese but the Chinese Communists protested this 'American interference.'

Below: Japanese sentries stand guard as American officers of the occupation force enter the gates of the American Embassy in Peking, 30 October 1945. Japanese troops in China were kept under arms but subject to American orders for a short time after the war.

renders, which were to be handled only by KMT commanders.

US relations with Chiang Kai-shek were generally more strained than cordial. It was difficult for Americans to forget that during Japan's great offensive in 1944 against the US air bases in South China, Chiang withdrew his best troops from the area rather than use KMT soldiers to defend the Americans. The US also had become aware during the war against Japan that the most effective fighting by Chinese forces usually was from CCP troops.

Nevertheless, the United States found it essential to keep the Koumintang armies in the Pacific war against Japanese forces and adopted a policy of giving the KMT the status of a 'great power' for postwar planning purposes.

China was promised the return of territory lost to Japan, including Taiwan and other offshore islands. Chiang was also given billions of dollars in aid and weapons for fighting the Japanese. It was obvious to some observers, however, that much of the US aid to Chiang during World War II was never used against the Japanese, but was instead hidden in caches for use against the CCP after the war with Japan ended.

Relations between the US and the Chinese Communists did not improve during the three and a half years of assistance to the Koumintang following World War II. Chiang's forces controlled most of the large cities of China, but the CCP controlled 175 small and medium cities plus about a quarter of the countryside.

While the situation superficially appeared to favor the Koumintang, the strategy of Mao Tse-tung since his 'Autumn Harvest Uprising' of 1927 had been to control rural areas and allow the Nationalist troops to hold the cities. From the rural bases the Communists could interrupt communications between cities, depriving them of rail and highway links, and denying them access to food, fuel, and other supplies. It was a technique used also by Communist insurgents in other countries, including the Berlin Blockade.

World War II had ended with 1,100,000 Japanese soldiers trapped between the Great Wall and the Yangtze River. By the autumn of 1945 about 400,000 Japanese still remained in China. Thus, in September 1945, to support the Koumintang troops in their efforts to clear out the remaining Japanese and prevent a clash between the KMT and the CCP, the US rushed the Third Amphibious Corps of Marines, headed by Major General Keller Rockey, to North China. The Corps included 53,000 Marines of the First and Sixth Divisions and various support units which were landed at Tienstin and Tsingtao with orders to secure the ports for the KMT and reopen the rail links between North China and Shanghai.

As the Japanese invaders were being dealt with, battles between the KMT and the Chinese Communist troops were reported continuing in 11 of China's 28 provinces. While the US Marines tried to keep the North China coal mines and railroads functioning, US troops occasionally became involved in the fighting against the Chinese Communist troops. In one incident, the Communists attacked a train carrying General Dewitt Peck, Commander of the First Marine Division based at Tienstin. General Peck ordered his marines to return the fire, and radioed his plight to General Rockey, who advised the Communist leaders he would order an air strike against the village from which they operated if they did not cease their guerrilla attacks against the US Marines.

By January 1946, the United States had supplied the KMT with equipment and training for 39 divisions. The USSR and Great Britain joined the United States in trying to arrange a truce between Chiang and Mao. Some observers expressed fear that an all-out civil war between the KMT and the CCP would erupt into a war involving the United States and Russia, and the US use of atomic bombs. A free election was proposed but the Communists claimed that the US feared the outcome of a popular vote by the Chinese people would be the election of the party of Mao Tse-tung. The truce, however, lasted only two months and ended with a full-scale attack by the Koumintang troops against the Communist forces.

During the early months of 1946 some 7000 US Army and 6000 US Navy personnel were sent to Shanghai. Nearly 24,000 other US Army, Navy, and Marine officers and men were involved in other facets of the American effort to support the Koumintang government in China. They included members of the Seventh Fleet under Vice-Admiral Daniel Barbey, who attempted to land KMT troops at Port Arthur and Darien in Manchuria. However, Russia, whose troops had still not withdrawn from the area, refused to allow the US transports to use those important harbors.

Some 60,000 Chinese Communists, reportedly armed with Japanese weapons captured by the Russian Red Army in Manchuria, seized other ports and forced the Seventh Fleet transports to withdraw from Yingkow harbor. In April 1946 the Russians agreed to allow US transport planes to ferry Koumintang troops to Changchun, but Chinese Communist troops surrounded the airfield and again opposed American efforts to help the Chiang government forces reestablish control of Manchuria.

Elsewhere in China, the US was more successful in supporting the anti-Communist KMT troops during April and May 1946. The 443rd Troop Carrier Group of the Tenth Air Force was sent to Chikiang to ferry Chiang's Sixth

Army to Nanking. This was the official return of the Chinese government to its former national capital. When the US C-46 and C-54 transports arrived, the American troops found Chiang's Sixth Army consisted of some 33,000 Chinese, most of whom were susceptible to air sickness and some of whom were superstitious about air travel.

The US Air Transport Command also ferried 26,000 men of the 94th Army from Shanghai to Peiping and the 92nd Army from Hankow to Peiping. Each flight could accommodate between 50 and 80 Chinese troops and the massive airlift continued for several weeks as Koumintang units raced the Communists to regain control of key cities and disarm Japanese soldiers. But Chinese Communist troops were quickly turning most of the nation into a giant battlefield. At Shantung, for example, 20,000 CCP soldiers surprised Koumintang troops by arriving in a fleet of fishing junks.

At Tangku, the Communists attacked a US Marine Corps ammunition depot in an attempt to seize its contents, but were driven off after a fire fight that lasted two hours. Attempting to stem the tide, in July 1946 Washington authorized $500 billion in aid plus $500 billion in equipment to help Chiang fight the CCP forces. The US also dispatched 100 military advisers. But the Communists eventually captured nearly all the US equipment sent to Chiang Kai-shek's armies in Manchuria. Mao Tse-tung later boasted that it was the gift of aid by Washington to the KMT that made the civil war possible.

By 1948, the US had given the Koumintang government four and a half trillion dollars to fight the CCP. But hundreds of thousands of KMT troops defected to the Communists. Many units were decimated by CCP tactics that later would be used against United Nations troops in Korea—decoy the enemy with small forces, then lure them into terrain where they could be trapped and destroyed. As Mao described the tactic: 'Force the enemy to come in like a fist, then open the fist so the fingers can be amputated one by one.'

Back in Washington, as Chiang's plight became desperate, US military leaders urged direct American intervention in the Chinese civil war to save the KMT. However, President Truman vetoed such a step. At the end of October 1948 when Chiang's forces became trapped in Mukden—which played into the Communist strategy of getting their enemy to defend the cities while exposing communications in the countryside to guerrilla attacks—the US airlifted food and supplies to the Koumintang troops. Then the US had to ferry Chiang's troops from other Manchurian cities to reinforce his soldiers holding Mukden. When Mukden fell on 1 November 1948, Chiang's US military adviser, General David Barr, advised Washington that it was 'the beginning of the end.' Barr blamed the Koumintang failure to best the Communists on 'the world's worst leadership and a complete loss of the will to fight.'

In the face of growing anti-American feelings in China, US troops withdrew from China in February 1949. The final showdown between Mao Tse-tung and Chiang Kai-shek came in April when Mao quietly moved 300,000 soldiers across the Yangtze River in a single night and surrounded the capital city of Nanking. The capital fell on 27 April 1949 and a month later Shanghai was taken.

From June until August 1949, in speeches and talks with US representatives, Mao Tse-tung indicated a willingness to establish friendly relations with the US and to accept American aid in rebuilding China. Rebuffed by Washington, Mao journeyed to Moscow in December 1949 for a series of meetings with Stalin. The USSR provided the needed aid for the newly formed Peoples Republic of China and gained an ally along its eastern frontier. In retrospect, some might claim the US made a mistake in backing Chiang Kai-shek against the CCP. During the early 1940s, the Chinese Communists had a better relationship with the Americans than they did with the USSR. Although the CCP received advice and instructions from Moscow during the early years of its war against the KMT, Mao Tse-tung often insisted he was 'not a Russian pawn' and declared the CCP 'did not make a revolution in order to hand the nation over to Russia.' But the US policy-makers later accused the Peoples Republic of China of being another Russian satellite country.

Stalin, meanwhile, had honored a friendship and alliance pact with Chiang Kai-shek, and even as American troops finally withdrew from China in 1949, Stalin continued to regard the Koumintang as the 'legal government' of China, maintaining relations with the KMT until Chiang fled to Taiwan. But meanwhile the USSR generally avoided direct contact with the Chinese Communists. The Russian Communists often referred to the CCP as 'margarine

Above: Men of the 1st Marine Division enter Tientsin on 1 October 1945, ending eight years of Japanese occupation.

Left: General Marshall meets with Generalissimo Chiang Kai-shek and Madame Chiang in Nanking at the end of 1945.

Communists,' making light of the Chinese form of Communism. But Stalin also had favored a weak KMT that would not challenge Russia's claims to Outer Mongolia. And it was reported during the Chinese Civil War that Stalin encouraged Mao Tse-tung to prolong the war in the hope that America could be 'bled white' through massive contributions to Chiang Kai-shek.

The 38th Parallel

General Order 1 was a directive issued by the US Government to the Japanese Government shortly after its surrender in August 1945. This document instructed Japanese commanders to surrender to designated Allied officers. The order required that in Korea Japanese forces south of the 38th Parallel surrender to the US commander. The text of the order, including that on Korea, had been approved by the United States' British and Soviet

allies. The artificial division of Korea at the 38th Parallel was to be temporary, intended to facilitate the surrender of Japanese troops. The US and the Soviet Union had never made a formal wartime agreement to divide Korea into two zones of occupation. Indeed, Soviet troops were already in Korea in August before the decision on the 38th Parallel was approved by President Truman. When the Japanese in the north zone surrendered to the Soviets, the nearest US troops were some 600 miles away on Okinawa.

Even before US troops arrived in Korea on 8 September 1945 to accept surrender of the Japanese, US planes had dropped leaflets with Korean translations of a declaration which stated that 'in due course Korea shall become free and independent.' This was an agreement made between Roosevelt, Churchill and Chiang Kai-shek at the Cairo Conference in late 1943. The Koreans took the words 'in due course' to mean 'almost immediately.'

The first US forces to occupy South Korea that second week in September 1945 were headed by Lieutenant General John R. Hodge, who had been assigned as US Commander in South Korea, and Major General Archibald Arnold, as the military governor. General Arnold's orders were to establish an administrative structure, the American Military Government, for the 25 million Koreans living south of the 38th Parallel beginning in September. His staff consisted of 109 war-weary combat officers and men. In the confusion of early efforts by the US to democratize South Korea, some Japanese administrators were assigned government positions, an error that antagonized the Korean people. The US had followed a similar policy in Germany, where former Nazis were sometimes given administrative jobs because they seemed better qualified than Germans who had no government experience during the Nazi years.

General Arnold discovered the Japanese had, during 35 years of colonial rule, neatly organized Korea into a self-sufficient entity with industry north of the 38th Parallel and agriculture south of that latitude. After the military division between the US and the Soviets, North Korea needed the 'rice bowl' south of the 38th Parallel but was separated from its traditional food supply by the artificial boundary. While South Korea controlled the food supply, North Korea controlled the production of coal and steel. The Soviet zone of Korea was managed in a manner more directly related to the Soviet version of a postwar world. As expressed by US General Matthew Ridgway, the Soviet concept of an 'independent' Korea was a Korea independent of any non-Communist influence. North Korean units had served with the Red Army and became the cadres of a North Korean army, equipped first with captured Japanese weapons and later with modern Soviet military equipment. A Democratic People's Republic of Korea, a Soviet-style of government, was established with headquarters at Pyongyang. All anti-Communist expression was suppressed, and the Soviets refused to allow a United Nations team to enter North Korea to supervise free elections.

The Soviets withheld coal shipments to Seoul until January 1946, except for several carloads delivered to the Soviet Embassy in Seoul. The South Koreans requested 240,000 tons of North Korean coal and 1000 tons of steel. The Soviets sent a 60-man delegation to discuss this request and other matters. The negotiations were conducted by Lieutenant General Hodge and Colonel General Terenty Shtykov, head of the USSR delegation. In March, the conference was declared a failure. It was agreed only that transportation and postal services between the zones would be resumed, and three carloads of coal to be traded for surplus South Korean rice were delivered. But later Colonel General Ivan Chistiakov, General Shtykov's superior, forbade the transportation of Korean passengers and most goods across the 38th Parallel.

During the negotiations between Generals Shtykov and Hodge, Americans first learned

Above: Former Army Chief of Staff, General of the Army George Marshall, is seen off by his successor General Eisenhower as he leaves to take up his post as ambassador to China in December 1945. Looking on are Admiral Stark and the Chinese Ambassador.

Right: Marines armed with Thompson submachine guns, an M1 carbine and a BAR help to keep the peace in a Chinese town in late 1945.

about Kim Il Sung, who was a 32-year-old Korean trained in Moscow since 1943 and who would become premier of North Korea. Sung was Chairman of the Interim Peoples Committee which met in Pyongyang and adopted a platform promising to 'exterminate pro-Japanese and anti-democratic elements' as well as 'imperialist ideas.' At a meeting in Moscow in December 1945 of the Council of Foreign Ministers, representing the US, Soviet Union and Great Britain, a plan was made to create a four-power trusteeship for Korea to last up to five years. The plan was denounced by Koreans, who demanded independence. When Soviet cooperation in setting up the trusteeship was not forthcoming, the US asked the United Nations to resolve the debacle. When the UN observers offered to sponsor free elections, the USSR objected to participation by South Korean parties which had rejected terms of a Moscow proposal on the matter. Since most political parties in South Korea had objected to the Moscow proposal, elections were held only in the south. The Republic of Korea was officially established with Syngman Rhee as president. The USSR responded by creating the North Korean government with Kim Il Sung as Premier. The US officially ended its military occupation of South Korea in September 1948. The USSR followed with an announcement that it would withdraw its Red Army troops by the

end of 1948. However, the USSR left behind a highly trained and well-equipped army of 135,000 Korean soldiers. On the other hand, the Republic of Korea (ROK) military force was largely staffed with inexperienced officers and very little military equipment.

The US policy by 1949 had become relatively simplistic: America would place its security in the hands of the United Nations; any future war would be a global war in which US superiority in air power and atomic weapons would dominate because conventional warfare with large armies had become obsolete. Although the US was aware of Communist troop activities beyond the US defense perimeter, they were regarded as a bluff in the diplomatic poker game of the late 1940s. Washington was certain that the Soviets would not risk a nuclear war by taking overly aggressive action.

The USSR exploded its first atomic bomb in September 1949. The nuclear parity achieved with the United States seemed well timed with the spread of anti-Western uprisings throughout Asia, which may have been inspired in part by the success of the Chinese Communists. Americans and other Western powers found 'go home' signs posted from Indochina to Indonesia. The Pentagon had not counted on the possibility of 'limited warfare' as a Communist card in the game. That card was now to be played in Korea.

THE KOREAN WAR

Hindsight reveals that the United States, as the rival superpower of 1950 to the Soviet Union, had indicated an absence of interest in the integrity of South Korea. A US attempt following World War II to secure a united Korea through the United Nations had failed. Between the surrender of Japan in 1945 and establishment of the Republic of Korea (ROK), the United States made a half-hearted effort to manage a military government of South Korea. While the Communists in North Korea organized an army of 135,000, including 25,000 Soviet-trained troops with experience in the Red Army or Chinese Communist forces in Manchuria, the US sent a few hundred military advisers to Seoul to establish an army of fewer than 100,000 lightly armed soldiers who had neither combat experience or heavy military equipment. The North Koreans were equipped with tanks, attack aircraft, and heavy artillery.

Further lack of interest was displayed by a series of public announcements during the late 1940s that the limits of the US 'defense perimeter' in the Pacific extended from the Aleutian Islands of Alaska to Japan and the Philippine Islands. Both Korea and Taiwan were beyond that perimeter, which was further restricted in January 1950 by US Secretary of State Dean Acheson. Acheson declared that it was 'neither sensible nor necessary' to guarantee the political integrity of South Korea or Taiwan. Asia in the late 1940s remained the same low priority political and military item it had been in the 1930s. The US provided token defensive forces for Pacific outposts but made generous contributions to the defense of Europe. Washington made no effort to conceal the fact that the Truman Doctrine and the Marshall Plan were created for the purpose of resisting Communist inroads into Europe. Aid to Chiang Kai-shek, meanwhile, was planned at the 'bare minimum' level needed to keep the Koumintang government in power in China.

Washington's public pronouncements may have given the 'wrong signal' to the Communist world. A Communist military observer also might have been misled by US military doctrine which in 1950 was focused toward a World War II type of attack on European terrain. Until the outbreak of hostilities along Korea's 38th Parallel, the typical US Army unit—notwithstanding American possession of nuclear weapons—was essentially the same as it was on the last day of World War II. The most significant change was an increase in bulk due to the addition of heavier equipment designed to increase the firepower of an infantry division. The number of infantry companies in an armored division had been increased from nine to 16 and infantry divisions were authorized an organic tank battalion plus one tank company per regiment.

The tank, which had become the World War II 'Queen of Battle,' was expected to play a major role in any future conflict. The European Theater military leaders of the US Army regarded the self-propelled antitank gun as outmoded and recommended that the best antitank weapon was another tank—one that would outmaneuver and outshoot any enemy tank.

As a result the US organized its ground forces in Europe so that armored divisions contained more infantrymen and infantry divisions contained more tank units.

North Korea's Surprise Attack

That was the policy of US ground forces on 25 June 1950 when Soviet-equipped North Korean forces with seven infantry divisions, a brigade of T-34 medium tanks, and supporting troops crossed the border in a two-column drive toward the South Korean capital of Seoul. North Korean Marshal Choe Yong Gun led the surprise attack.

General Matthew Ridgway, who served as commander of the Eighth Army in Korea, described the American military as in a state of 'shameful unreadiness.' Except for one army division stationed in Germany, every division had been skeletonized. Infantry regiments had been reduced from three battalions to two, and artillery battalions were reduced from three to two batteries. Despite the new emphasis on tanks, most of the tanks assigned to the first US units sent to Korea were in storage or had been deleted from the skeleton units. In addition to equipment problems, the troops generally were in poor physical condition and lacked sufficient training. All American planning had

Above: Men of a US artillery unit take what rest they can, 31 July 1950, 'somewhere in Korea.'

Previous page: The evacuation of Hungnam in December 1950, a truck convoy passes along the beach to embark on the waiting landing craft.

Right: Machine gunner of the 27th RCT (25th Infantry Division) in action near Taegu, 20 August 1950.

Below: US troops come under sniper fire in a Korean town during the retreat to the Pusan perimeter in July 1950.

25 June 1950
Korean attack
begins

FRONT LINES
- - - - 4 JULY 1950
.... 14 JULY
-·-·- 25 JULY
――― 5 AUG
-··-··- 26 AUG
――― 10 SEP
▨▨ PUSAN PERIMETER, 10-15 SEPT
➤ NORTH KOREAN ATTACKS

© Richard Natkiel, 1982

assumed the next war would be a global war, with the US and USSR slugging it out on a European battlefield. The concept of a 'limited war' with a Communist satellite nation on the Asian mainland 'never entered our councils,' General Ridgway commented.

The United Nations Security Council was called into an emergency session and ordered an immediate cessation of fighting and the withdrawal of North Korean troops. When North Korea ignored the UN demand, the international body adopted a US resolution on 27 June 1950 which called for members to help South Korea 'repel the armed attack.' On the same day President Truman ordered US forces to the aid of South Korea and General Mac-Arthur was made Commander in Chief of the United Nations units (the first commander of UN forces ever appointed.) Within eight hours, elements of the United States Far East Air Forces attacked Communist advance units which had driven nearly 75 miles down the East Coast of South Korea in the first two days of fighting.

A North Korean army column headed toward Seoul was unable to move rapidly in its southward drive because of two factors of foresight by members of KMAG, the US Korean Military Advisory Group. KMAG (pronounced Kaymag) had been able to train one ROK unit, the 6th Division, to combat readiness. And the KMAG leader assigned to that division, Lieutenant Colonel Thomas D MacPhail, correctly interpreting intelligence reports that a massive North Korean attack was imminent, had persuaded the ROK division commander to cancel all leave. As a result the 6th ROK Division, with units of the 1st ROK Division, was ready and held back the North Korean drive toward Seoul for three days. One infantry company defending the northern outskirts of the capital literally fought to the last man.

Elsewhere, however, the North Korean Peoples Army advanced quickly. Laesong was taken in the first four hours of the invasion. By the evening of 26 June, North Koreans had tanks on the highway to Seoul, 10 miles away. When it appeared that Seoul was becoming

Above: Infantry in a reserve position clean their weapons.

Above left: The first Communist offensive.

Left: Men of the 38th Infantry dig in. During its long periods of stalemate, conditions in the Korean War rapidly became reminiscent of the trench warfare of World War I.

Below: A member of the 27th RCT, 25th Infantry Division, in combat just north of Taegu, 29 August 1950.

surrounded, with ROK units retreating on both left and right flanks, the defenders of the capital were evacuated to positions south of the Han River. General MacArthur's staff in Tokyo had thought the Han River might be a suitable defensive barrier. But in the turmoil of the first days of the invasion, the ROK government lost control of the situation. South Korean troops fled southward across the Han, shoulder to shoulder in some cases with North Korean Army members infiltrating south. Masses of civilians jammed the roads, carrying belongings, some leading horses or cows, all racing to stay ahead of the advancing North Korean troops. In the confusion, the entire ROK Army Headquarters was moved to Sihung, south of Seoul, without the knowledge of the US military advisers, and communications were lost with ROK units still fighting in the Seoul area.

General MacArthur and seven members of his staff flew to Suwon, 20 miles south of Seoul, on 29 June for a personal inspection of the situation. MacArthur traveled by jeep to a hill overlooking the Han River and saw the columns of smoke still rising from fires burning in Seoul. Much of the jeep trip was a struggle to move against the tidal wave of ROK troops and civilians fleeing southward. MacArthur reported to the Joint Chiefs of Staff that ROK forces seemed 'incapable of gaining the initiative' and that the South Korean peninsula would be overrun by the Communist forces without immediate massive military aid. Washington's initial response was to authorize the use of one regimental combat team to assist the ROK troops. The nearest regimental combat team at that time was in Hawaii, more than 4000 miles away.

General MacArthur realized he could not wait for troops from Hawaii and organized a task force of 500 US soldiers from the 21st Infantry Regiment in Japan, including two rifle companies, a recoilless rifle crew, six bazooka teams, and two army platoons equipped with 4.2-inch mortars. The bazooka teams were equipped with old 2.3-inch weapons which had been replaced in many army units by 3.5-inch bazookas during World War II. The years of rapid demobilization and bulldozing thousands of tons of vital equipment into Pacific Ocean lagoons had taken their toll in terms of US military strength.

The makeshift US defense force was scheduled to be airlifted to Suwon to engage the North Koreans. But the front lines changed so rapidly during the early days of fighting that the first troops had to be ferried to Pusan, at the southeast tip of Korea, instead. The troops, given the code name of Task Force Smith for their commander, Lieutenant Colonel C B Smith, worked their way northward along highways and railroads to Osan, where they encountered an advancing North Korean infantry unit equipped with 30 medium tanks on 5 July 1950. For seven hours the outnumbered and outgunned Americans poured their fire at the Soviet-made tanks, knocking out five. The surviving US infantrymen were finally forced to withdraw and managed to reach additional

The Navy's Task Force 77, meanwhile, established a blockade around South Korea, eliminating North Korean efforts to mine harbors, land forces behind ROK lines, or interfere with surface communication routes between Korea and Japan. The US Air Force moved in early with leftover World War II fighters and bombers, P-51 Mustangs and B-26 light bombers. Some B-26s had been flown against Japanese targets in 1945 and had thousands of hours of service in their log books. In more than a few instances, the B-26s were flown by pilots who had used the same aircraft in World War II. The B-26s and P-51s were opposed at first by Russian YAK-9 fighter aircraft. Both sides deployed propeller aircraft. The US possessed jet fighters but the Korean targets were 400 miles from jet air bases in Japan and early model F-80 Shooting Star jets could not carry enough fuel to make an 800 to 1000-mile round trip plus time aloft to seek a target.

During the first weeks of the war, the fighting was reminiscent of early World War II battles before the US had organized its expertise at building forward airstrips overnight and moving airborne armies that could be dropped almost anywhere to encircle and annihilate an enemy. For the American soldier in Korea, it was a nightmare of rain and mud, slugging it out along tortuous hillsides, wading through calf-deep rice paddy water, running out of ammunition in undefendable gullies, and retreating after days without sleep through villages and countrysides where the local population might be pro- or anti-Communist.

US Army strength had dropped to nearly 600,000 on the eve of the Korean War. Congress,

elements of their regiment, which had followed by sea. Task Force Smith—composed mainly of poorly equipped soldiers hurriedly recruited from easy occupation duties in Japan—was then America's only combat unit engaged in fighting the North Korean Communist forces.

Virtually unnoticed in the early days of the Korean War was the safe evacuation of all American civilians by the US 7th Fleet, commanded by Vice-Admiral Arthur D Struble.

however, voted to extend the Selective Service Act and President Truman had the authority to order reserve units into active service. Beginning in July, four National Guard Divisions were called to active duty—the 28th (Pennsylvania), 40th (California), 43rd (Connecticut, Rhode Island and Vermont), and 45th (Oklahoma). Some 62,000 members of the enlisted reserve were called up for 21 months of service. Eight Army and one Marine Corps divisions were committed to the Korean fighting. A dozen other divisions were mobilized. More than one million officers and men were called up. Not all were needed in Korea, but the Truman administration worried that the USSR might take advantage of the US involvement there to move its own troops into some other area of the world.

In addition to the logistical problems of manpower and equipment, US forces in Korea were plagued by adverse weather conditions and terrain, and enemy tactics that had not been foreseen. The mountainous terrain of Korea obstructed the effectiveness of American mechanized equipment. North Korean troops also displayed expertise in infiltrating American lines through holes and exposed flanks, enabling them to establish positions to the rear of US units. This tactic enabled the North Koreans to strike at US command posts, artillery positions, and support units. The North Koreans also employed tactical guerrilla units of 12 to 15 men each. The guerrilla units were very successful in raids behind US lines.

In their first encounters, North Korean leaders sent up to four tank battalions ahead of

the main body of troops. The US ground troops had little to no success in using their 2.36-inch bazooka rockets against the T-34 tank armor. The 60 mm bazooka shells were described by observers as being no more effective against Russian T-34 tanks than 'pea shooters.' Often, the shells bounced harmlessly off the sides of the North Korean tanks because the ammunition was at least five years old and no longer capable of exploding properly. The US had

Above: MacArthur (seated) and General Almond (right), Commanding General X Corps, observe the Inchon landings from the headquarters ship *Mount McKinley.*

105-mm weapons but lacked ammunition for them. Antitank mines were not available either in Korea or Japan. Only light tanks were usable by the American forces because Japanese-built bridges were not strong enough to support the heavier Sherman tanks. Even after the arrival of light M24 American tanks, it was difficult for the US forces to deal effectively with the Russian-built armor, but the rate of American successes improved with the arrival of 3.5-inch rocket launchers, medium tanks, and attack aircraft.

Nevertheless, many American officers became casualties during the early weeks of fighting, in part because enlisted men recruited from the occupation forces were so poorly trained that company commanders were the only men capable of handling bazookas and other weapons. Because of communications problems, field grade officers had to make trips to the front lines to get information. (Major General William F Dean of the 24th Division was captured by enemy troops on such a mission.) There was suddenly serious concern in Washington that US troops might be driven into the sea by the North Korean army.

Left: A wounded soldier is evacuated to a mobile hospital. A real-life version of the familiar film and TV scene. The Korean War was the first conflict in which helicopters played a significant role though the rather limited payload of most of the types available confined them largely to scouting and casualty evacuation missions.

Right: Gun crewmen of the 780th Artillery cover their ears as their 8-inch howitzer is about to fire on Communist positions on Hill 983.

Below: A column of soldiers from the 5th Republic of Korea Division moves up to the front.

So much of previous US troop involvement had been in offensive tactics that few Americans knew how to handle a sustained defensive action against a large enemy force. Now US troops were forced to react to North Korean offensive tactics. Instead of conducting cohesive fighting withdrawals as ordered by their leaders, the first American troops to engage the North Koreans tended to panic when the enemy threatened to overrun their positions. In the panic withdrawals, described in official reports as 'mob movements rather than military movements,' American troops were 'cut to pieces' by enemy fire. As the US soldiers gained combat experience, however, they learned to remain in position until a tactical withdrawal could be planned. Casualties were sharply reduced in later engagements with the North Koreans.

American troops also suffered in the early fighting from an improperly perceived need to protect a wide front while short of manpower. This condition resulted in defense of an entire area with a thin line of troops and an inability to resist the massive manpower attacks employed by the Communists. In addition, it caused problems of command and control.

Shortly after the appointment of General MacArthur as UN Commander in Chief, US Lieutenant General Walton Walker was named to head the 8th US Army forces, which then included the 24th Division commanded by General Dean, and the 1st Cavalry and 25th Divisions which arrived piecemeal from Japan. General Dean fought a five-day delaying action at Taejon when the North Korean forces attacked his division from three directions, leading to the capture of the American general as he personally directed rear guard action of the 24th Division withdrawal. The 1st Cavalry and 25th Divisions then relieved the 24th and with reorganized ROK troops helped slow the continued advance of North Korean units.

Under the command of General Walker, UN lines became stabilized along a line extending from the Naktong River for a distance of about 90 miles northward from the Korea Strait, then eastward to the Sea of Japan at Pohang. The area included Taegu and the only port available to the UN, Pusan. The area became identified as the 'Pusan perimeter' and remained the only ground held securely by American and South Korean forces from the beginning of August until the breakout of 15 September 1950.

During the approximately six weeks of fighting around the Pusan Perimeter, North Korean troops continued a series of uncoordinated attacks along the front, probing for weak spots. Five of the reorganized ROK divisions were assigned to defend the northern battlelines, while the US troops, augmented during August by two additional infantry regiments and a brigade of US Marines, held the 90 miles of western front. On 3 September, the North Koreans launched a three-division attack along the northern side of the perimeter, requiring reinforcements by the 24th Division.

In the initial fighting, Americans seldom conducted night attacks, a tactic commonly used by North Korean units. As a result, US troops often began a successful daylight attack against the enemy forces but stopped the effort when night fell, with little or no pressure to continue the action or increase patrols. During the overnight lull in fighting, the North Korean troops dug in, strengthened their positions and were better able to resume the battle the following morning. Until US troops began night attacks or continuation of the battle after dusk, using flares, searchlights and other forms of illumination, they experienced an unnecessarily high rate of casualties.

Military observers credit the navy and air arms of the United Nations Command for stalling the North Korean advance beyond the rim of the Pusan perimeter. The US 7th Fleet

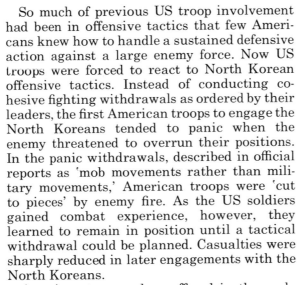

poured gunfire into Communist shore positions while blockading the peninsula against any attempt by the North Koreans to resupply their troops from the sea. Navy and Marine Corps aircraft, meanwhile, joined units of the US Far East Air Force in support of UN ground forces. The US air units were augmented in August by the arrival of an Australian Air Force Group. The North Korean Air Force was reduced to a token force while fighters and bombers of the United Nations Command became the dominant offensive arm. By mid-September, the navy and air units would establish an envelopment of the North Korean troops south of the 38th Parallel.

The South Rallies: the Inchon Invasion to the Yalu

The first phase of the Korean War ended on 15 September 1950 with General MacArthur's dramatic landing at Inchon, 150 miles north of the Pusan perimeter, with amphibious troops of X Corps. MacArthur had planned, almost from the establishment of the Pusan perimeter, a strategy for crushing the North Korean army by attacking from behind their own lines from the Yellow Sea, using combined army and marine units, while the 8th Army pushed northward from the Pusan perimeter. The 8th Army and X Corps would retake Seoul by approaching from different directions, thereby trapping the North Korean army below the 38th Parallel.

MacArthur's plan was rejected twice by the Joint Chiefs of Staff, who finally agreed to a third request by authorizing the use of a US Marine Corps division with amphibious training and a wing of aircraft. Amphibious experts also tried to discourage such an invasion when MacArthur revealed his plan at a briefing in Tokyo three weeks before the operation was put into effect. But MacArthur argued that it was necessary to go for a victory in South Korea before the start of winter, when the climate alone would cause more nonbattle casualties than the expected losses of the Inchon invasion, by now given the code name of Operation Chromite.

One objection to the plan was, again, the poor state of the US military establishment that had developed during the five years of the one-weapon doctrine. The Korean War already had begun eroding manpower and materiel faster than they were being replaced, and the Truman Administration, including the President himself, had reportedly indicated concern that the Korean fighting might merely be a prelude to a Communist move in Europe leading in turn to World War III. The US had put all its eggs into the atomic bomb basket and was

Right: MacArthur looks out from his personal aircraft while observing a paratroop drop behind Communist lines near Sunchon, 20 October 1950.

Below: A Marine helicopter employed in the casualty evacuation role, 3 October 1950.

simply not prepared to wage conventional war on a large scale.

Beyond Washington's concerns about taking some of the military's best troops when they might be needed on the other side of the world, Inchon was considered virtually impregnable. Perhaps because the Inchon landing was improbable—General Ridgway called it a 'daring 5000 to 1 shot'—it would surprise the Communists. It had to be approached through mile-wide mudflats in a tortuous channel where tides varied 30 feet per day and it was protected by shore batteries. Besides, the assault was planned during the typhoon season. To succeed, the operation would require a combination of perfect coordination, skill, and luck.

While the success of the Inchon landing generally is credited to the genius of General MacArthur, it would not have been possible

Below: The battleship *Missouri* bombards targets near Chonjin in the northeast of North Korea in October 1950. The *Missouri* was the only US battleship in commission at the outbreak of the Korean War.

Above: Infantrymen in a typical front line trench in Korea.

of the tremendous variations in tides at Inchon, landings were scheduled for either morning or evening high tides each day for several days to avoid stranding amphibious craft with personnel and equipment on lowtide mudflats.

Although the US 8th Army was scheduled to break out of the Pusan perimeter at the same time US Major General Edward Almond was directing the Inchon landings, General Walker's forces—never at full strength and weakened considerably by withdrawal of marine units for the Inchon landing—experienced unexpected delays in getting his forces northward to join X Corps in the battle for Seoul. Communist forces in the area south of the 38th Parallel refused to believe UN propaganda reports about the Inchon action that threatened to isolate them and so they continued to fight on there.

After nearly a week of counterattacks by North Korean forces holding the 8th Army within the Pusan perimeter, General MacArthur revealed plans for a second landing from the Yellow Sea, at Kumsan, nearly 100 miles south of Inchon. However, North Korean units suddenly began withdrawing to the north on 23 September, and units of the 1st Cavalry Division and the 7th Infantry Division broke through separately, meeting again for the liberation of Seoul on 27 September.

The battle for Seoul was not as easy as previously anticipated. From Kimpo Airport to Seoul, a distance of about eight miles, US Army and Marine regiments encountered tough resistance from North Korean soldiers. Seoul's liberation required nearly 10 days of house-to-house fighting. North Korean troops were barricaded in nearly every block with snipers, machine guns and antitank weapons. Marines were still flushing Communist soldiers from burning buildings on 28 September.

More than 125,000 North Korean troops were captured during the United Nations offensive. Many thousands also escaped capture by changing into civilian clothing and mingling with the population or fleeing into the rugged countryside. Most of the North Korean materiel below the 38th Parallel was abandoned by the Communist troops as they surrendered or

without the work of Navy Lieutenant Eugene Clark who was put ashore near Inchon on 1 September to obtain the information needed about details of Inchon harbor. For two weeks, working at night and hiding during the daylight hours, Lieutenant Clark located North Korean gun emplacements, measured the seawall, and compiled other vital data. Lieutenant Clark was so thoroughly familiar with the site when the first assault craft of Operation Chromite sailed into Flying Fish Channel from the Yellow Sea before the dawn of 15 September that he was able to turn on a lighthouse beacon to help guide the X Corps personnel to their beachheads.

The North Koreans should have suspected that an assault was imminent because American destroyers and cruisers, accompanied by British cruisers, had shelled enemy positions near Inchon for two days before the landing. However, as General Ridgway commented later, the Communists 'knew' Inchon was safe because 'no commander in his right senses' would attempt an invasion at that impossible site.

The US 5th Marines led the assault, storming Green Beach on the island of Wolmi that guarded the Inchon harbor. Some units scaled the seawall with ladders. Others rammed holes in the seawall with their LSTs or used dynamite to blast openings. The island was taken in 45 minutes. Artillery, tanks, and the 7th Infantry Division followed the marine assault into Inchon. On 16 September, the 5th Marines captured Kimpo Airport, South Korea's largest airfield, and were halfway to Seoul. Other marine regiments took Inchon areas designated as Red Beach and Blue Beach. Because

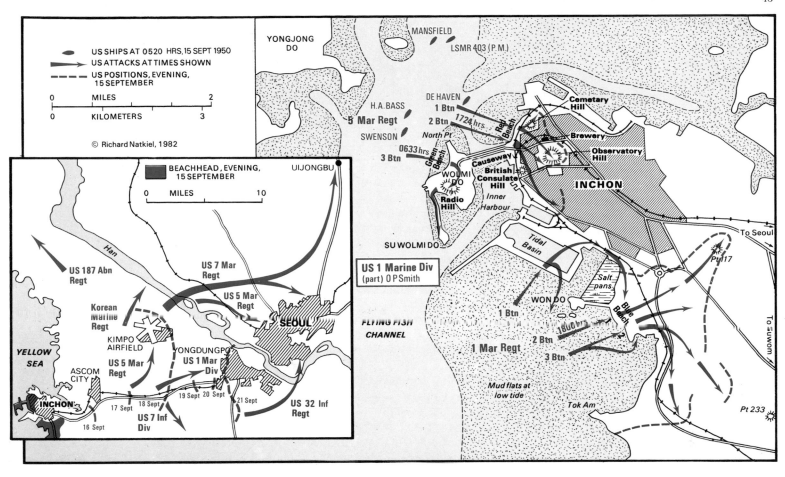

US SHIPS AT 0520 HRS, 15 SEPT 1950
US ATTACKS AT TIMES SHOWN
US POSITIONS, EVENING, 15 SEPTEMBER

0   MILES   2
0   KILOMETERS   3

© Richard Natkiel, 1982

BEACHHEAD, EVENING, 15 SEPTEMBER
0   MILES   10

UIJONGBU

US 187 Abn Regt

Han

US 7 Mar Regt

Korean Marine Regt

US 5 Mar Regt

SEOUL

KIMPO AIRFIELD

YELLOW SEA

US 5 Mar Regt

ASCOM CITY

YONGDUNGPO

US 1 Mar Div

INCHON

16 Sept   17 Sept   18 Sept   19 Sept   20 Sept   21 Sept

US 7 Inf Div

US 32 Inf Regt

FLYING FISH CHANNEL

YONGJONG DO

MANSFIELD

LSMR 403 (P.M.)

DE HAVEN

H.A. BASS

5 Mar Regt

SWENSON

North Pt

1 Btn

2 Btn   1724 hrs

0633 hrs

3 Btn

WOLMI DO

Radio Hill

SU WOLMI DO

Causeway

British Consulate Hill

Inner Harbour

Cemetary Hill

Brewery

Observatory Hill

INCHON

To Seoul

US 1 Marine Div (part) O P Smith

Tidal Basin

Salt pans

WON DO

1 Btn

1 Mar Regt

2 Btn   1800 hrs

3 Btn

Blue Beach

Pt 117

To Suwom

Mud flats at low tide

Tok Am

Pt 233

scattered. The successful outcome of this September action marked the end of the second phase of the war. Before the fighting for Seoul was ended, however, plans were made for the third and most dangerous phase of the Korean War—the pursuit and destruction of the remainder of the North Korean forces.

On 27 September, General MacArthur was authorized by President Truman to operate north of the 38th Parallel in pursuit of North Korean troops. To make it clear that the operation was only for the pursuit of North Korean troops, the authorization stated that 'no major Soviet or Chinese Communist forces' had entered North Korea, that there had been 'no announcement of intended entry' by the major Communist powers, and 'no threat to

counter UN operations militarily in Korea.' Although China had warned repeatedly that it might help the North Koreans resist a United Nations invasion north of the 38th Parallel, the warning was regarded by most US military leaders as a bluff. Thus ROK troops crossed the border on 1 October, followed eight days later by the US 8th Army. Two divisions were left behind to mop up the North Korean stragglers in the south and to secure communication lines with bases in Pusan and elsewhere.

Washington also ordered that under no circumstances were aircraft under the United Nations command to fly north of the Yalu River, separating Manchuria from North Korea. Air Force General Hoyt Vandenberg explained, among other reasons, that losses of US aircraft on missions to destroy Communist bases north of the Yalu would weaken America's ability to cope with any Communist aggression in Europe. The injunction automatically provided sanctuary for Communist aircraft or other forces beyond the Yalu River. Washington also had recommended that any UN troop movements near the Yalu River should be limited to ROK forces rather than US military units.

Except for the various restrictions on military activity, MacArthur was advised that he should 'feel unhampered tactically and strategically' in operations north of the 38th Parallel. A meeting was arranged between General MacArthur and President Truman on Wake Island, about midway between the Hawaiian and Philippine Islands, on 14 October to discuss the conduct of the war. General MacArthur reportedly assured the President that if China entered the war as threatened, it probably would not contribute more than 50,000 to 60,000 troops. A Chinese force of such size, MacArthur believed, could be controlled by the much larger United Nations contingents. Because reconnaissance north of the Yalu River was prohibited, the UN forces were unaware that some 300,000 Chinese Communist 'volunteers' were massing along the border.

Meanwhile, the UN units, augmented throughout the autumn by battalions and brigades of ground forces from Great Britain, Canada, Australia, Turkey, Thailand, the

Philippines, the Netherlands, France, Greece, Columbia, Ethiopia, New Zealand, South Africa, Belgium and Luxembourg, moved rapidly northward to consolidate gains in North Korea before deep winter snows could hamper activity in the mountainous terrain. In some instances, UN forces advanced ahead of MacArthur's original plans. The ROK 3rd Division, for example, captured the North Korean port of Wonsan, on the eastern coast, on 11 October; MacArthur had planned for the US Marine Division to take Wonsan in an amphibious landing on 20 October.

Actually, the US Marines did not reach Wonsan until 26 October because MacArthur's plans for transporting the division from Inchon around Korea to the east coast port failed to take into consideration the need for the Navy to remove some 2000 Soviet-made mines in the Wonsan harbor. The Marines then made what was called an 'administrative' landing, since the port had been in UN hands for two weeks. The Wonsan assault was to be coupled with an attack on Pyongyang, North Korea's capital city, followed by a linkup of UN forces across the narrowest part of North Korea. Pyongyang was overrun on schedule, 20 October, by combined forces of ROK troops and the US 187th Regimental Combat Team, which made an airborne assault on the city. And when the US 1st Marine Division moved into Wonsan, ROK troops were released to race toward the industrial Hamhung and Hungnam areas farther up the east coast of North Korea.

As the US Marines secured the port of Wonsan 26 October 1950, units of the ROK 6th Division reached the Yalu River and the US 24th Division was within 70 miles of the Manchurian border. As the ROK division's 7th Regiment reached the Yalu, they apparently stumbled upon a staging area for Chinese Communist troops massing for an attack on the United Nations forces. The Chinese force nearly annihilated the ROK troops.

On the same day, elements of the ROK 26th Division advancing from Hamhung toward the Chosin Reservoir encountered strong Communist resistance at Sudong. In the fighting, the ROK forces later discovered that 18 prisoners taken in battle were members of two regiments of the 124th Division of the Peoples Republic of China (PRC) army. Shortly afterward, US Marines attached to X Corps encountered a group of Chinese tanks and took prisoners identified as members of China's 126th Division. On 28 October, troops of the PRC 39th, 40th and 42nd Armies were reported to be in North Korea. General MacArthur's staff dismissed the reports as part of the great diplomatic poker game with the Communists playing a card in which a few Chinese 'volunteers' were 'showing support' for the North Korean cause.

The Chinese used tactics which tended to support the opinion that their presence was merely a rumor. They marched at night, avoided daytime use of roads, hid in mine shafts, tunnels, or village buildings to avoid aerial surveillance, carried cooked food so that fire would not be needed for preparing meals and occasionally started forest fires to provide concealment. Each Communist soldier functioned as a self-sufficient fighter, traveling by foot and carrying enough food and ammunition to last up to five days. Using such measures, the Chinese Communist troops could seemingly materialize on a hillside, attack an enemy, and then just as suddenly disappear into the rugged background of North Korea. On 1 November 1950, they began to appear in concentrations of several thousand in the area of Unsan, about 60 miles south of the Yalu River.

Within hours on 1 November, Chinese troops suddenly materialized east of Unsan and overwhelmed the 6th ROK Infantry Division. Before nightfall, General Walker reported that the ROK unit had been destroyed as an organized fighting force. PRC troops next at-

Above left: Men and tanks of the 7th Infantry Division in the final stages of the advance to the Yalu, 21 November 1950.

Left: By January 1951 the UN forces were on the defensive. Here men of a Raider company attached to X Corps await an attack.

Right: General MacArthur tours the Wonju sector in February 1951. Sitting immediately behind is General Ridgway.

tacked the US 8th Cavalry Regiment in a manner that would be repeated many times in the following months—with a multitude of brass horns and whistles blowing while mortar shells and Soviet Katusha rockets rained down on the UN forces. The US cavalry troops found themselves on the defensive again and surrounded by hostile forces. After fighting that raged through the night, the US troops tried an orderly withdrawal but found their escape route cut off. Troops that tried to withdraw along the main road from Unsan were ambushed. By morning, the US regiment was shattered. Many soldiers continued fighting as individuals or in twos or threes, moving into the surrounding hills with whatever wounded they could carry.

The US 8th Cavalry Regiment lost approximately half of its personnel as well as hundreds of vehicles and artillery pieces in its first engagement with the Chinese troops, later

identified as members of the PRC 39th Army. The fighting was described like the scenario of a Hollywood cowboy-and-Indian movie, with Chinese and American soldiers wrestling each other on the ground, firing handguns from the hip, crouching behind wrecked vehicles while firing rifles, throwing hand grenades at close range, and setting vehicles afire to produce illumination for sighting the enemy. Chinese Communists sometimes attacked in waves of hundreds, bugles blowing, while their bodies accumulated in heaps of three deep in some places. Between Chinese attacks, American troops crawled over the bodies of PRC soldiers mowed down in a previous wave to retrieve their weapons and ammunition so they could be used against the next wave.

After mauling the US and ROK troops, the Chinese forces withdrew northward. They also released some captured American soldiers and left wounded US troops on litters beside roads

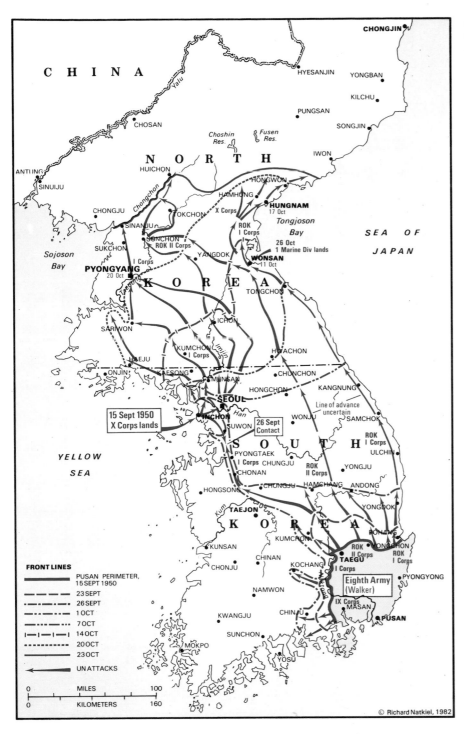

where they could be retrieved by UN medics. They were generally regarded at first as more humane in their treatment of prisoners than were the North Koreans, who had a reputation of executing captured troops. But the PRC soldiers also firmly believed that US troops were victims of a capitalistic and imperialistic regime and encouraged returned prisoners to turn their guns on their officers and lead their fellow soldiers in a Communist revolution.

As the war continued, however, a large percentage of American and British soldiers captured by the Chinese Communists died of torture or neglect. A number of young Americans held as prisoners were susceptible to ideological 'brainwashing' and other techniques, such as improved living conditions, used by the Communists, and some of these prisoners ended up cooperating with their captors. The effect of 'brainwashing' on American troops captured by the Communists was not fully realized until after the soldiers had been returned. The recognition resulted in, among other things, changes in the Army's training for possible capture by enemy forces.

The UN command was slow to comprehend Communist tactics and strategy, despite General MacArthur's claim to a superior ability to 'understand the Oriental mind.' US officers, for example, did not realize that the 'wave' effect of Chinese attacks was due to inadequate communications of command and control so that several different Chinese companies or battalions would attack a position from which hostile fire was originating without coordinating their assaults. The Communists also tried to get as close to an enemy position as possible to obtain some immunity from artillery and aircraft fire. However, the preference for close infighting also made the PRC troops more vulnerable to mortars, tanks, automatic weapons and small arms fire from the defending UN troops.

The Chinese, like their North Korean protégés, stressed the penetration of weak points and the encirclement of defensive positions of the United Nations units. When approaching an enemy position, the Communists used a

tactic of moving with two units forward and one back. As they encountered resistance, the formations were shifted to one unit forward and two back. After finding a weak point, the advance unit would try to penetrate deeply enough to engage the defender's reserve forces while the remainder began to encircle the forward defenders.

While on the defensive, the Chinese made superb use of camouflage and concealment so they often were invisible to UN use of aerial surveillance. The American forces, on the contrary, made little effort to conceal their positions, which usually were easily identified by their wealth of vehicles, weapons, bunkers and litter. Also, the US troops felt no urgency about using concealment or camouflage since the Communists were unlikely to use aircraft for surveillance or attack.

The Chinese Join Hostilities + Fighting Intensifies

The next move by General MacArthur's troops after the presence of Chinese troops was confirmed was to continue the original mission of locating and destroying the remnants of the North Korean army. The UN command was so

confident that complete victory was near when it resumed its northward push to the Yalu on 24 November that the drive became known as the 'Get The Boys Home By Christmas' offensive. General MacArthur flew to North Korea on 24 November to personally supervise the start of the drive to the Yalu.

General Almond's X Corps would advance on the right and General Walker's 8th Army on the left to envelop the enemy on the northern edge of its country. The US X Corps was essentially the army and marine units used in the Inchon landing and later ferried around to the east coast port of Wonsan. The US 8th Army included the US 2nd, 24th and 25th Divisions, the ROK 1st, 6th, 7th and 8th Divisions, the British 27th Brigade and a Turkish brigade. The US 1st Cavalry Division would be held in reserve.

Only one US unit, the 17th Regimental Combat Team of X Corp's 7th Infantry Division actually reached the Yalu River. The unit lacked winter footwear, gloves and other gear needed to withstand the climate which often dropped well below zero degrees Fahrenheit in November. The troops suffered frostbitten fingers and coped with inadequate manpower, food, and ammunition, only to be ordered to withdraw within a few days of their objective as bugle-blowing PRC units suddenly appeared in an attack on the right flank of the 8th Army. It was the start of a major offensive involving an estimated 200,000 Chinese Communist troops.

After virtually annihilating the ROK II Corps, the PRC units attacked the US 2nd Army Division. Only one unit of the 2nd Division escaped without major losses by withdrawing toward the Yellow Sea. The 5th and 7th Marine Regiments of X Corps were diverted to the west to try to take some of the pressure

off the 8th Army but were jumped by the Chinese Communist 79th and 89th Divisions. That battle raged through the night as the PRC troops took advantage of the darkness to mount a massive assault. As in the earlier engagements with the PRC forces, the Chinese seemed to have an endless supply of manpower and sent wave after wave of Communist soldiers into the marine positions. The Marines used the light from a burning building to aim their weapons at the Communist troops, which were rapidly turned into layers of Chinese bodies around the perimeter of the US defensive position.

General Oliver Smith, who had led the US 1st Marine Division in the drive toward the Yalu River, was authorized to abandon his equipment in order to withdraw his men safely. However, Smith rejected the offer, choosing to fight his way out with the help of any equipment that could be moved. Working around the Chosin Reservoir in temperatures so cold that carbines and BARs could not be used, General Smith's Marines fought their way through the PRC 59th and 58th Divisions to reach Hagaru, at the south end of the reservoir, where the men could be supplied with air drops of ammunition, food and drinking water. At Hagaru an airstrip was hacked out of the frozen earth so that the wounded could be airlifted to safety. To cross a reservoir spillway, a temporary bridge was dropped in sections and assembled by the Marines so that all equipment could be moved farther south.

After fighting off the Chinese 58th Division on their western flank, the marines were attacked by the Chinese 76th Division from the east. At Koto-ri, the US Marine units were attacked by the Chinese 60th Division from the west and the 77th Division from the east. Finally, after nearly two weeks of continuous

Above: Tanks of the 1st Marine Division move past a group of North Korean prisoners, 26 September 1950.

Opposite: Paratroops of the 187th Airborne RCT rehearse a combat jump behind the lines in Korea, 25 April 1951.

Below: Troops of the 25th Division fight off Communist attacks near Chorwon in April 1951.

started the trek to the 'roof of Korea.' The US 1st Marine Division had suffered 4000 of the casualties, in addition to 6000 who survived but were temporarily disabled by cold weather injuries. More than 4300 of the casualties had been airlifted out of the Chosin Reservoir area via the emergency airstrip at Hagaru.

The US 8th Army, on the western side of the Korean peninsula, withdrew below the Chongchon River and a week later abandoned the capital, Pyongyang, and moved toward the 38th Parallel. The US 2nd Division had suffered so many casualties that it was declared combat noneffective for 30 days until it could be reoutfitted with personnel and materiel. Many of the 2nd Division casualties had occurred near Kunu-ri, between Unsan and Pyongyang, when Communist gunners disabled vehicles in a retreating column on a narrow valley road. In the ensuing gridlock of wrecked and burning vehicles, many of the UN troops became helpless targets for Communist forces in the surrounding hillsides.

The US Far East Air Force aided in the evacuation of men and materiel during the southward push by Chinese Communist troops. In one major operation, transports evacuated 3600 troops, 200 vehicles and 1300 tons of cargo to South Korean bases. C-47 transports and C-119 Flying Boxcars ferried ammunition and medical supplies to UN troops in advance positions and evacuated sick and wounded. At Haguru, 1580 wounded were airlifted from the battle zone in a single day. To help evacuate General Smith's men and equipment across the Chosin Reservoir after Communists had destroyed the original route, C-119s were used for the first time in history to transport an entire eight-span 16-ton bridge.

In contrast to the United Nations forces' sophisticated navy, aircraft, and motorized weapons, the Communist Chinese soldier often went into battle with a rifle and grenades. He had no gloves and wore a cotton-padded uniform and canvas shoes in winter. The fact that a peasant army of poorly fed, poorly clothed, and poorly equipped soldiers could threaten to annihilate the troops of a highly industrialized superpower with nuclear weapons stunned observers throughout the world in December 1950.

US aircraft had neutralized 18 major industrial targets in North Korea in the first 90 days of the war. B-26 bombers had flown 53,000 sorties against Communist forces, destroying an estimated 38,000 vehicles, 407 locomotives and 3700 railroad cars, as well as 168 bridges. US F-51 fighter planes were credited with eliminating the equivalent of four tank divisions and 100,000 troops. But the US X Corps was not 'home by Christmas' 1950. On 25 December, its troops were back in Pusan where they had been driven three months earlier by a similar army of foot soldiers.

The strategy and tactics of the Chinese Communists continued to influence the nature of the war in Korea. While the self-sufficient Chinese soldier could find effective concealment and could operate in rugged terrain where mechanized equipment could not, his

battles with seven different divisions of Chinese Communist troops, General Smith reached the Hungnam defense perimeter. Only the troops killed in battle were left behind; the severely wounded were carried back in the division's vehicles.

Within a few days, even the Hungnam beachhead was evacuated. In a scene reminiscent of Dunkirk, the USS *Missouri* bombarded the harassing enemy troops as a fleet of 109 vessels under the command of Rear Admiral James H Doyle moved the entire X Corps and its equipment from the Hungnam perimeter. Doyle's Joint Task Force 90 evacuated 91,000 Korean civilian refugees from the beachhead, in addition to 105,000 UN troops, more than 17,000 vehicles and 375,000 tons of supplies. Cargo that could not be evacuated was destroyed on the beach and docks.

X Corps losses were approximately 5500 killed, wounded or missing out of 26,000 who

Left: MacArthur and South
Korean Leader Syngman
Rhee.

Below: Sherman tanks
bombard a Communist hill
position, September 1951.

rate of advance was limited to how far he could walk in a day or a night. In the UN withdrawal from the Yalu frontier, PRC troops often could not keep up with the southward 'advance to the rear' movement of the US 8th Army and X Corps units. The separate soldiers or units of troops also lacked the benefit of close communication with each other, resulting in costly tactical errors. Communist units often would continue probing attacks at a strengthened point on the UN perimeter without being aware that a weak neighboring point could be penetrated with relative ease. The Chinese also wasted manpower and time in pursuing ambush and encirclement strategies when they could have had a greater adverse effect on the United Nations forces by capturing advance airstrips and supply dumps which were vital to the enemy operations, as at Hagaru.

Nevertheless, the PRC troops were able to regroup, rebuild, and resupply their forces quickly after their November offensive against the US 8th Army and X Corps. (X Corps, in a reorganization move, was made a part of the strategic reserve of the 8th Army.) On 23 December 1950, while X Corps was being evacuated from Hungnam and the 8th Army was planning the defense of Seoul against a new Communist invasion, General Walker was killed in a jeep accident. General Matthew Ridgway was notified in Washington that he had been selected to replace Walker and left

immediately for Korea. General MacArthur gave General Ridgway command of all ground forces in Korea. MacArthur, meanwhile, assumed overall command of ground, air, and sea operations for the United Nations forces.

The Communist forces opened their second major offensive on 1 January 1951 with a force of 400,000 Chinese and 100,000 North Korean troops. The newly reorganized US 8th Army, with 200,000 men, was almost immediately pushed back to the outskirts of Seoul. On 3 January, Communist troops overran positions of the ROK troops, exposing the flanks of the US 2nd Division. The severe fighting required commitment of the 3rd and 7th Divisions from the strategic reserve to help the 2nd Division withdraw with a minimum of casualties.

On 3 January, General Ridgway ordered evacuation of Seoul again. The orderly evacuation of ROK government offices and withdrawal of UN forces was complicated by the rush of thousands of Korean civilians and retreating ROK troops across the Han River bridges. Many of the South Korean soldiers had thrown away their rifles and handguns and were fleeing southward in whatever vehicles they could find. Civilians on foot, their worldly belongings carried on A-frames on their backs, clogged the bridges leading from Seoul. General Ridgway ordered the main bridge closed to all but military traffic in order to get all the 8th Army men and weapons, which included big eight-inch

howitzers and British Centurion tanks, safely across the river ahead of the Communist advance.

The UN forces established a new defense perimeter about 50 miles south of the 38th Parallel, along a line running roughly from Pyongtaek on the Yellow Sea to Samchok on the Sea of Japan. From that position, patrols and reconnaissance flights made daily searches for signs of Communist troops' presence. Although nearly 200,000 were reported to be north of the UN defense perimeter, no evidence of their presence was found and General Ridgway ordered the 8th Army to begin moving north again on 25 January. Communist counterattacks stopped the drive at Chipyong and Wonju, in central Korea, 11 February, but UN troops were able to advance to the south bank of the Han River on the west. In the Chipyong-Wonju fighting, the 2nd Division again bore the brunt of the battle. The division's 23rd Regimental Combat Team with the aid of a battalion of French soldiers fought a total of five Chinese Communist divisions until 18 February, when 1st Cavalry Division tanks

arrived. The Chinese retreated, leaving behind 2000 of their dead.

The UN forces did not immediately attempt to retake Seoul, which had psychological and political importance, but no military value. The more important objectives were the port of Inchon and the airfield at Kimpo, west of Seoul. Those objectives were taken in the next stage of General Ridgway's counteroffensive (a drive whose original code name of 'Operation Killer' was changed to 'Operation Ripper' on the recommendation of Washington officials who felt that 'Ripper' had greater 'public relations value' than 'Killer'). However, one purpose of the campaign was to inflict heavy casualties on the Communist forces. Others were to retake Seoul and other key points near the 38th Parallel and to capture a large Communist supply base at Chunchon, northeast of Seoul. Field artillery battalions received special training in the United States for use in the offensive, which got underway 7 March.

Seoul, which the Communists had captured twice, was again retaken on 14 March 1951. ROK troops first entered the city and advanced

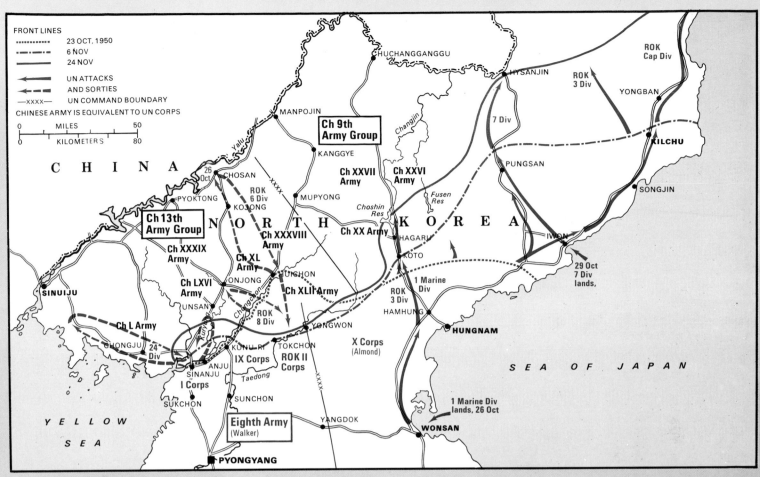

several miles, encountering only light fire. Other patrols found the city nearly abandoned, except for some 200,000 civilians of an original population of 1,500,000. Chunshon also was taken with little difficulty. And when the 187th Regimental Combat Team made an airborne drop in an effort to trap Communist troops at Munsan, more than 20 miles north of Seoul on 23 March, the enemy simply withdrew farther north. As a result, the plan of 'Operation Ripper' to inflict heavy casualties on Communist troops failed to achieve that objective. There were few serious engagements, although in one fight between battalions of ROK and PRC troops, the ROK forces killed 230 Chinese without suffering a single casualty of their own. By 31 March 1951, the 8th Army had pushed beyond the 38th Parallel and was ready for the next move—to take the so-called Iron Triangle, a triangular-shaped area formed by lines linking Chorwon and Kumwha at the base and Pyongyang at the apex.

Following the entry of Chinese Communist troops into the Korean War, General MacArthur made a series of public statements which were considered contrary to US foreign policy in the Far East, including recommendations that UN forces should pursue a more aggressive campaign by attacking military bases in Communist China. Both the US Department of State and the UN opposed such a move. The

Left: BAR team of the 179th Infantry, 45th Division, keeps the Communist positions under observation, west of Chorwon, 2 January 1952.

Below: The 6th Tank Battalion gives fire support to the 19th RCT (24th Infantry Division), 10 January 1952.

controversy came to a dramatic conclusion when, on 11 April 1951, President Truman exercised his prerogative as Commander in Chief by relieving General MacArthur of his combined command of United Nations and United States forces in the Far East. The basis for dismissing General MacArthur was a charge that he had ignored presidential orders made on 6 December 1950 to clear public statements on national policy through the State Department. Particularly troublesome was a letter to Republican Congressman Joseph Martin which was read into the Congressional Record on 5 April. In it MacArthur expressed his dissatisfaction with Washington caveats against violating the Chinese Communist sanctuary beyond the Yalu River. MacArthur had also recommended aid to Chiang Kai-shek in invading the Peoples Republic of China from his Taiwan bastion; suggested that if the USSR wanted to risk war there was no better time for the US; and had demanded that the Chinese Communist military leader in Korea surrender or face possible naval and air attacks against the Chinese mainland.

Washington's reasons for not adopting General MacArthur's recommendations were many and included: (1) a 'gentleman's agreement' with China that if the US did not attack bases in Manchuria, the Communists would not attack US bases in Japan and South Korea;

(2) it would be useless to bomb transportation facilities in Manchuria unless US forces also destroyed the USSR's Trans-Siberian Railway, by which Chinese Communist equipment reached Manchuria; (3) a US naval blockade of the China coast would not be effective unless it could be extended to Soviet ports of Darien and Port Arthur and the British Crown Colony of Hong Kong, points through which China could still conduct trade with the outside world; and (4) the US could not support an invasion of mainland China by Chiang Kai-shek's troops based in Taiwan, an invasion that would probably fail even with US logistical support.

Thus, MacArthur's proposals went far beyond the Truman Administration's policy of merely trying to restore the status quo of South Korea. Also, Washington's attitude that Europe's welfare had priority over that of Asia was directly contrary to MacArthur's concept that Western Europe was 'relatively unimportant.' With MacArthur's dismissal, General Ridgway was summoned to Tokyo as his replacement, and Lieutenant General James A Van Fleet was rushed from the United States to take command of the 8th Army.

The Communist 1951 Spring Offensive began with a night attack 22 April on a ROK 6th Division position at one of the reservoirs near the center of the UN perimeter. The ROK forces fell back in confusion as the bugle-

Right: MacArthur and his wife leave Tokyo airport to return to the USA after he had been dismissed by President Truman in an important assertion of the rule that the government and not the military should decide the nation's policy.

Below: A scout from the 2nd Infantry Division and a South Korean soldier who had accompanied him on patrol receive aid after being wounded, near Kumhwa, 14 February 1952.

blowing and grenade-hurling Chinese broke through their lines, exposing the flanks of the US 24th Division on the left and the US 1st Marine Division on the right. General Van Fleet ordered a pullback to one of the prepared phase lines while other troops were moved into the gap left by the retreating South Korean soldiers. The maneuver foiled the Communist forces in their attempt to divide and encircle the US troops.

On 26 April, Chinese troops cut a main highway linking Seoul on the western side of Korea with Kansong on the east coast. UN forces then fell back to the Hangchon River, a tributary of the Han River. The Chinese mounted another attack in an attempt to retake Seoul, but General Van Fleet established a new defense line just north of Seoul and the Han River. On 29 April, the Chinese made two attempts to cross the Han River and outflank the UN forces. Both attempts failed. In one effort, 6000 of the Communist forces boarded small boats at a point on the Han west of Seoul. They were strafed by UN planes and the few who survived the attack were mowed down by troops of the 5th ROK Marine Battalion. The second attempt, east of Seoul, was stopped by units of the US 24th and 25th Divisions.

General Van Fleet made greater use of air power and artillery, partly because aircraft and big guns were in better supply than during the first months of the war. During the last week of April 1951, UN fliers averaged nearly 100 missions a day against the Communist forces while the 8th Army's IX Corps fired 15,000 artillery rounds at the Chinese in the first three days of their April 1951 offensive.

April 1951 also was a turning point in aerial combat history for it marked the first jet fighter dogfights. The US F-80 Shooting Stars had been flown from Japan originally to eliminate the Russian fighter aircraft YAK-9s supplied by Russia and to harass North Korean ground forces. While escorting B-29 bombers on runs to the Yalu River, the F-80s encountered resistance from Soviet MiG-15s, with Chinese pilots. The MiG-15s were superior in performance not only to the F-80s but in some ways to the later model US jet fighters, the F-84 Thunderjets and F-86 Sabres. But the UN pilots with better training and more experience demonstrated an upper hand in air-to-air combat, averaging 13 MiG-15 kills for every US jet lost. The UN lost nearly 10 times as many planes to antiaircraft fire as to MiG fighters. Because they sometimes flew as low as 30 feet above the ground in attacking Communist troops, UN planes were often the targets of sticks and stones thrown by enemy soldiers. Many UN jets returned to their bases with damage caused by explosions of their targets, holes produced by their own shells ricocheting, or fuselage rips and tears caused by accidentally flying into wires.

The Communist Spring Offensive lost momentum after the failure to cross the Han. The North Korean and Chinese troop losses were set at 70,000, compared to about 7000 UN casualties. The Communist troops withdrew beyond UN artillery range on 30 April.

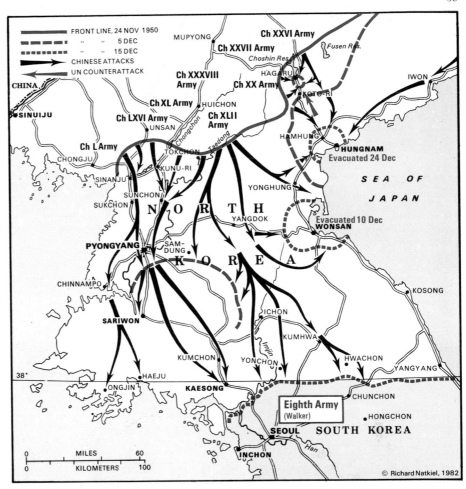

Above: The Chinese advance toward Seoul.

Renewed Offensives Stalemate as an Uneasy Peace is Reached

General Van Fleet attempted to move the 8th Army northward when the Communist attack ended. Tank patrols were able to advance about 12 miles before encountering stiff enemy resistance. At the same time, around 10 May, intelligence reports indicated a large Communist buildup of troops and equipment despite attacks by UN aircraft deep into North Korean territory. To meet the second phase of the Spring Offensive, General Van Fleet ordered 500 miles of barbed wire strung across his lines, plus land mines supplemented by drums of gasoline and napalm that could be ignited by remote controls. The new attack started on the night of 15 May 1951 as 30 divisions of Chinese and North Korean troops drove toward the center of the UN perimeter, an area defended

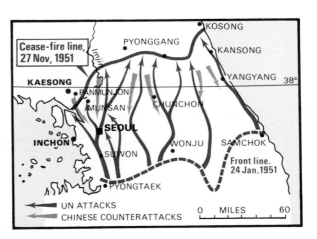

Left: The final important movements of the war. Fierce fighting continued at times until the ceasefire in 1953 with both sides angling for an advantage to bring to the peace talks but there was little major change to the front.

Above: President-elect Dwight D Eisenhower during his visit to Korea in 1952.

was cut until US infantry units assisted by French and Dutch battalions counterattacked and restored the vital link.

After three days of battle, the 2nd Division withdrew to a line five miles to the south. The 2nd Division had suffered 900 casualties in the battle, but Chinese and North Korean forces had lost an estimated 35,000. Total Communist losses in the second phase of their offensive increased to an estimated 90,000 before it was halted on 20 May 1951.

While the Communist forces were over-extended, their supplies nearly exhausted and under almost constant strafing and bombing by UN aircraft, General Van Fleet launched a counteroffensive on 20 May. By 31 May, the UN forces had advanced as far as Kansong on the east coast, Munsan on the west, and the Hwachon Reservoir in the center of the line. By 11 June, the UN troops had taken both towns at the base of the Iron Triangle, Chorwon and Kumhwa, and were advancing toward the apex at Pyongyang. But Communist troops resisted the advance from high ground near Pyongyang and the UN tanks and infantry withdrew.

On 25 June 1951, the first anniversary of the original North Korean attack, General Ridgway was advised that Soviet Ambassador Jacob Malik, the USSR delegate to the United Nations, had called for an armistice between the two sides. The move was approved by representatives of the Peoples Republic of China. On 30 June, General Ridgway made a radio broadcast directed to Peiping's military leaders with an offer to send representatives to a mutually satisfactory location to discuss a cease-fire. Vice-Admiral C Turner Joy was named to head the United Nations delegation while Lieutenant General Nam Il of the North Korean Peoples Army represented the Communist forces at the first meeting held at

by the US X Corps and ROK III Corps. In the second day of fighting, ROK positions were overrun and Communist troops poured through the gap as US units were shifted to close the hole. In the fierce fighting, one UN field artillery battalion fired 10,000 rounds of 105-mm shells at the Communists. Units of the US 2nd Division became trapped with Chinese and North Korean troops attacking them from all sides. The main supply route of the 2nd Division

Kaesong, near the 38th Parallel, in early July 1951.

One of the first matters agreed upon by both sides was that hostilities should be allowed to continue during peace negotiations. It soon became apparent that the Communist forces wanted time to recover from their 1951 losses. The meetings, which continued until late August, were marked by trivial arguments and propaganda statements. The Communists and United Nation units both used the period to improve their positions and fight minor skirmishes for high ground or other key military objectives.

Summer fighting in Korea had difficulties that could match those of winter combat on the peninsula. US soldiers, stripped to the waist for comfort on a sunny hillside, would suddenly find themselves trapped by downpours that could wash out a supply road. Battles, some lasting several days, were fought over sites known as Hill 1179, Bloody Ridge, Heartbreak Ridge, or the Punch Bowl, which was the rim of an extinct volcano crater between the Iron Triangle and the Sea of Japan. The Communist troops now built long tunnels through the hills with camouflaged entrances. Some of the tunnels had entrances on either side of a hill, enabling the troops to withdraw from heavy bombardment on the side facing UN troops and surface on the other side of the hill.

After the first round of cease-fire talks had broken off, General Van Fleet began a series of drives to force the Communist troops back from the Seoul-Chorwon rail line, the Hwachon Reservoir, and part of the Iron Triangle. The advance was followed by a Communist request to resume negotiations for a ceasefire. A new site for talks was established at Panmunjon, between the lines of the opposing forces. The new round of discussions began 12 November 1951. On 23 November, both sides agreed to a ceasefire along a demarcation line that would be considered permanent if a full armistice agreement was not reached by the end of 1951.

While negotiations continued at Panmunjon through 1952, the Korean War settled into a trench warfare stalemate similar to the condition that developed in Europe after the first year of World War I. Minor raids and skirmishes were fought from bunkers along the demarcation line. The Communists continued to build up forces north of the demarcation line and at one time had 800,000 troops stationed in North Korea, most of them Chinese. They also acquired the latest in Soviet ground-weapons, including radar-controlled antiaircraft guns.

The repatriation of prisoners became a point of dispute during the Panmunjon negotiations. Washington officials had promised that no Communist prisoner of war would be forced against his will to be returned to his country of origin. Every prisoner would be screened to determine how many wanted to be returned or wanted asylum. The Communist negotiators insisted on total return of the nearly 170,000 POWs held, but 50,000 of the prisoners rejected repatriation. The screening seemed to harm the political position of the Communist negotiators and led to demonstrations by some Communist prisoners in the POW camps in South Korea. In one incident, Communist prisoners attacked members of the US 27th Infantry Regiment sent to maintain order during the screening. One US soldier and several Communist prisoners were killed in the riot and more than 100 were injured.

In a related event on 7 May 1952 on the island of Koje, a prison camp in the Sea of Japan where 80,000 Communist POWs were held, a group of prisoners requested a meeting with Brigadier General Francis T Dodd to discuss grievances. The request was a ruse used to take General Dodd hostage. The POWs threatened to kill Dodd unless their demands were met. The demands included not only a cessation of screening and asylum for prisoners who did not want to be returned to Communist control but an agreement by UN leaders to cease the use of a variety of alleged atrocities that included the

Below: The battleship *Iowa* off the Korean coast. Among the rearmament measures which were taken after the outbreak of the Korean War was the recommissioning of a number of battleships including three of the *Iowa* class which had been taken out of service.

use of poison gas, germ warfare, and atom bomb experiments. The uprising at the Koje POW camp delayed the transfer of General Ridgway, who had been appointed Commander of the North Atlantic Treaty Organization, and General Mark Clark, his successor. General Dwight Eisenhower had resigned the NATO command to seek the Republican nomination for president of the US.

In order to free General Dodd from the POW captors, Brigadier General Charles Colson agreed to 'correct' alleged abuses. General Dodd was released on 11 May 1952, four days after the siege began. When the POW demands were exposed as part of a Communist propaganda campaign manipulated from North Korea to support their negotiations in Panmunjon, General Clark ordered Brigadier General Haydon L Boatner to Koje Island on 12 May to take control of the Communist POW situation.

There were further POW disorders, including an uprising 10 June when the Communist prisoners dug trenches and made Molotov cocktails from stove gasoline for use against General Boatner's men. The UN prison command was reinforced with troops from the 187th Airborne Combat team. In the ensuing 90-minute battle, 150 Communist prisoners were killed or wounded while US casualties included one killed and 13 wounded. An attempted mass escape from a second POW camp, at Pongnam, in December 1952, ended with 185 Communists killed or wounded.

Events that seemed to propel the Korean War to a conclusion included the election of General Eisenhower as President of the US in November 1952, and the death of Joseph Stalin on 5 March 1953. Although the USSR did not commit troops to the fighting in Korea, some Communist soldiers had identified themselves as 'honorable fighters of the Great Stalin.' The loss of Stalin and the election of a military hero by the American people resulted in visible unrest in the Communist world. A request was made by General Peng Teh-huai of the Chinese 'volunteer army' and North Korean Premier Kim Il Sung for resumption of the armistice negotiations at Panmunjon.

The Communist representatives announced they would accept an earlier offer to exchange sick and wounded POWs at a meeting on 28 March 1953. This action led to the release of 684 UN personnel, including 149 Americans, by the Communists and 5800 Communist POWs by the UN in an 11 April exchange called 'Little Switch.' But movement toward an armistice was again delayed after the prisoner exchange by objections from South Korean President Syngman Rhee to a division of Korea, and the decision by leaders of the Communist forces to score a great propaganda victory by ending the war with a defeat of the United Nations forces.

In early 1953, the Communists had built up their forces to a total of nearly one million, including seven Chinese armies and two North Korean corps massed along the barbed wire and mine fields of the UN line. There were 11 more Chinese armies and one North Korean corps in reserve. Ground forces on the UN side numbered nearly 800,000, including 12 South

Korean Divisions and eight divisions of troops from the US and other UN member nations. In an initial attack, Chinese troops drove through their own mortar and artillery fire against a Turkish brigade. The two-day battle ended with more than 3200 Chinese and 575 Turkish soldiers killed or wounded. On 10 June 1953, the Chinese began their greatest offensive against the UN forces since the April 1951 campaign. The fighting raged back and forth across the Iron Triangle and Punch Bowl areas until mid-July at a cost of 70,000 Communist casualties.

On 19 July 1953, a final armistice agreement was reached at Panmunjon and a *de facto* boundary was worked out along the existing battle lines. The boundaries outlined the area that would become the DMZ, or demilitarized zone. On 27 July 1953, Lieutenant General William K Harrison, Jr, and General Nam Il signed the armistice agreement. The shooting ceased at 10 pm, 12 hours after the signing. The agreement was technically a truce that was mutually beneficial. Neither side surrendered and neither side won the war. But after more than 37 months of fighting, both the United States and the Peoples Republic of China, the major non-Korean combatants, had realized that the alternative to a truce was an expansion of the war which could eventually involve attacks on their own soil.

The Korean War was unique in military history in that it was an action authorized by an international organization, the United Nations. Although a total of 17 member nations contributed troops for fighting the Communist armies, 90 percent of the frontline soldiers were supplied by the Republic of Korea (ROK) and the United States. The ROK and the US forces also sustained most of the casualties.

For a 'limited war,' the Korean War cost more than six million dead and wounded, about half of them South Korean civilians. On the Communist side, approximately 900,000 Chinese and 520,000 North Korean soldiers were killed or wounded. An additional 120,000 were taken prisoner. ROK casualty figures include 415,000 killed, 429,000 wounded, and 460,000 missing. US total casualties were 157,530, with 54,246 killed, 103,284 wounded, 760 missing, and 5133 prisoners. Total casualties among the other participants on the United Nations side were 17,260, of which the United Kingdom suffered 5017, Turkey 3349, Australia 1591, Canada 1396, and France 1135 dead, wounded or missing.

The Korean War was the first major conflict of the nuclear age. While no atomic bombs were used, there was always a threat that expansion of the fighting to areas beyond the Korean peninsula would inevitably lead to World War III and a nuclear holocaust. Except for the learned experience that large ground forces with light weapons can balance the superiority of the fire power of modern mechanized armies in rugged terrain, the war accomplished very little. North Korea was still north of the 38th Parallel and South Korea was still south of the boundary. The political ideologies of the opposing nations were unchanged. More than 30

Above: President-elect Eisenhower eats chow with men of the 15th Infantry Regiment. Lieutenant General Reuben Jenkins, commander of X Corps, in the background, checks up on everyone's table manners.

Above right: Meetings of the Korean Armistice Commissions continue to the present day.

years later, armed forces of the two sides would still face each other across the DMZ. And the United States had made only a slight change in its Pacific Defense Perimeter—to include South Korea within a line extending from the Ryukus to the Philippine Islands.

Combat innovations of the Korean War included not only the first jet fighter dogfights in April 1951, but the introduction of eight-pound body armor jackets, and helicopter use for airlifting troops and cargo. The first integration of black soldiers into previous all-white military units also occurred during the war.

Body armor had been available for US soldiers since the Civil War when heavy steel breast plates were produced for members of the Union Army. The development of plastic materials in the 1940s led to the invention of a sleeveless lightweight body armor made of multiple layers of glass fiber and nylon. When used by US troops in Korea, the plastic jackets reduced fatal chest and abdominal wound cases by 70 percent.

The US Marines were credited with 'discovering' the helicopter as a combat vehicle in the early weeks of the Korean War. Troops of the 1st Marine Division exploited the versatility of helicopters by using them in August 1950 for observation, rescue, casualty evacuation, liaison, and even such mundane chores as laying communication wires. As the war progressed, the Army, Navy and Air Force added helicopters to their equipment arsenals.

The first integration of whites and blacks in the US Army was started during the summer of 1952, following discussions by General Ridgway in Tokyo and General Maxwell Taylor, the Assistant Chief of Staff in Washington, on methods of improving the *esprit de corps* of US troops in Korea. The process began with the breaking up of all-black combat units in the 9th, 15th, and 24th infantry regiments, and assignment of those troops to all-white military units. The same procedure was followed by

integrating soldiers from all-black artillery and armored supply units in Korea.

US military doctrine was changed only slightly during the Korean War. Perhaps the most important tactical innovation was the 'fight-and-roll' method introduced during the large-scale mass attacks by the Chinese Communist forces during their 1951 offensive. Using the fight-and-roll technique, based on the premise that an inflexible defense line had little or no effect against a mass attack, the defending troops remained in their positions until the enemy had paid the maximum price—but before the defenders were engulfed. The defenders then conducted an orderly but rapid withdrawal to a defensive position. The defenders might have to fall back, but eventually the attackers would lose momentum.

At critical times during fight-and-roll action, counterattacks would be launched with massive concentrations of artillery fire. In Korea, as many as 14 artillery battalions were used, each firing five volleys per minute. In one battle in Korea, the 38th Field Artillery Battalion averaged nearly 1000 rounds of 105-mm shells per hour for 12 hours. Additional firepower came from tanks kept behind the crest of a hill and moved forward to prepared positions when a target appeared. Armored personnel carriers also gained a more important role, being used to move supplies and reinforcements.

However, the official position of the US Defense Department at the end of the Korean War was that no real changes in doctrine had resulted from the experiences along the 38th Parallel. An Army Field Services bulletin prepared after the Korean War was originally titled 'Lessons Learned.' The army changed the title to 'Training Bulletin' and explained that the fighting in Korea had provided 'few items' that could be described as 'lessons learned.' A 1954 study of the US Army infantry school suggested that a more appropriate title would have been 'Lessons *Relearned* In Korea.'

RESTIVE STRAINS OF THE INTERWAR PERIOD

Before his death in 1965 Winston Churchill said of the Korean War that 'its importance lies in the fact it led to the rearming of America.' The Korean War also led to the rearming of Western Europe and an abrupt termination in efforts to ease tensions by negotiating disarmament treaties. The Eisenhower Doctrine of the 1950s would replace the Truman Doctrine of the 1940s with generous military and economic commitments to nations seeking protection from possible encroachments of international Communism.

As self-appointed peace-keeper of the world, an idealistic America had introduced the Marshall Plan in 1947; its premise was that international tensions were caused by poverty, a symptom that could be remedied with US financial aid. When the Soviet Union announced its development of an atom bomb, America modified its policy of 'nuclear deterrence' to one of 'massive retaliation,' suggesting that the US could always outproduce a potential enemy with more and better nuclear weapons. The one-weapon military doctrine was the subject of debates that embroiled political and military leaders for much of the decade between the Korean and Vietnam Wars.

The foreign aid programs of the Truman Administration were not undertaken easily. They required a continuation of wartime federal tax levels in order to shore up the faltering economies of other countries. Meanwhile, the USSR and her family of satellite neighbors shunned the Marshall Plan, charging it was a 'capitalist plot' to undermine Communism—which was at least partly true. Washington planners feared that European countries would prefer Communism to poverty.

In addition to the cost of supporting the economies of other nations, America's own peacetime military budget suffered from inflation. Between the end of World War II and 1950, the price of equipping an infantry division had risen from $19 million to $91 million. For an armored division, according to US Defense Department reports, the cost had jumped in five years from $40 million to $293 million. The heavy antiaircraft gun needed in 1945 cost $160,000; the bill for a replacement was $250,000. And the price for a jet bomber was $8 million per plane, compared to a mere $600,000 for a propeller-driven B-29. Thus, economic reasons alone favored a reduction in international tensions and a desire by some to believe that US-USSR differences were simply a matter of interpretation of the various agreements made at Teheran, Yalta, Moscow, and Potsdam.

International Peacetime Alliances and Treaties

Because England and France were apprehensive about a resurgence of German military power, as occurred after the end of World War I, they signed a defense treaty in March 1947. The 50-year Anglo-French agreement became known as the Dunkirk Treaty of Alliance. Two years later, on 19 March 1949, the Dunkirk Treaty was extended to include Belgium, the

Netherlands, and Luxembourg. Because the new pact was signed in Brussels, it was called the Brussels Treaty. The signatory powers were identified as the 'Western Union.'

A next step occurred as a result of a US Senate resolution, approved on 11 June 1948, authorizing the United States to enter into 'regional and collective arrangements' with other nations for 'effective self-help and mutual aid.' On 8 April 1949, the 'Western Union' met in Washington with representatives of the United States, Canada, Italy, Portugal, Norway, Denmark and Iceland to sign a document that came to be called the North Atlantic Treaty. The US Senate approved America's participation in the North Atlantic Treaty Organization (NATO) on 21 July 1949. And on 20 December 1949, members of the Brussels Treaty powers approved a merger of its military arrangements with those of NATO.

Like the earlier Dunkirk and Brussels Treaties, the North Atlantic Treaty was not specifically directed toward Communism or the Soviet Union. The stated purpose of the treaty was the preservation of peace and a willingness to provide for the security of the other signatory nations. However, the treaty carried an implied warning that a military attack on one member of NATO would be considered an attack on all. It also implied that the protection was extended beyond the homelands of the signatory powers to include the British, French, and US military garrisons in Berlin.

The North Atlantic Treaty was unique in several ways. For the United States, it was the first peacetime commitment to a military alliance. Each of the signatory powers was given the right to veto actions of other members in NATO matters. No member, however, was required to supply any particular military unit, nor required to participate militarily. Nevertheless, the formation of NATO had a sobering effect on USSR attitudes in Germany. The

Previous page: M48 tanks move on to the beach to reinforce the units committed to Lebanon, 6 August 1958.

Right: French troops halt in a Vietnamese village during a sweep against Communist forces in January 1953. The progress of the Communists in Vietnam inspired considerable but eventually unavailing US aid to the French.

Below: Presidential candidate General Eisenhower and his running mate Richard Nixon acknowledge the cheers of the Republican Convention in 1956. Nixon was Eisenhower's vice-president in both terms.

REPUBLICAN NATIONAL CO

Berlin Blockade was lifted shortly after the creation of NATO even though Soviet Deputy Premier Viacheslav Molotov warned at a Prague meeting of East European nations that Russia would not tolerate participation by West Germany in NATO activities, a warning ignored by the NATO members.

Despite the apparent ease of organizing NATO, the organization existed as a paper tiger for several years and had no practical reality. Ratification was delayed by some member countries because of internal considerations. The US Congress wanted assurance that it was not surrendering its right to declare war. France wanted the treaty to cover Algeria, which was facing a rebellion. There was a question of the term 'North Atlantic' if Italy, and later Greece and Turkey, joined the pact. The North Atlantic region was generally considered to be Europe and 'ships and islands north of the Tropic of Cancer,' which in effect could also have excluded Canada and the United States, and such US interests as Puerto Rico and the Virgin Islands.

An immediate effect in Europe of the Korean War was a change in attitude about West German participation in NATO. The 'easy solution' to East-West tensions—that the USSR would behave impeccably if left alone—died with Soviet support of the North Koreans. West German Chancellor Konrad Adenauer was among European leaders who were convinced that the Korean War was a Kremlin-orchestrated diversion to conceal a planned massive push by the USSR into his country. Adenauer offered to raise a German defense

force of 150,000 to prevent what he described as a possible 'Korean-type aggression by Soviet-zone police.' France, which had opposed US recommendations to train German units within NATO member divisions, announced that since Germany 'benefits from the security of NATO, it should participate.' On 19 December 1950, NATO members agreed to rearm West Germany and accept the US proposal to in-

Below: Eisenhower and retiring President Truman in conversation in November 1952, just after Ike's election.

Above: John Foster Dulles in August 1954. As Secretary of State Dulles was the moving force behind the policy of 'massive retaliation' which threatened that aggression by the Soviet Union on even the smallest scale might be met by an all-out US response.

Tough-talking President Truman, meanwhile, used his 1951 State of the Union address to Congress to warn Russia that the US was 'preparing for full wartime mobilization, if necessary.' US military strength would be more than doubled to a budgeted 3,500,000 officers and men in 1951 and US factories would be asked to produce 50,000 aircraft and 35,000 tanks annually. (America's peak output of warplanes in World War II was 96,000 a year and the auto industry produced 49,000 tanks plus 156,000 gun-carriages and related battle vehicles a year.) Nor were tensions relaxed when NATO commander Eisenhower appeared 1 February 1951 before members of the US Senate and declared he would use nuclear weapons 'instantly' in a war if he thought the 'net advantage of their use was on my side.'

On 27 April 1951, NATO events advanced with the signing of an agreement between the United States and Denmark for US use of bases in Greenland for the duration of the North Atlantic Treaty. Eleven days later, on 7 May 1951, the US sent the first contingent of 200 troops to Iceland under terms of the treaty. An advance force of 5000 men of the US Army 4th Division embarked from New York on 24 May 1951 to become the first American troops committed to NATO. They were followed a month later by the US Army 2nd Armored Division. Meanwhile, the US Air Force dispatched two fighter-bomber wings and one troop carrier wing to Germany, and four wings—one each of F-84 Thunderjets, F-86 Sabrejets and B-29 and B-50 bombers—to England.

tegrate German combat teams of 6000 to 8000 men into divisions of member nations.

General Dwight Eisenhower, who had become president of Columbia University in New York City after World War II, was called back into uniform to serve as commander in chief of NATO. Eisenhower left Washington 6 January 1951 for Europe and a meeting with British Field Marshal Viscount Montgomery, Commander of the Brussels Treaty forces. Montgomery was named Deputy Supreme Allied Commander Europe for NATO. Although President Truman assured Eisenhower when he left for Europe that he had the 'wholehearted backing of the American people' in the NATO venture, he didn't. Congressional debate over US participation in NATO raged for months, but Congress finally approved the treaty although limiting the US contribution to NATO to four divisions.

On 23 July 1951, General Eisenhower formally opened his SHAPE (Supreme Headquarters, Allied Powers Europe) offices at Marly, 15 miles west of Paris, and appointed French Vice-Admiral André Lemonnier as deputy commander for NATO naval forces. With Eisenhower ensconced in his command post, the US extended its NATO commitments with an agreement covering military use of bases in the Azores, which were already included in the NATO protective umbrella. Negotiations also were begun with the Franco government in Spain, over the objections of other NATO members because of Franco's ties with the Axis powers during the Spanish Civil War of the 1930s. That dispute was resolved when Portugal extended its own commitment to include Spain in an Iberian Peninsula 'defense unity.'

The summer of 1951 also saw America extend its interests through the Mediterranean to the Middle East. During July, the US negotiated an agreement with Saudi Arabia in which the US was allowed to station military aircraft at Dhahran while the oil-rich Arab nation in return was allowed to purchase US military equipment. The US also secured rights to six air bases in French Morocco and began to woo Yugoslavia away from the USSR hegemony while convincing other NATO members to admit Greece and Turkey to the pact. By November 1951, Belgrade was receiving US military aid for use in frontier skirmishes with its Soviet-supplied neighbors.

While America was showing its flag in the Mediterranean and Middle East, NATO flexed

its muscles in West Germany by staging eight days of maneuvers with 160,000 troops in a mock campaign to drive a theoretical invader from West German soil. The NATO troops displayed for the first time the SHAPE flag and shoulder patches featuring two arched swords against a background of golden leaves and the motto *Vigilia Pretium Libertatis* ('Vigilance is the price of liberty'). On 20 October 1951, the US 43rd National Guard Division arrived to augment America's contributions to NATO forces. It was the first time in American history that a US National Guard division was assigned to overseas duty during peacetime.

In a congressional resolution signed by President Truman, the state of war between the United States and Germany was formally ended on 24 October 1951. The document was not a peace treaty and was worded so it would not alter the right of the US to station occupation

Above: Eisenhower in talks with General Paul Ely, Chairman of the French Chiefs of Staff and Admiral Arthur Radford, Chairman of the American Joint Chiefs.

Below: The USS *Tunny* off Point Mugu, California, with a Regulus I guided missile in the launching position on the foredeck. The photograph was taken in August 1954.

forces in Germany. But the status of Germany had changed since America's declaration of war on 11 December 1941, and an interim 'peace contract' would be negotiated with West Germany until the matter of eventual reunification of the two Germanies could be accomplished.

Cold War border incidents continued through 1951, including the seizure on 18 October 1951 of the village of Steinstuecken in the US sector of Berlin by the East German People's Police. East German Communists explained that Steinstuecken was 'historically' a part of the Brandenburg Province in the Soviet zone. The three-mile square suburb and its 194 residents were returned to American control after US Major General Lemuel Matthewson threatened reprisals. On 19 November 1951, Soviet fighter planes intercepted a US C-47 plane on a courier mission to the US Embassy in Belgrade and forced it to land in Hungary. Hungary charged the plane had violated that nation's air space, confiscated the plane and levied 'fines' totaling $123,605.15 against the four captured USAF fliers. The Truman administra-

tion paid the fines for the release of the Americans while members of Congress demanded retaliation.

The US continued to talk tough through ominous-appearing press statements about development of an atomic-powered warplane capable of circling the globe 80 times at 2500 mph speeds without landing to refuel; the development of jet-powered robot bombers with speeds of 1000 mph; an announcement that all four-engined commercial aircraft in the US had been placed on a standby mobilization alert for transfer to the Military Air Transport Service on 48 hours notice; and display of a prototype model of the new eight-jet B-52 Strategic Air Command bomber. The US Defense Department also revealed its development of a 280-mm howitzer designed to fire shells with nuclear warheads, and progress in the manufacture of atomic-powered engines for submarines. Because the various examples of American preparedness had no immediate practical value in the event of a sudden Soviet attack, the various announcements were viewed at home and

Right: Vice-President Nixon formally opens the American section of an international exhibition in Moscow, 24 July 1959. Nixon and Soviet leader Nikita Khrushchev, standing to Nixon's right, were soon involved in the famous 'kitchen debate' as to whether standards of living were higher in the US or USSR.

Below: Loading an Honest John nuclear artillery weapon on to its launch platform during training in West Germany in 1957.

abroad as futile public relations gestures. While the US did eventually produce a fleet of B-52 bombers, nuclear-powered submarines, and radar-guided missiles; commercial airliners were not commandeered for use as military transports and atomic-powered airplanes never went beyond the drawing-board stage.

Demands of the Korean War and the NATO buildup resulted in an increase in US military manpower from 2,400,000 in 1951 to 3,475,000 in early 1952. Defense Department figures showed a growth from 1,100,000 to 1,600,000 for the Army, 590,000 to 810,000 for the Navy, 540,000 to 850,000 for the Air Force, and 170,000 to 210,000 for the Marines. Nevertheless, US Army Chief of Staff Lawton Collins revealed that the continental United States had been stripped of all regular army infantry divisions. Eight army divisions were in Korea or Japan and five were in Europe. Collins said the US mainland was being protected by four National Guard divisions plus two airborne and one armored division of the regular army. Because of the military manpower crisis, Collins asked Congress to extend the period of activation of National Guard units. Defense Secretary Robert Lovett disclosed at the same time that the United States was running several years behind the Soviet Union in the production of new military equipment because the USSR

'never let down' in arms manufacture when World War II ended. And General Alfred Gruenther, Chief of Staff to SHAPE, said NATO still lacked the 'necessary forces to stop a determined Soviet attack.'

On 28 April 1952, the peace treaty between the US and Japan became effective with the simultaneous start of a US-Japan mutual security agreement. Supreme Headquarters, Allied Occupation Forces, Japan changed its name to Headquarters, Far East Command. The USSR declared the American action was illegal and that it would continue to maintain an 'occupation mission' in Japan indefinitely. General Mark Clark became Far East Commander effective with the end of the official US occupation of Japan, replacing General Ridgway who left Tokyo to succeed General Eisenhower as NATO commander. Eisenhower announced his resignation effective 1 June 1952 to become a candidate for the Republican nomination for President. On 30 April 1952, Eisenhower conducted a 'farewell review' of US troops in Germany and reported 'everything is up' in the condition of the American forces in NATO.

Steps to solidify the NATO alliance were taken 26 May 1952 when the US, Great Britain and France signed a 'peace contract' with the Bonn government. Like the US-Japan peace

treaty, the contract was accompanied by an agreement between former World War II enemies—in this case, between West Germany and members of the Brussels Treaty powers—to form a new defense alliance. The European Defense Community (EDC) in effect created a joint European army. The US Senate ratified America's 'peace contract' with West Germany on 1 July 1952.

The USSR (as they had in the case of the US-Japan treaty) claimed the American agreement with Germany was illegal, and specifically a violation of the Potsdam agreement. However, the USSR reacted with more than words to the US-Germany war settlement. Hundreds of Communist sympathizers from East Germany invaded the US sector of Berlin and fought with the police. The East German police increased its guard of the frontier between East and West Germany, and announced that no travel to or from West Berlin or West Germany would be allowed after 30 May 1952 without special permission. A month later, East Germans were observed building a 500-mile-long barbed wire fence along the 'no man's land' between East and West Germany. Meanwhile, in Berlin, the US increased jeep patrols to curtail kidnappings of prominent West Germans by raiding parties coming across the border from Communist East Berlin.

Challenges Around the World

A sign of things to come for Americans occurred in 1952 when Cuban ex-president Fulgencio Batista staged a 77-minute revolution and overthrew the government of Carlos Prio Socarras. Socarras was allowed to leave for Mexico with his family and several cabinet members. Batista announced he would honor a bilateral military agreement signed with the United States three days before his coup, on 10 March 1952. A month later, on 3 April 1952, the USSR declared it was severing diplomatic relations with Cuba because Batista's customs officers insisted on searching the baggage of Soviet diplomatic couriers. Batista explained the searches were necessary because under the Socarras regime the Russian legation in Havana had become a center of Communist espionage and propaganda activities for Latin America.

The early involvement of the United States in the war against Communist insurgents in Southeast Asia was hardly noticed during the last years of the Truman administration, because of the priority concerns about the Korean War and protection of Europe against possible Soviet aggression. US 1st Fleet Commander Vice-Admiral Arthur D. Struble met 15 May 1951 in Singapore with General Sir John Harding, commander of the British Far Eastern Ground Forces, and General Jean de Lattre de Tassigny, commander of the French forces in Indochina. The meeting was to discuss joint strategy on the defense of Southeast Asia.

The meeting was followed by a French-US meeting in Washington where General de Lattre asked for enough military equipment to arm eight divisions of Vietnamese to fight the Viet Minh guerrillas. President Truman assured the French that he regarded the wars being waged in Korea and Indochina as 'the same fight for liberty.' Brigadier General Francis Brink was named Chief of the US Military Aid Mission to Indochina.

The US State Department issued a statement affirming the Truman position while adding that Indochina was 'a close second' to the Korean War, which would have top priority for American interests. On 24 September 1951, the French carrier *Arromanches* arrived in Indochina waters with American propeller-driven Hellcat fighters and Helldiver light bombers. A week later, the US delivered to the French at Saigon enough Garand rifles to outfit four Vietnam army divisions.

On 9 October 1951, the French commander in Indochina asked the United Nations not to accept a truce with the Chinese Communists in Korea unless there could be a simultaneous settlement of the war in Indochina. France warned that the Peoples Republic of China would shift its military resources to Southeast Asia after reaching a separate peace arrangement in Korea. The request was ignored but the US continued shipping military supplies to Saigon. At the beginning of 1952, the US State Department reported that 100,000 tons of American military equipment had been delivered to the French forces fighting Communist guerrillas in Indochina.

Left: An AJ-1 Savage bomber ready to take off from the carrier *Midway* as another Savage flies past. The Savage was the US Navy's first nuclear-capable attack aircraft.

Above: US Marines peace-keeping in Lebanon, 26 July 1958.

Below: Marine tanks and landing craft during a joint exercise with Turkish forces held in October 1957.

But trouble was brewing elsewhere as well. In January 1952 Winston Churchill returned to the United States on a mission to recruit a 'token force' of United States troops to aid Great Britain in the defense of the Suez Canal. The US had held earlier discussions with Great Britain, France and Turkey about a Middle East Defense Plan but implementation of the plan had been delayed because of other commitments.

Egypt had closed the canal to Israeli shipping on 19 May 1950 during one of the series of Arab-Israeli skirmishes that had been going on intermittently since the 1947 decision of the United Nations to partition Palestine into separate Jewish and Arab states. The action at Suez was coupled with Egyptian determination for independence from British control. Egypt, meanwhile, had indicated it would support a Middle East Defense Plan with the US, Britain and France if the English would first withdraw from the Suez area. The situation boiled over into January 1952 rioting in which tens of thousands of Egyptian nationalists sacked and burned companies operated by or for Americans. Although the US had thus far avoided direct involvement in the Suez controversy, it was gradually drawn into the vacuum caused by the decline of British and French colonialism in the Middle East—as well

as in Southeast Asia. American prestige in the region suffered because of its close ties with the European colonial powers.

America's relations were also affected by its open support of an independent state of Israel, carved from the area of Palestine in 1947. The US action was regarded domestically as an expression of humanitarian goodwill but it was viewed by the Arab world as an example of American hypocrisy and injustice since interests of the Arab world were not given equal consideration. The US involvement in the partition of Palestine also represented a policy departure in that it was not a step taken for purposes of America's national security, whereas Truman Doctrine aid to Greece and Turkey, and US opposition to Soviet moves in Iran were presumably strategic security moves.

With the Egyptian Revolution in July 1952, plans for a Middle East Defense Command linking the US with Great Britain, France, Turkey, Egypt and possible other Arab states were forgotten. The US instead kept its foot in the Middle East door by offering Point IV aid to Egypt, Lebanon, Jordan, Turkey, Iran, Iraq, Israel, Libya and Saudi Arabia, as part of a Mutual Security program. In addition to Point IV—a Truman administration program designed to help Third World countries through investments of $4.5 billion in public and private

funds—the United States made a $40 million economic assistance grant to the new Egyptian government headed by General Mohammed Naguib and Colonel Abdul Nasser. Syria rejected Point IV aid as a new approach to colonialism; and while Egypt was receptive to American financial aid, Nasser revealed that his country was also trading its rice and cotton crops in exchange for Soviet military equipment and supplies.

Below: Matador tactical nuclear missile of the 11th Tactical Missile Squadron during maneuvers at Fort Polk, LA, in 1955. The Matador could carry a 200 kiloton warhead a distance of 650 nautical miles.

The election of Eisenhower as president in 1952 resulted in a few changes in US military doctrine, with increased emphasis on the 'massive retaliation' concept. The stockpiling of tactical nuclear weapons by the United States and Great Britain was accompanied by plans of those countries to reduce their conventional ground forces. Other NATO countries, meanwhile, were expected to continue their buildup of conventional ground forces. When the USSR announced its possession of tactical nuclear weapons, European defense planning became confused and the feeling of security once provided by the US nuclear umbrella was suddenly lost.

The United States agreed to provide tactical nuclear weapons to other NATO members under a 'double key' arrangement, which meant that permission to use the weapons would have to be given by the host country as well as the US. However, Germany protested that it actually had little or no control over nuclear weapons based there under terms of the Washington-Bonn peace contract.

The Republican administration extended the Truman Doctrine by introducing the Eisenhower Doctrine, which offered military and economic assistance to any nation believed to be in danger from Communist-directed invasion or subversion. The new policy was more generous than the Truman Doctrine and was criticized by some observers for making commitments around the world without determining first if those commitments could be honored. The Eisenhower Doctrine promised the contribution of 'armed force' by the United States if requested, yet President Eisenhower also

pushed for cutbacks in federal spending for defense. Draft calls were reduced; 40,000 Defense Department employees were fired; the number of military equipment manufacturing plants was reduced; Navy manpower was cut by 55,000; and the US Air Force budget was trimmed by some $5 billion, all in the first few months of the Eisenhower administration. The Air Force cuts were described by a former AF Secretary Thomas Finletter as a 'reversion to ground soldier thinking' while the USSR was building up its air power and navy strength.

The death of Joseph Stalin on 5 March 1953 was followed by a more conciliatory attitude of the USSR toward the United States. Georgi Malenkov, Stalin's immediate successor, introduced a policy of 'peaceful coexistence' with the western powers. However, Malenkov also demanded in return the acceptance of the Peoples Republic of China as an equal partner with the US, USSR, Great Britain and France in a 'Big Five' power structure and the banning of 'atomic and other arms of mass destruction.'

American foreign policy appeared to be one of vacillation during the first year of the Eisenhower presidency. On April 16, in a speech broadcast worldwide and translated into 45 languages by the Voice of America, President Eisenhower urged that the East European nations be given 'full independence,' and a 'broader European community, conducive to the free movement of persons, of trade and of ideas.' Eisenhower also called for a 'free and united Germany, with a government based upon a free and secret ballot.' Yet when 100,000 East Berliners staged an uprising two months later, rioting and burning buildings, Eisenhower

said the US would not intervene when Soviet and East German troops attacked the demonstrators with tanks, machine guns and automatic weapons. Similar uprisings in Leipzig and Jena were put down by East German Volkspolizei.

The Malenkov reign in the Kremlin was short-lived. War Minister Nikolai Bulganin and Presidium member Nikita Khrushchev rose rapidly in the Soviet hierarchy after the death of Stalin. Malenkov was replaced in 1955 by Bulganin who was in turn replaced in 1958 by Khrushchev as the Soviet premier. During this post-Stalin era, the USSR attitude toward the Western allies appeared to have mellowed. Although the Soviets still hoped for a reunified Germany, the new leaders were willing to accept the fact of a nation divided between the East and the West. Some observers also theorized that the successor to Stalin wanted to put on a friendly face for the benefit of Third World countries that had been reluctant to deal with an aggressive Soviet Union.

On 8 August 1953, Malenkov announced in a speech to the Supreme Soviet that Russia had developed a hydrogen bomb, stating that 'the US has no monopoly in the production of the hydrogen bomb.' Although the US had tested H-bombs at Eniwetok as early as 1952, the first official confirmation had come in President Truman's final State of the Union address in January 1953, when Truman warned Russia against adhering to the Leninist philosophy that a war between Communist and capitalist nations was an inevitable 'stage in the development of a Communist society.' Truman said that Lenin was a 'pre-atomic man' and with

both sides possessing nuclear weapons, a war between the US and USSR 'cannot be a stage in the development of anything save ruin' for the Soviet Union leaders and their homeland.

On September 1953, NATO began a mock 'atomic' military maneuver near Frankfurt, Germany, using 175,000 US, British and French troops in a simulated battle with tactical nuclear weapons. In the exercise, called 'Operation Monte Carlo,' the NATO troops were under the command of US Lieutenant General William Hoge, former US military commander in South Korea. At the same time, 'Operation Weldfast,' involving 100,000 Greek, Italian, Turkish, British and US army, navy and air force personnel conducted a test of NATO defenses in southeastern Europe; and 'Operation Mariner,' the largest peacetime air and sea maneuver ever staged, was held in the North Atlantic with 500,000 men, 1,000 aircraft, and 300 warships. At year's end, NATO members agreed on the design of a new .30 caliber small arms bullet. However, NATO did not have a standard rifle that could use the ammunition.

In the meantime, other once-remote concerns were growing in importance to the US. On 29 December 1953, US Secretary of State John Foster Dulles said the American press had exaggerated the significance of a Communist threat to Indochina. But the fact was that Communist leader Ho Chi Minh's troops had driven a wedge between the southern and northern portions of Indochina at its narrowest part—a 100-mile waist bordered by Thailand

on the west and the Gulf of Tonkin on the east. The Viet Minh guerrillas had surrounded the French garrison at Dien Bien Phu, but the French were hoping to interrupt, using aircraft, the movement of a large Communist supply convoy moving toward Dien Bien Phu. Also, a column of French-Laotian troops was trying to advance from Luangprabang to relieve the Dien Bien Phu garrison. However, France also minimized the importance of the attack and announced plans to cut the size of forces in Indochina from 180,000 to 165,000 in 1954.

The Ho Chi Minh forces overwhelmed the French forces at Dien Bien Phu in 1954, and France withdrew from Indochina after signing an armistice with the Viet Minh on August 11. The French phase of fighting Communist forces in Indochina had lasted seven years. The French High Command estimated its casualties at about 150,000 killed, wounded or missing, compared to 620,000 Viet Minh killed or wounded and 230,000 captured. The US had provided hundreds of millions of dollars in aid to the French— $400 million in 1953 alone—and nearly 100 shiploads of military equipment.

The French-Indochina war eventually affected US military operations both in Europe and in Asia. Beyond America's direct fighting role against Ho Chi Minh's Communist soldiers in Vietnam following the French withdrawal, the French National Assembly revealed that the US had paid nearly 80 percent of the cost of anti-Communist fighting in Indochina. When the French defenses at Dien Bien Phu collapsed

Above: Men of the 2nd Battalion, 2nd Marines march through the dock area of Beirut prior to being evacuated from the city, 13 August 1958.

Below: President Eisenhower visits SHAPE headquarters in September 1959. Eisenhower was the first Supreme Allied Commander at SHAPE. General Norstad, the Supreme Commander in 1959 is at the President's left.

in May 1954, France's own resources were so seriously drained that the country's continued participation in NATO was questioned.

During negotiations for an armistice during the summer of 1954, France was reluctant to be a part of any aggressive NATO activities that might irritate Ho Chi Minh's backers in the Kremlin. Also France was faced with a new colonial war in Algeria. The US turned down a French request to help finance another fight against colonial rebels. Most NATO members faced economic problems. The threat of a war in Europe with the USSR seemed diminished because of a new Soviet peace offensive. There was renewed pressure in the US to take its troops out of Europe. The total impact of those factors threatened the demise of NATO in 1954.

During the final phase of fighting in Indochina, US Marines were alerted for possible action in Vietnam. Part of the 7th Fleet was dispatched to the waters of Southeast Asia but no direct action was taken. At almost the same time, on 17 May 1954, the US State Department reported a 'development of gravity' in Guatemala where a shipload of Soviet military equipment had arrived. That event was hardly surprising to Latin American observers who had been reporting for more than a year such activities in Guatemala as the training of 'Caribbean Legion shock troops,' the expropriation of hundreds of thousands of acres of United Fruit Company lands for distribution to landless peasants, and the arrest of US citizens who protested the dismissal of Guatemalan Supreme Court judges by the government of President Jacabo Arbenz Gusman. On 16 October 1953, US Senate Foreign Relations Chairman Alexander Wiley had charged that 'Communism has established a strong beachhead in Guatemala.'

On 18 June 1954, an insurgent force headed by Colonel Carlos Castillo Armas invaded Guatemala from Honduras. The US and nine other Western Hemisphere governments convened the Council of the Organization of American States to consider the threat to peace and security of the region. With US Marines standing by and the Armas forces supplied with American arms, the existing government was overthrown. Colonel Armas then became the new president. The US offered the new Guatemalan government $6,425,000 in economic aid and in June 1955 signed a military assistance pact with the Armas administration.

Continued Polarization of the Superpowers: a World Rearmed

With the controversial and heavy-handed US involvement in Guatemalan affairs at an apparent conclusion, the US turned its attention back to the Southeast Asia region and met in Manila 8 September with delegates of seven other nations to form a SEATO pact, or Southeast Asia Treaty Organization. The other participants were Australia, Great Britain, France, New Zealand, Pakistan, Thailand, and the Philippines. Taiwan was specifically excluded from SEATO, whose members pledged joint action against aggression to any member country.

With the inclusion of Pakistan in SEATO and Turkey in NATO, the US was beginning to forge a wall along the southern border of the USSR. Secretary of State Dulles spent much of 1954 traveling to various Middle East capitals, filling in a few missing pieces of the wall. In April 1954 Iraq agreed to accept $58,600,000 in military and economic assistance in a treaty

Below: Eisenhower and Soviet leader Khrushchev during a meeting at Camp David.

that was eventually expanded to include Turkey, Pakistan, and Iran and was known as the Baghdad Pact. However, the US failed in repeated efforts to bring Egypt into a Middle East Defense Command. Colonel Nasser attended the Bandung Conference in April 1955 and reportedly was persuaded by Communist China's Chou En-Lai to deal with the Soviet Union. Thus, US efforts to prevent the USSR from establishing a foothold in the Middle East in the 1950s failed. The failure was not entirely due to anti-American antagonism, but in part to a US refusal to supply arms to Egypt unless Egypt agreed to a mutual security pact.

In January 1955, the Eisenhower administration appropriated $216 million in aid to South Vietnam, Cambodia and Laos. Although Taiwan had been excluded from SEATO, the US also pledged a defense of Taiwan and the neighboring Pescadores Islands. A demand by the Peoples Republic of China to withdraw US Navy forces from the Taiwan area was ignored.

On 14 May 1955, the European nations of Poland, Czechoslovakia, Hungary, Albania, Rumania and Bulgaria officially created the Warsaw Pact as a response to NATO. The Peoples Republic of China and the German Democratic Republic (DDR) were present at the ceremonies as observers. The German Democratic Republic was later admitted to the Warsaw Pact, with the USSR declaration that West Germany's participation in NATO had set a precedent. Although the Warsaw Pact was represented as a defensive organization created to counter alleged 'expansionism' of NATO countries, observers noted that the organization was essentially the same as the Soviet satellite forces in existence at the end of World War II, with USSR military officers in key command positions in each of the member nation armies.

In June 1955, the US Congress voted to extend the life of the Selective Service law for an additional four years. Later, authorization was voted to increase the size of the US military reserve from 800,000 to 2,900,000. The US was reported to have accumulated a stockpile of 4000 nuclear weapons, compared to 1000 for the USSR. Secretary of State Dulles announced the adoption by the United States of an official 'massive retaliation' policy, made possible by having the largest number of nuclear weapons.

But 'massive retaliation,' which had been mentioned before by other political leaders, had a less startling effect on the world than Dulles' pronouncement in 1956 of a 'brink of war' policy. The Secretary of State explained the brink of war concept as the 'ability to get to the verge without actually getting into a war.' Dulles was a major influence in the changes in American foreign policy after he was appointed to the Eisenhower Cabinet. While the Truman administration had followed a course of 'containment' of Communism, Dulles sought the 'liberation' of regions already within the Communist world. However, the Dulles 'brinkmanship' was again more a matter of talking tough than acting tough.

In contrast to the US policy expressed by Dulles, Khrushchev declared in his 'de-Stalin-

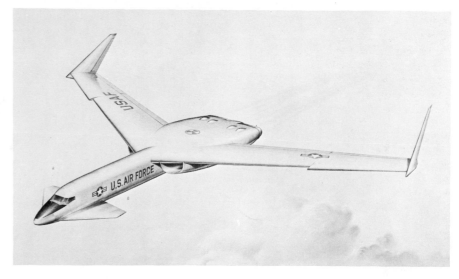

ization' speech at the 20th Communist Party Congress in February 1956 that the struggle between Communism and capitalism could be conducted by economic and political methods and need not include the use of military force. Khrushchev also spoke of 'many different roads to socialism,' apparently hoping to lure Yugoslavia back into the Soviet orbit. The speech had unexpected results for the USSR both in Asia and Eastern Europe.

While the Peoples Republic of China accused Khrushchev of 'deviationism' in abandoning the Stalinist hardline against capitalism, workers in Poland and Hungary began agitating for reforms. The 1956 Polish revolt began 28 June when workers at the Stalin Engineering Works in Poznan went on strike. Hundreds of demonstrators joined the strikers in riots that continued for several days, resulting in the release of political prisoners from jails, burning of military vehicles, and the seizure of a radio station and Communist Party Headquarters. The Soviet leaders threatened to intervene with Soviet troops unless Polish 'democratization' was stopped. Quiet was not restored until 26 October 1956 and with the Gomulka regime in control of Poland.

In Hungary, meanwhile, rioting followed a silent demonstration by 200,000 persons who participated in a memorial service 6 October for four Hungarian leaders executed during the Stalin regime for alleged 'Titoism' and links to US agents. Former Premier Imre Nagy was readmitted to the Hungarian Communist Party and Communist Party leader Erno Gero went to Belgrade to reestablish Hungarian-Yugoslavian relations. On 23 October, students and workers demonstrated openly for the removal of Gero from office and formation of a new government headed by Nagy. The demonstrators also demanded the removal of Soviet troops from Hungary. When Soviet troops tried to quell the rioting, insurrection spread throughout Hungary with thousands of Hungarian army officers and men fighting alongside civilians against Russian tanks, armored cars, artillery, and jet aircraft.

On 28 October 1956, it appeared the rebels had caused a withdrawal of Soviet troops. But on 1 November, USSR troops and tanks advanced on Budapest in force. Premier Nagy

Above: The 1950s and early 60s were a particularly fertile period for the production of far-fetched futuristic designs of military equipment. The illustration shows a General Dynamics proposal for a nuclear powered aircraft dating from 1960.

Right: Davy Crockett tactical atomic weapon system, designed to give heavy firepower to the smallest infantry units, a photograph dating from 1961.

Below: US and Chinese Nationalist forces during joint amphibious maneuvers off Taiwan.

renounced Hungary's Warsaw Pact membership and asked for United Nations protection. As the USSR battered Budapest, the UN and NATO ignored the Nagy plea, despite American promises to 'liberate' the people of Communist-controlled countries. A final teletype message from Hungary on 4 November read: 'All Budapest is under fire. The Russian gangsters have betrayed us.'

As guerrilla warfare and labor strikes continued in Hungary through the rest of November, refugees streamed across the border to Austria at a rate of several thousand per day. Hungarian Communist and USSR troops tried to block the flow of refugees whose numbers soon exceeded a total of 100,000. Although the Eisenhower administration failed to intervene in the crisis, it did mobilize military transport planes to aid the refugees. The US dispatched C-118s and C-121s from bases in the US, England and Germany with bedding for 500, meals for 5000, medical supplies—and even baby diapers and lipstick—for the Hungarian refugees. The mission, dubbed 'Operation Safe Haven,' also provided transportation for 9700 refugees to the United States and other countries willing to accept them. American personnel often worked within the sound of Soviet gunfire at Hungarian-Austrian crossing points.

The timing of the Polish and Hungarian revolts worked to the disadvantage of the United States, which was faced almost simultaneously with the outbreak of hostilities in the Middle East. On 19 July 1956, the US withdrew an offer to help finance the Aswan Dam in Egypt, an action followed by a British cancellation of a $14 million grant and nullification of a $200 million World Bank Loan. Egyptian

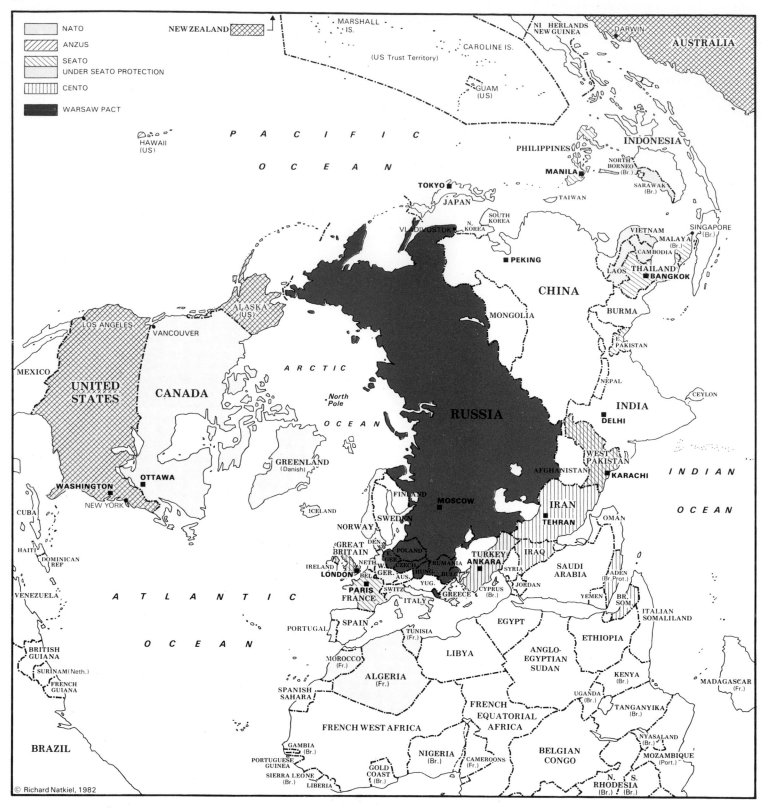

President Nasser reacted by announcing the nationalization of the Suez Canal in order to finance the Aswan Dam project with revenues assessed from ships using the canal.

Nasser's action was followed immediately by a call for a Western Big Three meeting on the Suez crisis, and during the first week in August, French and British forces were deployed to the Mediterranean. Nasser rejected a proposal for international control, as recommended by President Eisenhower on 29 August. Five hundred pilots and other employees quit their jobs on the waterway in September as Egypt took over full control of the canal. When Soviet pilots were hired to replace those who had

quit, the US announced it would not permit them aboard US warships in the Canal.

On 26 October 1956, Arab and Israeli fighting suddenly evolved from border skirmishes into a fullscale war. Israel called for total mobilization with women as well as men ordered into the fighting. Two days later, the US State Department ordered the evacuation of all Americans 'not performing essential functions' in the Middle East and on 2 November ordered a halt to arms shipments to Israel. Tensions increased further when Britain and France issued an ultimatum for Israeli and Egyptian forces to cease fighting and withdraw 10 miles from the Suez Canal Zone.

Above: A map illustrating the various alliances developed by the US during the 1950s in an attempt to confine the spread of Communism. In fact they had rather an unfortunate effect in increasing Soviet fears of Western aggression.

Right: A member of the US Military Assistance Advisory Group supervises a training lecture for Chinese Nationalist troops.

When Egypt rejected the ultimatum, Britain and France attacked Egypt despite protests by the United States. Port Said was captured 7 November 1956 by the British and French paratroopers and amphibious forces. The Soviet Union announced in the United Nations that it was 'prepared to use force to crush the aggressors and restore peace in the Middle East,' and suggested it might send 'volunteers' to the region. President Eisenhower responded by stating the US would oppose any Soviet intervention in the Middle East.

The Suez crisis was cooled through the United Nations. Israel scored an impressive victory in the '100-hours war' by decimating four Egyptian divisions and taking most of the Sinai Peninsula at a cost of 184 Israelis killed or captured. Israel, meanwhile, claimed 1000 Egyptians killed and 6000 captured. Nearly 40,000 Egyptian survivors fled back across the Nile River, abandoning their weapons in retreat.

In the fighting, much of the Suez Canal became blocked by sunken ships and destroyed bridges. The British reported 118 troops killed or wounded. French losses were 44 dead, wounded or missing. The British and French counted 125 Egyptians killed in the battle for Port Said, but Egypt claimed its losses were closer to 3000. President Eisenhower stated on 27 November 1956 that US 'differences' over the Suez Canal had not weakened America's NATO partnership with England and France.

The Eisenhower Doctrine, extending economic and military assistance, including US troops, to any Middle Eastern nation fearing 'overt armed aggression from any other nation controlled by International Communism,' was in full swing in 1957. In April King Hussein of Jordan felt threatened by a freely elected but pro-Nasser government and imposed martial law. Hussein claimed Egypt was behind a 'Communist plot' to annex his country. The United States immediately dispatched its 6th Fleet to 'protect the independence and integrity' of King Hussein with American paratroops. The US also airlifted some $10 million worth of weapons to Jordan.

A second 1957 crisis involving the United States did not materialize. On 29 November 1956, the United States had warned that it would regard 'with the utmost gravity' any threat to members of the Baghdad Pact—Turkey, Iran, Iraq or Pakistan—by the sub-

Below: A Strategic Air Command B-52 bomber launches a Hound Dog Missile. The Hound Dog came into service in 1961 and could carry a four megaton warhead.

stantial shipment of Soviet military equipment to Syria. Turkish troops were reported mobilizing on the Syrian frontier with US military advisers present. Egypt sent a token force of soldiers to Syria, and the Soviet Union threatened the use of nuclear weapons 'if necessary' to prevent US aggression. When no political or military activity happened, it was rumored that the US had lost a round of brinkmanship, but there was never any hard evidence that the Americans actually had planned an attempted overthrow of the pro-Nasser Syrian government.

A more visible US presence in Southeast Asia was observed in early 1957 when American interests appeared threatened by fighting in the Malaya Peninsula area. The carrier USS *Princeton* was dispatched to Sumatra with a US Marine infantry regiment and a squadron of transport helicopters aboard.

Later in 1957, the US military was involved in a domestic crisis as President Eisenhower ordered 1000 US Army troops to Little Rock, Arkansas, to enforce the integration of black and white high school students. In the same month, September 1957, the US began underground testing of nuclear weapons in Nevada to circumvent restrictions on the experimental detonation of nuclear bombs in the atmosphere.

On 4 October 1957, the Soviet Union lobbed its first artificial satellite into space and changed NATO security planning forever. The ability of the USSR rockets to put a Sputnik into orbit around the world was a realistic demonstration that no nation on earth—particularly the United States—was safe from

Soviet weapons. And if the mainland of the United States had become vulnerable to Soviet nuclear warheads, Western Europe was for practical purposes beyond the ability of NATO to defend from a Soviet attack.

America's policy of 'massive retaliation' no longer offered the sense of security it formerly did. Indeed, the reality of Sputnik induced the French to begin dissolving its ties with NATO and to scrap its other hopes for a unified Western Europe. The US itself began to think in terms of defending the continental US against a Soviet attack for the first time, rather than serving in the outfield with weapons that could be used to back up frontline troops some 4000 miles to the east.

In an apparent effort to allay fears of the Western powers, Khrushchev introduced in early 1958 the concept of a 'nuclear-free zone' in Europe. The zone would have extended from the Baltic through Germany, and the Balkans to the Mediterranean. US diplomats expressed interest in the plan initially but then rejected the Soviet plan when analysis of the details showed it would weaken NATO and actually move the frontier westward to the French border.

By playing catch-up, the US was able to launch its own artificial satellite, *Explorer I*, within a few months. On 3 January 1958, the 1st US Missile Division, which evolved from the World War II 1st Bombardment Division, was transferred to the control of the USAF Strategic Air Command. The division included two squadrons of intermediate range ballistic missiles (IRBM). At the same time, the Strategic

Air Command was assigned responsibility for America's intercontinental ballistic missiles (ICBM). The AF's ICBM arsenal included the 5500-mile range multistage Atlas and a similar version called Titan. The Air Force also announced possession of Bomarc surface-to-air interceptor missiles, the 1500-mile range Thor IRBM, a Snark SM-62 pilotless aircraft with a 5500-mile range, a Rascal air-to-ground missile with a 100-mile range, a Matador surface-to-surface 500-mile missile and the Nike surface-to-air antiaircraft missile. A B-70 supersonic bomber capable of flying at an altitude of 75,000 feet for several days was on the drawing board but would be cancelled by the end of the decade because of the proliferation of operational missiles.

The US Navy, meanwhile, demonstrated the capability of its nuclear-powered submarines with a series of underwater endurance tests. The *Nautilus* surfaced on 5 August 1958 after 96 hours under the polar ice. On 22 September 1958, the Navy revealed that *Skate* had survived 31 days under the polar ice cap. And on 6 October 1958, the *Seawolf* completed a 60-day underwater tour without surfacing. The Army was testing a new *Davy Crockett* tactical nuclear weapon to replace the four-year-old *Honest John* nuclear warhead. The DEW line, a defensive ring of radar stations designed to detect incoming Soviet missiles, was in place along the latitude of 70° North. The Air Force had enough B-52s equipped with nuclear bombs to maintain a continuous alert with part of the fleet airborne while other B-52s were on the ground for servicing. Thus, the US was ready for any kind of military action anywhere in the world.

The USSR was also in a position to fight a limited war, a major war, a cold war or any other kind of encounter. Not only had it expanded its navy—which was virtually non-existent at the end of World War II—to a fleet second only to that of the United States, but had also acquired the world's largest fleet of submarines. The USSR military strength was estimated to include 175 army divisions, compared to 14 army divisions for the US.

During the summer of 1958, the Peoples Republic of China appeared ready to attempt an invasion of the Taiwan stronghold of former Chinese Premier Chiang Kai-shek. The Chinese Communists had been shelling the offshore islands of Quemoy and Matsu since the fall of the Koumintang government on the mainland in 1949. Although Quemoy and Matsu were within artillery range of mainland China, they were held by Nationalist Chinese troops and served as somewhat questionable observation posts overlooking mainland China's harbors at Amoy and Minhow. Whether Quemoy and Matsu were intended to be included in the US agreement to protect Taiwan and the Pescadores Islands was never fully resolved. In fact, the subject became an issue in the 1960 presidential campaign debates between Senator John Kennedy and Richard Nixon. However, the US became indirectly involved in the 1958 fighting over the islands when the US Navy provided Chiang Kai-shek's air force pilots

with air-to-air missiles for use against Communist Chinese observation planes. The missiles apparently were sufficiently effective to end the mainland Chinese threat to Quemoy and Matsu.

In July 1958, the Eisenhower Doctrine got its second test in the Middle East when it appeared that Lebanon would fall victim to a suspected plot by the USSR and the newly formed United Arab Republic, a union of Egypt, Yemen and Syria. Syria had requested union with Egypt in February 1958, partly as protection against Soviet influence which Egypt's Nasser seemed well able to resist. The formation of the United

Above: An early test of a Nike Zeus missile in 1960. The Nike Zeus was the first US antiballistic missile but was only a limited success.

Below: B 52 Stratofortress armed with four Skybolt missiles at Eglin Air Force Base, Florida, in 1962.

Arab Republic (UAR) was welcomed by the Moslem population of Lebanon, a part-Christian, part-Moslem nation ruled under an old agreement by which the president has to be a Christian, the premier a Sunni Moslem and the president of the Chamber of Deputies a Shiite Moslem.

Lebanon's president, Camille Chamoun, had accepted the US offer to be a recipient of Eisenhower Doctrine aid despite opposition from other Lebanese political leaders who wanted no ties with the NATO powers following the experience of the Suez crisis. Because the Lebanese constitution forbids a president succeeding himself for an additional six-year term, many suspected that Chamoun was shopping for a reason to suspend or amend the constitution. As the anti-West pan-Arab sentiment in Lebanon swelled following formation of the UAR, demonstrations in Lebanon grew into riots which continued into March and April. When a popular anti-Chamoun newspaper editor was assassinated 8 May 1958, violence in Lebanon reached a fever pitch and Chamoun accused the Syrians of supporting an insurrection. Rioting in Beirut and Tripoli, with hundreds of casualties, was reported, and contents of a US Information Service Library were burned.

The United States reacted by airlifting antiriot arms and ammunition into Beirut by USAF transports on May 14. Three days later, the US State Department announced that tanks were being sent to Lebanon. Meanwhile, the US Fleet Marine Force, Atlantic, was ordered to move its headquarters from Camp Lejeune, North Carolina to the Mediterranean, where the US and British military commanders began a series of staff meetings to consider various deployment plans that might be used if an invasion was ordered. Various contingency plans for US military operations in the Middle East had been prepared in January 1956 when the Suez crisis first threatened to become serious. One plan, 'Operation Bluebat,' had been rehearsed by the 24th Infantry Division in Germany the previous November.

The signal event for troop deployment was the assassination 14 July 1958 of King Faisal and Crown Prince Abdul Illah of Iraq in a pro-UAR army *coup*. It was rumored that King Hussein of Jordan would be the victim of a second Arab world *coup* and Lebanese President Chamoun feared he also was on the pan-Arab hit list. Within 48 hours Chamoun asked for US military intervention.

Within eight hours President Eisenhower was meeting in Washington with Pentagon leaders, and a worldwide US military alert was declared. After Joint Chiefs of Staff Chairman General Nathan Twining assured Eisenhower that the USSR would not intervene, the President ordered American forces to establish a beachhead at Beirut by 9 the following morning, 15 July 1958. The date and hour were important because President Eisenhower planned to go on network television at that time to announce that the US Marines had landed on the beaches of Beirut.

However, in a scenario somewhat reminis-

cent of the first days of the Korean War, only one of the three Marine battalions selected to lead the invasion was within striking distance of Beirut when the order came to execute Operation Bluebat. And that unit, the 2nd Battalion of the 2nd Marine Regiment, lacked an LSD that contained the unit's artillery battery, two of the unit's five M-48 tanks, an underwater demolition team, shore party detachments and heavy equipment. It was en route to Malta for repairs. The nearest LSD with a similar load, assigned to the 6th Marine Regiment, was at Rhodes, hundreds of miles across the Mediterranean Sea. But by running at maximum speed, the various LSDs and LSTs assigned to the operation were able to get an advance contingent of Marines on the Beirut beach as President Eisenhower went before the American TV cameras.

Fortunately, the US Marines encountered no real resistance. By afternoon, Company G had taken control of Beirut airport and restored air traffic which had been interrupted. A roadblock of Lebanese tanks provided the most dramatic encounter as more US troops poured ashore. After a conference with the tank commander, who said his assignment was to prevent the US Marines from entering the city, it was agreed that the Lebanese army could escort the US troops into Beirut. By the evening of the second day, Beirut was relatively calm and the city was patrolled by joint American-Lebanese military teams. Two Marines who lost their way in Beirut were captured by a group of rebels, but were released after a lecture on American imperialism.

Meanwhile, additional American troops were

Above right: French paras land at Dien Bien Phu, site of the battle which confirmed the French defeat in Vietnam and led to the division of the country into North and South.

Right: Tanks in the streets of Budapest during the Hungarian Revolt in October 1956. The brutal Soviet suppression of the revolt did nothing to improve US-Soviet relations and the US inability to make a meaningful response went some way also to discrediting the massive retaliation doctrine.

en route by air and sea from Bremerhaven, Germany, and air bases in Germany and France. At one time so many C-124s and C-130 transports were arriving at Adana Air Base in nearby Turkey that they had to be put in holding patterns until ramp space could be found for them. The aircraft then had to be squeezed into the Beirut Airport where they were unloaded at a rate of one every four minutes and serviced for a return trip. Five days after the start of Operation Bluebat, nearly 14,000 American military personnel were on duty at Beirut and 10,000 of them were concentrated in an area of less than four square miles around Beirut Airport.

US Army troops relieved the Marines near the end of July and all American military units were withdrawn by 15 October 1958. US casualties were remarkably few, with one killed and several wounded by sniper fire. But small arms fire was sporadic, generally occurring in the Bast section of Beirut, the stronghold of pan-Arabism.

The 1958 Lebanon mission was variously described as 'not war, but like war' by a Pentagon spokesman, and as an 'American bridgehead to secure Lebanon from a Syrian invasion that never was' by the National Union Front, an anti-Chamoun political faction. If President Chamoun had hoped to use the Eisenhower Doctrine as a ruse to remain in office, it failed. Chamoun lost the political contest to his opponents, who also repudiated the Eisenhower Doctrine.

It was Egypt, the nation suspected of trying to undermine its fellow Arab governments, that helped resolve the embarrassing situation for the US by asking the United Nations to intervene with a withdrawal resolution. On the plus side for the US, the invasion demonstrated to the Arab world that America would honor its commitments in the Middle East, even at the risk of a possible major war with the Soviet Union. By not involving itself in the domestic politics of Lebanon, the US gained some respect among the Arab nations that had feared American interests were a form of neo-colonialism.

A later US Army study of the 1958 intervention in Lebanon concluded that a similar operation today 'would be fraught with danger and of dubious utility.' While regarded as a model of unilateral joint military operation for the 1950s, the success of the Lebanese invasion was something of a military anomaly in that the action was virtually unopposed. If the Lebanese army or armed forces of neighboring Arab countries had chosen to interdict the Americans on the beaches of Beirut, Operation Bluebat might have been a model of military disaster.

In any case, Operation Bluebat was the largest US troop deployment between the Korean and Vietnam Wars. American commands around the world were affected by the operation and several participated in it. During the 102 days between the execution of the operation and final withdrawal of American troops, only one man was lost to hostile fire. The real nature of the crisis was considerably different from what the military commanders had been led to expect, but—as in other military operations—the real nature at the time did not become obvious until later.

THE KENNEDY YEARS

The Dawn of the Confrontational Sixties

As the 1950s came to a close, the Soviet Union's new leader, Nikita Khrushchev, became a major consideration in US military planning, including the deployment of troops and the continual question of the role of nuclear weaponry. Berlin once again became the central issue of European East-West negotiations and a pawn that would be linked to broader issues. Seldom as subtle as Stalin had been, Khrushchev attempted to resolve the conflict of a divided Germany by issuing an ultimatum to the western powers on 10 November 1958. The USSR leader called for the withdrawal of all foreign troops from Berlin by May 1959, at which time Berlin would become a 'free city,' under Communist control. If the western allies did not agree, the USSR would sign a peace treaty with East Germany, giving the East German government police control over West Berlin.

The United States and Great Britain replied to Khrushchev's proposal that they were sincerely interested in finding a 'peaceful solution' to the problem of divided Germany, and agreed to a meeting in Geneva during the summer of 1959 with the Soviet Union and representatives of the East German government—an event which in itself was regarded by West Germans as a *de facto* recognition of East Germany. However, the western powers found that unless they recognized East Germany as a Communist state, they could not include it in a European mutual security system, which they refused to do as part of a Soviet proposal for a nonaggression treaty between NATO and the Warsaw Pact.

President Eisenhower had met with Khrushchev during the autumn of 1959 at Camp David, where again the Soviet leader attempted to insert Communist terms in the solution to the divided Germanies, but remained unsuccessful in gaining agreement. In March 1960, Eisenhower pledged to the West Germans that any future agreement on Berlin would 'preserve the freedom of the people of West Berlin and their right to self-determination.' Nearly 18 months had passed since Khrushchev's ultimatum of November 1958, and there still was no settlement of the problem which had continued since the end of World War II.

As the 1960's began, US military deterrent power came under scrutiny, with the rate of growth of Soviet nuclear missile power uncertain. But concern over a possible problem with strategic targeting under the authority of the three services was relieved by a plan to have a new interservice strategic planning committee headquartered at the Strategic Air Command (SAC) outside Omaha, Nebraska.

During the early months of 1960, plans were firmed for an East-West summit conference scheduled for 16 May in Paris, where disarmament would be discussed, although Khrushchev continued to demand that the western powers unify Berlin and Germany on Soviet terms. President Eisenhower, mindful of the fact that the Japanese Navy attacked Pearl Harbor while Japanese diplomats were in Washington to negotiate a peace agreement, ordered an overflight of the USSR by a U-2 'spy plane' to determine if the Russians were conducting any warlike military preparations to coincide with the summit meeting. Defense of the United States by its armed forces had to consider the possible worldwide extent of the battlefield, and make use of global surveillance.

Always essential in military operational planning, the gathering of information against surprise attacks had become more elaborate as military technology advanced. The Central Intelligence Agency (CIA) was then the best-known component of the US Intelligence-gathering community, but other agencies or

Previous page: A typical US exercise in Germany. This is during Exercise Southern Arrow at Frankfurt, May 1966. Frequent exercises are seen as essential to demonstrate the enduring commitment of the US to fight with the NATO alliance in Europe in the event of an attack.

Left: Francis Gary Powers, the unfortunate pilot of a US spy plane shot down over the USSR on 1 May 1960. A number of US aircraft had in fact been downed during similar missions in previous years but none with as much attendant publicity.

Below: U-2 spy plane of the type flown by Powers. The U-2 is still in service with the USAF albeit in extensively updated forms.

staffs also operated within it. The Defense Intelligence Agency was founded the next year, in 1961.

The U-2 was sometimes called the 'winged Mata Hari.' Development of the U-2, the first US high-altitude surveillance plane, had begun in 1953, and by 1955 it was successfully tested. The US Air Force had requested a design for a single seat reconnaissance jet aircraft, capable of very long-range missions at altitudes beyond the reach of enemy fighter-intercepters, for use by the US intelligence-gathering system. A U-2 could fly 3000 miles at an altitude above 70,000 feet and at a maximum speed of approximately 600 miles per hour. As a spy plane, the U-2 could produce sharp photographic images of military installations or collect enemy intelligence data in 'black boxes' designed to detect nuclear, infrared or electronic radiation. The U-2's military role was concealed by giving it a cover as a weather research plane. These spy missions were so secret they were classified as 'black,' meaning there would be no written record of the activity, and communication about them would be limited to word of mouth in a debugged environment.

From early 1956 until May 1960, the U-2 was able to fly reconnaissance missions over the Soviet Union in safety. Flights were almost routine, with continual processing and interpretation of photos at the Photo Intelligence Division, which had been set up in 1953. With the high-flying U-2, intelligence on missile and nuclear weapon sites, atomic production, submarines, and other military information outside the US could be gathered. As the May summit conference approached, a suspected new Russian ICBM site was considered important enough to send aloft 'Operation Overflight.'

On 7 May 1960, Soviet Premier Khrushchev announced that a United States U-2 reconnaissance plane had been shot down over the Soviet Union six days earlier. The US cover story, prepared in advance: a US weather plane apparently had strayed over Soviet territory. The fact: it was determined that a Soviet SAM (surface-to-air missile) near Sverdlovsk, in the Ural Mountains of central USSR brought the first U-2 down, as Soviet MiG pilots had been unable to reach the high-flyer. However, the pilot, former Air Force officer Francis Gary Powers, had been captured (and was later tried on a charge of espionage in Moscow and sentenced to 10 years of 'deprivation of freedom.')

As later reports revealed, the USSR had been trying to bag a U-2 for several years, and had protested to the US repeatedly about the overflights. On a single day, according to the USSR, 17 U-2 flights over Soviet territory had been recorded. President Eisenhower was advised by Secretary of State Christian Herter to deny knowledge of the incident, but Eisenhower later decided to take personal responsibility.

Khrushchev's reaction was furious. He denounced US policies and threatened to send Soviet missiles to destroy airfields in any country permitting the use of their facilities by US spy planes. He also demanded the US

Right: Kennedy and Khrushchev during their meeting in Vienna in June 1961.

President make a public apology for the overflight, declaring he would walk out of the scheduled summit conference otherwise. The US responded with no apology, but a statement that the U-2 flights had no aggressive intent and were carried out 'to assure the safety of the United States and the free world against surprise attacks by a power which boasts of its ability to devastate others by missiles with atomic warheads.' Without Khrushchev in attendance, the Paris summit conference adjourned indefinitely three hours after it was scheduled to begin, and once again the German reunification question went unanswered, to remain a problem for future US military planning.

Other conflicts plagued the early 1960s as well. After Belgium granted the Congo independence on 30 June 1960, trouble began immediately. When civil strife erupted and European lives were endangered, Belgium sent in paratroopers. A call for international military aid to restore order was made by the new Republic of Congo, with a similar request on 12 July 1960 to the United States that US troops be sent as the violence continued. The

request was turned down on the grounds that the matter was being considered by the United Nations. On 28 July, a UN force, with a strength of 18,000, was assembled mostly from African nations, but the US Air Force supplied C-130s and C-124s to fly troops from North Africa and elsewhere into Leopoldville. The US also furnished supplies, communications, and medicine. The USAF's airlift structure extended almost 11,000 miles. The total cost was $14 million. Although US military personnel were not directly involved in the fighting, which continued for many months, in September 1960, when a USAF *Globemaster* arrived in Stanleyville from Canada, carrying supplies and Canadian personnel, a mob attacked the eight American crew members with rifle butts and sticks, under the impression they were Belgian.

Tensions around the world continued to claim the attention of US strategists, as the country found its international responsibilities multiplying in an increasingly complex global arena. While the violence in the Congo was going on, a new 'spy plane' case erupted when the USSR announced it had shot down a USAF RB-47 reconnaissance plane on 1 July 1960 in

Above, far left: American missionaries and their families arrive in Washington aboard an Air Force transport after being evacuated from the Congo, July 1960.

Above left: Test launch of the Atlas intercontinental missile from Vandenberg AFB, California.

Above: Launch of a Titan II.

Left: The Cambridge Bay station on the Distant Early Warning Line.

Soviet air space near Svyatoy Nos Cape off the northern coast of Russia. Four of the crew members, including the pilot, were killed and two were taken prisoner. Britain and Norway were also denounced as 'accomplices' by the USSR for having permitted the plane to use their bases, and reference was made to previous threats to attack any spy plane bases with nuclear rockets. The US and Britain rejected the Soviet version of the incident and declared the plane had been over international waters.

And across the world, after the French withdrawal from Indochina, the United States had continued to provide support for the Laotian army in the form of arms and cash, but by October 1960, when the amount exceeded $250 million, the US suspended military aid. Meanwhile, the USSR declared it could not 'ignore in silence the crude interference in Laotian affairs' by the United States and the SEATO powers. With the indication that Soviet influence might be stepped up in that arena, US aid was resumed, and a US attack carrier and transport steamed from Taiwan to the South China Sea with a force of 1100 US Marines to patrol Indochina. A month later, an agreement in principle was reached to end the long civil war there, but the provision for a coalition government aroused the concern of the US State Department that it would result, as in the East European countries, in 'increased Communist influence in the internal affairs' of the country. This concern would become paramount in years to follow.

As Americans went to the polls in November 1960 to elect a new president, rifts were beginning to appear in the NATO network. General DeGaulle had complained that within NATO 'everything is commanded by Americans' because America possessed the major arms. At the same time, the British reacted adversely to the announcement that United States Polaris-armed submarines were to be stationed on the Scottish coast, fearing they might provoke an attack as threatened by the USSR over the U-2 and RB-47 incidents. British Prime Minister Harold Macmillan gained little support with his argument that the US and Great Britain had 'an understanding' that the missiles would not be fired without consultation between representatives of the two governments. And in Coventry, when US Lieutenant General Lauris Norstad, NATO Supreme Commander, attempted to explain the United States position to a jeering crowd, police required 45 minutes to disperse anti-nuclear demonstrators.

With the election of John F Kennedy as President of the United States, the Kennedy administration took over the various diplomatic and military responsibilities in January 1961. It quickly discovered it had inherited a vast global complex of overt and covert military operations. These included command of some 250,000 troops stationed in West Germany which required constant training exercises and maneuvers along the frontiers of Communist states; a space program with military potential; the 24-hour airborne missions of Strategic Air Command bombers requiring one-third of the aircraft to be on alert at all times; a steadily growing arsenal of nuclear-armed missiles, and with it a great national 'missile gap' debate as to whether the US was ahead of or behind the USSR in the development of more and better nuclear weapons.

Despite the controversy, advances had been made in US weaponry. A week before the failed Geneva parley, on 10 May 1960, the USS *Triton*, a nuclear submarine, surfaced at Rehoboth, Delaware, as the first submarine to completely circle the earth underwater. Its skipper declared that the voyage proved that US submarines could travel 'anywhere in the world in secret.' The vessel had left New London, Connecticut, on 16 February 1960, with 183 officers and men aboard, on a trip which closely paralleled the route once taken by Ferdinand Magellan in the 1500s. In September 1960, the first atomic-powered aircraft carrier, the USS *Enterprise*, described by the Navy as the largest ship ever built—1,101 feet long with a possible crew of 3,300—was launched. It was able to cruise 20 times around the world without refueling.

The US also announced in the spring of 1960 the launching of a new type of 'hunter-killer' submarine, the 273-foot *Tullibee*; the production of an all-weather carrier-based nuclear attack bomber, the A2F-1 *Intruder*; and the Army's development of a new radar system for photographing enemy territory from the airspace over friendly nations. However, in terms of manpower, Army draft calls by the Selective Service system were steadily dropping in the first half of 1960, going from 7000 to 5500, the lowest number since the beginning of the Korean War.

On 20 July 1960, a US Navy task force called Special Projects, which was begun in 1955, had a successful first underwater test five years earlier than planned, with the launch of the intermediate range (1200 miles) Polaris missile. Two missiles were fired off from the Fleet Ballistic Missile submarine, the USS *George Washington* near Cape Canaveral. And in November, the nuclear submarine sailed from Charleston, South Carolina, armed with 16 thermonuclear Polaris missiles on the world's first underwater missile patrol.

As an answer to the 'missile gap,' in 1960 the installation of the first of the solid fuel Minuteman ICBM missiles began at launching sites in Montana. The Minuteman would be able to hit with the equivalent of some 500,000 tons of TNT within a mile of a target some 6000 miles away. By 1961, the US Air force was in charge of the largest US military construction program in peacetime. The installation of underground launching sites for the Atlas, Titan, and Minuteman was ongoing in a total of 18 states, with a cost of $7 billion. And by the end of 1962, some 200 combat-ready, nuclear armed, intercontinental ballistic missiles would be in place, ready to strike, with 126 liquid-fueled Atlases, 54 liquid-fueled Titans, and 20 Minutemen, each with a range of 6000 or more miles and an assigned target in the Soviet Union.

The Bay of Pigs Debacle and the Berlin Wall

President Kennedy also inherited a secret plan begun by the Eisenhower administration to overthrow the Castro regime in Cuba by training and supporting Cuban refugees for an invasion of the Caribbean island. After Fidel Castro overthrew the Batista government in Cuba in 1959, the Communist influence in Castro's government had become apparent within a year. Shortly after the U-2 incident in Russia, on 13 May 1960, Cuban Premier Fidel Castro announced on television that a Cuban patrol boat had attacked the US submarine *Sea Poacher* and charged that US Navy craft had violated Cuban territorial water on eight other occasions. Castro also declared in speeches in August 1960 that OAS members had been 'bought by US promises of hundreds of millions of dollars in foreign aid funds and that Cuba would depend upon Soviet 'rocket support' for its protection.

Harassment of US citizens in Cuba had become a problem during 1960, and the US State Department in October urged some 4000 nonessential Americans to return to the US

Right: Cuban exiles captured during the Bay of Pigs incident go on trial in Havana in 1962.

Below: Cuban soldiers celebrate the Bay of Pigs victory, posing beside a launch supposedly captured from the US-sponsored attackers.

'as a precautionary measure.' When the Cuban government seized and nationalized 166 US-owned businesses, the US retaliated by declaring an embargo on most exports to Cuba. The US Ambassador, Philip Bonsal, was recalled for 'an extended period of consultations,' while discounting rumors of a planned invasion as a 'hoax.'

As the US continued to plan its secret proxy invasion of Cuba, Khrushchev had reportedly advised Castro to 'ease up' on anti-US attacks, particularly threats to use Soviet missiles against the United States. During November, after Castro had put Cuba on a military alert, claiming a US threat to Cuba, the US considered an attack on the US Navy base at Guantanamo possible, and brought in additional Marines. Cuba asked for Soviet reassurance that a promise of Russian rockets would be kept. On 16 November 1960, Eisenhower ordered the aircraft carrier *Shangri-La* and five destroyers to patrol the central American coast from Yucatan to the Panama Canal to protect the area from a possible Cuban invasion, after urgent requests for help from Guatemala and Nicaragua. But, the USSR charged the following day that the Eisenhower action was probably a 'prelude to US military action against Cuba.'

On becoming Commander-in-Chief, Kennedy had the option of halting the planned invasion,

Above: Attorney General Robert Kennedy (left) and his brother the President pictured in 1963.

Opposite, top: Soviet soldier in a tunnel extending from the American into the Soviet sector of Berlin. The Soviets claimed, when they announced the existence of the tunnel in 1956, that it had been built for spying uses by the Americans.

Opposite, bottom: Berlin scene, August 1961. In the background an East German Police watercannon while in the forground are American soldiers on duty on the border.

The invasion at Bahia de Cochinos, or literally, Bay of Pigs was probably the most mismanaged military operation in US history. White House adviser Walter Rostow later described the mission as 'the most screwed-up operation.' CIA personnel planning the invasion ignored the advice by Cuban refugees against landing in the 'Blue Beach' area of the Bay of Pigs where the coral reefs beneath the surface of the water would rip open landing craft; CIA agents interpreted the coral reefs in aerial photographs as either seaweed or cloud reflections. A pre-invasion bombing attack on three Cuban air bases was carried out by three US-built B-26 bombers piloted by Cubans who said they had defected from the Cuban Air Force. When, on 17 April 1961, the anti-Castro rebels began landing on the swampy beaches of Cuba's southern Las Villas Province, Castro declared a state of national alert.

Problems continued to plague the invading Cubans. Motor launches intended to land the troops were equipped with untested outboard motors that failed to work. The aircraft used by the invaders were slow World War II planes that were vulnerable to groundfire. The US Navy jets from the carrier *Essex* were allowed to fly over the invasion area but were forbidden to join in the fighting. One squadron reportedly had no military maps of the area and had to depend upon an oil company map of Cuba for orientation.

Fidel Castro, on the other hand, was personally familiar with the Bay of Pigs area, his favorite fishing spot, and was able to direct defense from a nearby sugar mill which had the only telephone line. Other invaders were parachuted inland while smaller amphibious landings were made in Oriente and Pinar del Rio Provinces. The popular uprising by the people of Cuba predicted by the CIA did not happen. Instead, Cubans rallied to the defense of their island and inflicted heavy casualties on the invading rebels. President Kennedy had told a news conference on 12 April 1961 that the United States would not use military force to attempt to overthrow the Castro regime, but evidence presented at the United Nations indicated that the United States was deeply involved in the invasion. Captured equipment reportedly included US-made Sherman tanks.

The invasion was over by 20 April 1961. Castro announced in a television speech that Cuba had lost 337 men. The rebel losses were estimated at more than 1000. A Cuban radio station reported an additional 1000 invading rebels had been captured. During the next 24 hours, thousands of Cubans were arrested and dozens executed for alleged support of the invaders. Two of those executed were Americans who had been charged with smuggling arms into Cuba by boat on the day before the invasion. And though the B-26 bomber crews were Cuban, there were at least four Americans who died in combat when American pilots, all volunteers, were authorized to fly combat missions to relieve exhausted Cubans. The four Alabama airmen killed during the Bay of Pigs invasion were not admitted at the time to be CIA employees.

but instead chose to go ahead with the Eisenhower program. During 1960, a force of some 5000 Cuban exiles had been gathering for military training, most of them in camps in Guatemala and Louisiana. What began as a possible guerrilla operation became, under the CIA, a plan for the Cuban Brigade to establish a military foothold on the coast of Cuba, where it was believed an uprising of Cuban citizens would follow and overthrow the Castro regime. Among the preparations for the proposed invasion, a 'Democratic Revolutionary Front' headed by Cuban exiles met in secret in Miami, Florida, and selected Cuban ex-premier Jose Miro Cardona as president of a 'government in arms.'

Six freighters were leased by the CIA to transport the ground troops of the invaders. Other Brigade members had been trained by American pilots, some of them from the Alabama National Guard, to fly the B-26 bombers to be used in the military operation. The US Navy aircraft carrier *Essex* was to take aboard a squadron of AD-4 Skyhawk jet fighters. The jet squadron was intended for reconnaissance only, and forbidden to engage in combat. Along with five destroyers, the *Essex* was to escort the freighters to a rendezvous point outside the Bay of Pigs. From there, two of the destroyers, the *Eaton* and *Murray*, would escort the Brigade's ships into Cuban waters. The US destroyers were not, however, to get involved in any fighting.

After conferring with former Vice President Nixon on 20 April about the Cuban debacle, President Kennedy called former President Eisenhower to a meeting at Camp David on 22 April. Then, on 24 April 1961, President Kennedy issued a statement taking full responsibility for the US part in the attack on Cuba.

Soviet Premier Khrushchev warned that the arming of Cuban exiles by the United States could have resulted 'in a new global war,' but repeated his interest in meeting with Kennedy to discuss disarmament and 'all other questions relating to peaceful co-existence.' The USSR, said Khrushchev, was even willing to forgive the United States for the U-2 overflight—the affair that became the Soviet's excuse for aborting the Paris summit conference the year before. Kennedy and Khrushchev then announced that they would meet in Vienna, 3 June 1961, following the American President's planned visit to Paris at the end of May.

After President Kennedy's troubled early months in 1961, a shift in defense doctrine appeared. General Maxwell Taylor called it a 'graduated' or 'flexible response' doctrine, which meant that although the US nuclear striking power would remain as the ultimate defense, it would not be used against an enemy's limited aggression. The change in doctrine led to increased Army manpower and an increased use of air mobility.

The United States and the USSR both reported space achievements in the spring of 1961. On 12 April 1961, Soviet Major Yuri Gagarin became the first human to circle the

earth in a space capsule. The single orbit flight lasted a total of 108 minutes. On 5 May 1961, US Navy Commander Alan Shepard, Jr., became the first American astronaut by taking a 302-mile suborbital flight from Cape Canaveral, Florida, to a watery landing in the Atlantic ocean. Shepard's flight reached an altitude of 115 miles and lasted 17 minutes. The two flights evoked a bit of East-West controversy, the US accusing the Soviets of the use of secrecy and misinformation about space achievements whereas the US allowed public television coverage of its events. The USSR rejoined that such publicity was not necessary as the Soviets had claimed in advance that they would send manned space ships into orbit.

In advance of his scheduled conference with Khrushchev, Kennedy conferred with de Gaulle of France, Adenauer of West Germany, and Willy Brandt of West Berlin. The US revealed a British-French-US contingency plan to be used in the event of a renewed Berlin Blockade; it involved a 'war alert' to be followed by the capture of Helmstedt on the autobahn of East Germany, and a 'limited penetration of East German territory' using only non-nuclear weapons unless the USSR responded with nuclear weapons. Release of the plan before the meeting apparently was to warn Khrushchev that the West would not negotiate from a weak position.

A series of proposals was submitted to Kennedy by Khrushchev, including a requirement that East and West Germany be given six months to agree on a method of unification, after which the US, USSR, France and Great Britain should sign peace treaties with representatives of both East and West Germany. Khrushchev also proposed making Berlin a demilitarized 'free city' with all access routes to Berlin controlled by the German Democratic Republic (East Germany). Kennedy described the talks as a 'full and frank exchange,' adding

Above: American tanks and armored personnel carriers on the streets of Berlin at the height of the Berlin Wall crisis.

Top right: Workmen clear away debris from a newly-built section of the Berlin Wall, a picture taken in December 1961 when the Soviets were strengthening sections of the wall established earlier in the year.

Right: Interested Berliners watch maneuvers of the Berlin garrison in October 1961.

that Khrushchev's Berlin proposals would 'be the subject of further communications.'

However, after his return to Washington, President Kennedy authorized an increase in the strength of US combat divisions in Germany to 200,000, flying in a 40,000-man reinforcement to the US 7th Army in Europe, and allocating $3.5 billion for new conventional weapons and US civil defense measures. It appeared that Kennedy intended to hold West Berlin against any Communist aggression. Robert Kennedy, the US Attorney General, meanwhile, advised USSR Ambassador Mikhail Menshikov in Washington that President Kennedy 'believed the Berlin issue was worth going to war over.'

The Kennedy action was followed by panic in East Germany. The exodus of East Germans migrating through Berlin increased from 1500 daily to over 4000. The Warsaw Pact Nations were called to a meeting in Moscow in August 1961 and there were rumors of Soviet troop movements along the frontier between the two Germanies. Barbed wire and concrete posts were stockpiled at the barracks of the East Berlin garrison. On the night of 12 August 1961, subways and trolleys quit running between the East and West Berlin. Then motor vehicle and canal traffic between the two Berlins was halted. At 3 am on 13 August 1961, the East Berlin radio announced that the border between East and West Berlin was being sealed because of an 'expected military attack by NATO forces.' Work battalions began tearing up streetcar tracks and stringing barbed wire on concrete posts along the border. The 53,000 East Berliners with employment in West Berlin were notified that their work passes had been cancelled. West Germans waited anxiously for the Western powers to retaliate.

As if testing the resolve of the West, the Communists allowed the barbed wire barricades to stand for 10 days. When no retaliatory action occurred, the fence was gradually replaced with a high concrete wall and the number of crossing points was reduced from 13 to four. The Berlin Wall was technically a violation of the four-power agreement as viewed in the context of a unilateral action that integrated East Berlin into East Germany. From the Soviet perspective, the Berlin Wall was logical because the alternative to continued friction caused by the movement of East Germans through West Berlin would have been strong cordons of police and troops. The USSR also hoped the wall would be accepted as an implied recognition of East German sovereignty.

Both sides were cautious to avoid an escalation in the Berlin Wall confrontation. However, President Kennedy ordered the first partial mobilization of US military forces since the Korean War. A total of 22,000 members of the Air National Guard and 5600 Air Force Reserve officers and men were called to active duty. The Berlin garrison of US troops had been reinforced earlier by a dispatch of 1500 men along the 110-mile stretch of East German autobahn earlier. Following the Air Force call-up, the Defense Department ordered 46,500 Army reservists, mainly members of logistics and support units, to active duty, and four National Guard divisions were classified as 'top priority' units required to undergo intensive 'combat readiness' training. The Navy call-up ordered 6400 to active duty to man 40 destroyers and 18 antisubmarine aircraft squadrons.

USSR Premier Khrushchev announced he was still willing to try to 'find solutions' to the crisis but added that 'because of war threats' it had decided to resume testing of nuclear weapons. The response from Kennedy was that the US had 'no other choice' but to resume its own testing of new nuclear weapons. During September 1961, in a tunnel, deep underground below Rainier Mesa, Nevada at 1:00 pm, the US completed its first nuclear weapons test in three years. In contrast, the US Navy blimp program, used extensively during World War II, with some 168 blimps, was suspended in mid-1961. Only two Navy blimps were still in service by the end of the year, and their use on shore patrols and early-warning defense missions would be over by the spring of 1962.

But the smoldering confrontation between the two superpowers had a bit of fuel added when Khrushchev declared he 'would not promise' that the USSR would refrain from being the first nation to use nuclear weapons

in the event of a war. However, the Berlin Crisis of 1961 became a stalemate. USSR Deputy Premier Anastas Mikoyan expressed his country's attitude in an 21 August speech: 'You may not like East Germany, but you will have to ask them for a pass if you want to enter Berlin.' The East Germans made the Berlin Wall higher and thicker and dug trenches behind it. An East German official declared that it would 'last 1000 years,' a statement once made about the Third Reich.

President Kennedy sent Vice President Lyndon Johnson to West Berlin to reassure the anxious population that the US intended to guarantee their security. General Lucius Clay, the US military commander in West Berlin in 1948, also was sent to the city for morale-building purposes. Kennedy did not retreat from his position, but neither did he put additional pressure on Khrushchev to force a move by the Soviet military.

The Cuban Missile Crisis

In the next major move, the USSR in 1962 announced an agreement whereby the Soviets would supply arms to Cuba and also establish a Cuban base for a Russian fishing fleet in the Atlantic Ocean. The Bay of Pigs fiasco a year earlier had strengthened rather than weakened Fidel Castro's role as Cuba's revolutionary hero. The invasion had given Castro an opportunity to demonstrate his courage and leadership as a defender of his nation against one of the world's superpowers. The later revelations that Kennedy and his associates wove a fabric of lies and deception, misleading even their own UN Ambassador, Adlai Stevenson, regarding the true role of the United States in the Cuban invasion, further increased the stature of Castro among Cuba's Latin American neighbors and Third World countries.

Until 1962, the USSR had not allowed its nuclear missiles to be based anywhere beyond the borders of the Soviet Union. But in that year, Fidel Castro reportedly requested the protection offered by nuclear missiles. At least that was the claim of Nikita Khrushchev when he explained to the Supreme Soviet in December 1962 that 'We carried weapons there at the request of the Cuban government.' It was reported that negotiations for delivery of nuclear missiles to Cuba took place in early July 1962 when Raul Castro, the brother of Fidel, went to Moscow for a meeting with Khrushchev. Although President Kennedy had

Above: A vital part of US intelligence during the Cuban crisis was provided by photo-reconnaissance flights. Here pilots pose in front of an RF-101 aircraft. Note the panel in the aircraft's nose behind which one of the cameras is mounted.

Top left: President Kennedy looks out over the Berlin Wall during his famous visit to the city in June 1963. Note how, in the background, the arches of the Brandenburg Gate have been hung with drapes by the East German authorities to prevent Kennedy being seen from the east. Accompanying Kennedy is Berlin Mayor Willi Brandt.

Far left: American forces moved to full alert status throughout the world during the Cuban Crisis. These M48 tanks are serving with the Berlin garrison.

Left: A typical product of the reconnaissance missions over Cuba, showing MiG-21 fighters on Cienfuegos Airfield.

27 OCTOBER 1962
SAN JULIAN AIRFIELD.

UNCRATED FUSELAGE AND TAIL SECTION

BEAGLES BEING ASSEMBLED

Left: USAF reconnaissance photo showing Il-28 Beagles being assembled on San Julian Airfield, Cuba.

pursued a policy of isolating and ignoring Castro after the Bay of Pigs fiasco, Castro was convinced that the US planned another invasion of Cuba. The US, for its part, had repeatedly warned that it considered the Monroe Doctrine to be a valid unilateral policy despite political changes that had taken place in the Western Hemisphere since 1823.

Khrushchev had stated in a 12 July 1960 news conference that 'the Monroe Doctrine has outlived its time and has died a natural death.' The Doctrine, he added, had been used by the US to 'perpetuate the reign of colonialism and monopolies in Latin America.' It was during one of the near flashpoints of East-West tensions, a week in which the USSR had shot down a USAF RB-47 reportedly on a spy mission over northern Russia. Khrushchev had warned a few days earlier that 'figuratively speaking, in case of necessity, Soviet artillerymen can support the Cuban people with their rocket fire.' Because the USSR had missiles capable of reaching the US directly from Soviet soil, the White House did not consider the possibility

Below left: The Soviet merchant ship *Kasimov* en route to Cuba with suspicious crates on deck. Following the imposition of the US blockade a number of such vessels opened crates on their deck to prove that the contents were not missiles.

Below: Marines patrol the perimeter of the US Navy base at Guantanamo, Cuba, in November 1962. A US Navy helicopter flies in support.

Above: Nuclear-capable Ilyushin 28 Beagle medium bomber of the type supplied to Cuba.

western Province of Pinar Del Rio. The sophisticated equipment would have required Russian control because Cuba in 1962 lacked even the personnel to operate SAM anti-aircraft missiles.

President Kennedy's reaction was immediate and one of urgency. Elements of the 1st and 2nd US Marine Divisions began arriving at el Guantanamo Naval Base on Cuba on 21 October while dependents at the base were evacuated. Air Force Reserve units released only a few months earlier after the cooling of the Berlin Crisis of 1961 were recalled to active duty. The mobilization was on a 'no notice' basis, meaning there was no 30-day alert provided for 14,000 members of Tactical Air Command crews, most of them based in the southeastern United States.

Then, on the evening of 22 October 1962, President Kennedy announced on television the discovery of 'offensive missile sites' in Cuba, and what steps were being taken in response. One was instituting a quarantine around Cuba. His use of the term 'quarantine' was purposeful: a blockade was against international law. However, ships of the Atlantic Fleet's Task Force 136 under the command of Vice-Admiral Alfred Ward established a 'blockade' extending from Jacksonville, Florida, to San Juan, Puerto Rico, to intercept any Soviet ships that might be carrying missiles to Cuba. In addition to the Atlantic Ocean screening force of 60 ships, the US Navy deployed a picket line of ships around the coast of Cuba, reinforced by aircraft carrier patrols. Chief of Naval Operations George W Anderson ordered that all ships headed for Cuba would have to be stopped and boarded. Any ship that failed to heave to would be subject to attack. Any ship that carried embargoed material would be turned away.

that Russia would install medium or intermediate-range missiles in the Western Hemisphere. The Kennedy administration was further deceived by a Soviet statement on 11 September 1962 that the USSR 'had no need to find missile sites outside the Soviet Union.'

Although Kennedy had ignored Cuba politically, it was not forgotten. CIA operatives had continued to work in and about the Caribbean island, and intelligence feedback indicated a sudden increase in military activity around Havana. Ships were arriving from Eastern Europe with arms, Soviet technicians, and equipment for building surface-to-surface missile bases. President Kennedy requested Congressional authority for a call-up of military reservists, and ordered U-2 surveillance flights over Cuba. The first U-2 photos indicated only the installation of antiaircraft sites and new airbases for Soviet MiG fighter planes. But on 14 October 1962, the U-2 photos revealed in clear detail the presence of equipment for a battalion of Soviet medium-range ballistic missiles in the area of San Cristobal, in the

Below right: USAF reconnaissance photo of the SS-5 launch site at Guanajay, Cuba, 17 October 1962.

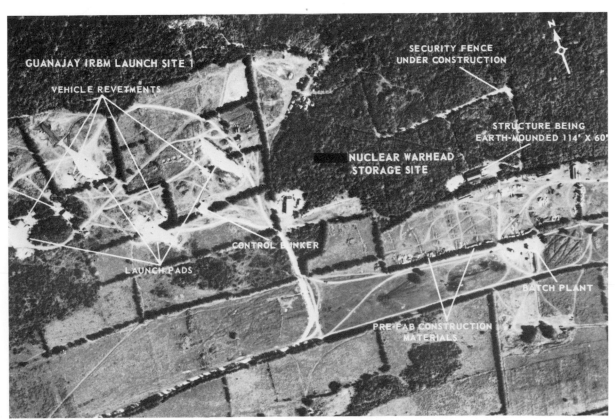

25 OCTOBER 1962
MRBM LAUNCH SITE 1
SAN CRISTOBAL, CUBA
22-40N 83-18W

OXIDIZER TRAILERS

FUEL TRAILERS

MISSILE TRANSPORTER & PRIME MOVER

MISSILE SHELTER TENTS

FIRING TABLE

THEODOLITE
HARDSTAND FOR ERECTOR

MISSILE TRANSPORTERS

ERECTORS

Anderson also ordered that any submarine detected in the area would be given the international code signal IDKCA, a command to surface or be destroyed. USAF fighters were ordered to intercept any Cuba-bound cargo aircraft and force it to land at a designated US airport for inspection.

Ships carrying non-military cargoes of petroleum, chemicals, paper, and trucks were inspected and allowed to continue to Cuba. But several Soviet ships known to be carrying arms steamed on toward the screening line as the world waited to see whether the USSR would defy the US Navy blockade. At the last moment, the Soviet ships turned back toward their home ports. As the US Secretary of State Dean Rusk described the situation, 'We were eyeball to eyeball and the Soviets blinked first.'

Before President Kennedy established the US quarantine of Cuba, the Soviets already had installed a number of 52-foot medium-range missiles. Reconnaissance photos showed many of the 1200-mile range projectiles with one-megaton warheads on their mobile launchers, angled up and pointing toward the US mainland. They were capable of reaching targets as far away as Washington, D.C., and St. Louis, Missouri. The photos also revealed at least 25 Ilyushin-28 bombers capable of carrying

nuclear weapons, and a half dozen bases with emplacements for 2500-mile range missiles that could reach any major city in the United States.

Khrushchev offered to dismantle the Cuban missiles and bases if the US would remove similar weapons from Turkey, where the United States had installed intermediate-range Jupiter missiles two years earlier as part of the NATO defense system. Kennedy rejected the Khrushchev demand, but did agree not to invade Cuba nor to destroy the Russian bases and armaments if the USSR would remove the war materiel within 30 days.

With that agreement, the quarantine was lifted 20 November 1962, and the military reservists were released from active duty. However, the United States continued its aerial surveillance after Castro refused to permit a United Nations team to conduct on-site inspections, a condition to which Khrushchev agreed, to guarantee the removal of Soviet weapons. US Secretary of Defense Robert McNamara expressed the theory that the Cuban Missile crisis was fostered by the USSR as a test of American willingness to go to war over an important issue. If the United States had backed down rather than risk the threat of a Soviet attack, the USSR would have

KRONSTADT PC

4 KOMAR PGMG

Above: The arms build-up in Cuba also included a wide range of conventional weapons. *Kronstadt* and *Komar* class ships are shown photographed at Banes on 3 November 1962.

Left: The San Cristobal missile launch site, pictured on 25 October 1962.

Below: The Soviet vessel *Metallurg Anasov* photographed returning to the Soviet Union on 21 November 1962.

felt free to make a bold move in Europe. But if there should be a test, it would be better to conduct the confrontation in the frontyard of the United States than in the backyard of the USSR. And if there were hostilities, the battle-field would be Cuba. Cuba was expendable and Castro was treated as a stooge who would not even be consulted at any stage of the crisis negotiations between Kennedy and Khrush-chev.

Among the effects of the confrontations be-tween the two superpowers during the early 1960s was a method to keep control of the far-reaching weapons system in time of war: the National Military Command System was set up in 1962. For the first time a central, overall command center was in the Pentagon. Included in the system was a seaborne top-command center in the heavy cruiser *Northampton*, three airborne command centers in converted KC-135 turbojet tanker aircraft, stationed at Andrews Air Force Base outside Washington, and a number of underground replicas of the Penta-gon command center. During 1962 the cost of research and development for defense and space ran up to $12 billion, more than 'in the entire interval from the American Revolution through and including World War II.'

Disarmament was also very much on the agenda in 1962. Throughout the year, the 17-nation Disarmament Conference in Geneva met to work out an agreement on halting nuclear weapons tests. A previous moratorium had been broken by Soviet tests in the fall of 1961. In the 1962 effort to reach a treaty, the US was willing to forgo on-site inspection. Under-ground tests would be permitted, but all others, in the atmosphere, water, and space, would be forbidden.

On 7 January 1963, the United States and the Soviet Union submitted a joint statement to the United Nations Secretary-General U Thant stating the two superpowers had resolved the crisis between themselves. Relations between the US and USSR improved perceptibly after the Cuban missile confrontation. There was a de-escalation of tensions over the divided Germany and Berlin. And on 5 April 1963, Khrushchev accepted a proposal by President Kennedy for a direct communications link, called the 'hot line,' between the White House and the Kremlin. There was a new moratorium on atmospheric testing of nuclear weapons, replacing the earlier agreement broken by both sides during the 1961 Berlin Crisis. Three-power talks were held in Moscow by representa-tives of the US, USSR and Great Britain, lead-ing to a treaty on the control of weapons in space and underwater as well as in the atmo-sphere. The NATO links were weakened by Charles de Gaulle's veto of the British applica-tion for membership in the European Common Market. But that episode was balanced by a deepening rift between the Soviet Union and the Peoples Republic of China.

Fidel Castro had offered to release the surviving prisoners of the Bay of Pigs invasion in return for US payment of 500 bulldozers or tractors. As the United States was not 'officially' involved in the invasion, it could not nego-tiate directly for the prisoners release. How-ever, Attorney General Robert Kennedy per-suaded American pharmaceutical and baby food manufacturers to make a 'private dona-tion' of $53 million worth of their products as a ransom payment.

Kennedy, in a retrospective interview, com-mented that if it had not been for the Bay of Pigs invasion 'we would be in Laos now.' He referred to the fact that the US was becoming deeply involved in resisting Soviet and Chinese military aid to subversive forces in Laos; he had ordered the US 7th Fleet, including three aircraft carriers and 1400 US Marines, to the Indochina area when the Bay of Pigs invasion occurred. The Cuban incident diverted the attention of the Kennedy administration from the turmoil in Southeast Asia.

VIETNAM: THE EXPLODING WAR

During World War II, the American military commitment to Indochina had been minor. Ho Chi Minh was then the recognized head of the leading resistance group against the Japanese occupation forces. At his request, he had received some American arms to help rescue downed Allied pilots and fight the common foe. He had built his own organization, the Viet Minh ('League for the Independence of Vietnam'), out of a gathering of many groups fighting against not only the Japanese, but the return of the French.

At the end of World War II in 1945, when the US turned away from his proposal for an independent Indochina and the French were once again in control, Ho Chi Minh declared himself President of an independent Republic of Vietnam, headquartered in Hanoi. The French were at first willing to accept this situation within a framework of an Indochina Federation and French Union. However, as early as 1946, the Viet Minh were already fighting the French, and by 1949, when China became Communist under Mao Tse-tung's armies, the Communist influence in the Viet Minh also became clear.

After eight years of fighting, the French were defeated decisively at Dien Bien Phu on 7 May 1954. Although the US military had not intervened directly, hundreds of millions of dollars in US financial aid to the French, in addition to shiploads of armaments and supplies had been provided. Between 12 May and 11 June 1954, the US even considered options for entering the fighting in Indochina. One option, called 'Operation Vulture,' would send hundreds of USAF bombers over Viet Minh targets. For land warfare, General Ridgway estimated the

Above: A plane piloted by a South Vietnamese rebel makes a bombing attack on the Presidential palace in Saigon in May 1962.

Left: US Special Forces soldier gives grenade instruction to a group of Vietnamese, Nui Ba Den, 1964.

Previous page: Men of the 173rd Airborne Brigade ready to defend the Bien Hoa base. They are armed with an M16 rifle and M79 grenade launcher.

Top right: US advisers coach a Vietnamese Ranger in the use of a Thompson submachine gun early in 1962.

Right: French troops advance cautiously hoping to flush Viet Minh snipers from the jungle thicket ahead, a picture taken in 1953 but a scene typical of the fighting in Vietnam for the following 20 years.

US would need at least eight divisions of ground troops, which was decided could not be spared from NATO commitments or mainland defenses.

However, in July, a Geneva peace conference was held and the Geneva Accords, which brought the war in Indochina to an official close, were accepted by the participating powers. Although the US declined to sign, the assurance was given that the US would not disrupt the Accords with the use of force, but the implied intent was that any return to fighting or aggression against the newly created South Vietnam would cause the US to come to its defense.

But two basic mistakes had already been made at the Geneva peace conference. One was the selection of Ngo Dinh Diem to lead the new government of South Vietnam. The Vietnamese resented the selection of another puppet ruler, Diem. Second was the recommendation that Vietnam be partitioned along the 17th Parallel. In urging the 17th Parallel for a DMZ, the US ignored French advice that the 18th Parallel was a better natural defense line because it contained a ridge of limestone hills extending from Laos to the East Coast of Vietnam with the Giang River just to the south. The Americans believed the 17th Parallel might have advantages because it was near Colonial Route 9, providing handy access for mechanized equipment.

Vietnam, under French rule, had been divided into three colonial areas: Tonkin—the Song Coi or Red River delta in the north, with the city of Hanoi and the port of Haiphong; Annam—the central mountainous area; and Cochin—the Mekong River delta in the south

with the city of Saigon. After the terms of the Geneva Accords split Vietnam into two countries at the 17th Parallel, the Tonkin lowlands were then completely within North Vietnam, while South Vietnam took in Cochin and much of the former area of central Vietnam.

The US Sinks Deeper into Vietnam Mire

September 1954 is sometimes cited as the beginning of American troubles in Vietnam. When US consular officials in North Vietnam insisted that accreditation by the Saigon government was sufficient, Ho Chi Minh's government regarded the US attitude as 'arrogant' and cordoned off the consulate so it could not be supplied. The US finally closed its Hanoi consulate in November 1954.

After the division of Vietnam, thousands in the population exchanged places, with northerners fleeing south, and Viet Minh going north. However, many thousands of the Viet Minh went underground in South Vietnam with the intention of an eventual takeover, using either persuasion or terror. Later, many North Vietnamese Communists crossed the border covertly into South Vietnam for the same purpose. And all were organized into the Ho Chi Minh directed National Liberation Front.

The term 'Viet Cong' (from the Vietnamese term for Communist, *Cong-san*) was used to identify these Viet Minh subversives. Ngo Dinh Diem had good reason to suspect the Viet Cong—based on the repeated discoveries of Communist arms caches during raids on their hideouts. The caches included not only rifles and ammunition, but machine guns,

Above: A Laotian soldier under instruction from US advisers, 1962.

Right: Troops of the 5th Vietnamese Division run to US transport helicopters during fighting in Tay Ninh Province in October 1962.

Opposite, top: Vietnamese troops with a captured Viet Cong suspect. Viet Cong taken prisoner by the South Vietnamese could expect little mercy. Prisoners taken by the US forces were usually handed over to the South Vietnamese after interrogation.

Opposite, bottom: Male and female members of the South Vietnamese Civil Defense Guard parade at Hao Cain in June 1962. In the final analysis US attempts to strengthen the South Vietnamese were vitiated by the corruption and inefficiency of the South's government.

mortars and land mines, all neatly packaged in greased wrappers for future use. Also captured in the raids were stores of non-military items, such as typewriters and electric generators, for use by political cadres in future Communist offices south of the DMZ. However, US military advisers discounted the seriousness of the Viet Cong threat and planned instead on meeting a possible confrontation with the 350,000 Viet Minh troops, which then constituted the North Vietnamese army. But by the end of 1960, the Viet Cong had been systematically killing village political leaders, usually those loyal to Diem, and killing hundreds of South Vietnamese troops in single attacks.

After the election of President Kennedy, one of the first casualties of the Kennedy administration's intervention in Indochina occurred 23 March 1961 when a specially modified SC-47 intelligence-gathering plane en route from Vientiane in Laos to Saigon was shot down over the Plain of Jars while checking radio frequencies used by USSR cargo planes delivering arms to the Pathet Lao forces. At the suggestion of President Kennedy, reconnaissance flights beginning in April 1961 were RT-33s borrowed from the Philippine Air Force and repainted with Laotian markings. Realizing that the US and USSR were on a collision course because of the Communist versus anti-Communist fighting in Laos, Kennedy and Khrushchev agreed to a conference in Vienna, Austria, in early June 1961, and agreed in substance to convince their 'clients' in the area to maintain the declared cease-fire; in fact, the warring forces in Laos continued their fight for some years.

On 11 October 1961, Kennedy sent General Maxwell Taylor and a group of advisers to Sai-

Left: A female Viet Cong suspect captured in May 1962.

Right: Prisoners of a Vietnamese airborne unit await questioning, December 1962.

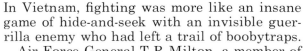

Below: A South Vietnamese patrol searches a country hamlet in May 1962. The soldier nearest the camera is armed with a Thompson submachine gun and has a pack of spare magazines strapped to his chest.

gon to discuss the possible use of US troops to support the Diem government. The US Military Advisory Group in South Vietnam was then a reported 685 men. But there was no plan for dealing with an enemy that moved freely through Vietnam, Cambodia and Laos. Any American action would be limited to South Vietnam. Areas beyond the South Vietnam frontiers would remain sanctuaries for the North Vietnamese and Viet Cong armies. One major difference between the Korean War and the Vietnam War would be the absence of massed armies facing each other along a 100-mile front, withdrawing to prepared trenches and bunkers, with aircraft dogfights overhead.

In Vietnam, fighting was more like an insane game of hide-and-seek with an invisible guerrilla enemy who had left a trail of boobytraps.

Air Force General T R Milton, a member of the Taylor mission, recalled later that the group had 'no clearcut objectives—just go over there and straighten things out.' Beyond recommending more money and military advisers for South Vietnam, the group thought the situation would provide an opportunity to try out a couple of the New Frontier ideas: Defense Secretary McNamara's 'flexible response' to replace 'massive retaliation,' and the new Special Forces counterinsurgency troops that became popularly known as the 'Green Berets.' Soon after, USAF Globemasters began shuttling in more American instructors and advisers to bolster the South Vietnam government's will to defeat the Viet Cong.

Following President Kennedy's decision in December 1961 to expand military assistance to the Diem regime, some 300 US helicopter pilots in 'Eagle Flight' units were among the early arrivals in Vietnam. Their assignment was to ferry South Vietnamese troops. The first unit of the US ground forces to arrive in Vietnam was a communications unit, the 39th Signal Battalion, beginning in February 1962. By early May 1962, there were some 5000 US troops serving in South Vietnam, including the US Special Forces.

The counterinsurgency-trained Special Forces, the Green Berets, were described originally as 'guerrillas with a specialized capability for dealing with guerrilla warfare.' They served as instructors to the Vietnamese and could lead them into combat, but were not to participate in the fighting except in self-defense.

A Green Beret 12-man detachment was trained to teach as many as 1,500 South Vietnamese guerrillas. The Special Forces were training all of South Vietnam's Ranger companies, teams of South Vietnamese paratroopers, for raids behind the lines, and also all of the loyalist troops in Laos.

However, the Army's Green Berets were not the only US military trained in guerrilla warfare. The Air Force had its counterinsurgency group, 'COIN,' with its Air Commandos. The Navy had its 'SEALS' for 'unconventional warfare' on sea, air, and land. And the Marines, who had always considered themselves able to engage in counter-guerrilla operations, stepped up their training in this area. With the buildup of US involvement in South Vietnam, the Special Forces, the Air Commandos, and the SEALS were all being used to advise the South Vietnamese troops.

On the day Kennedy announced the departure of the Taylor mission in October, he also authorized the sending of SC-47s, B-26s and T-28 fighter bomber trainers to Bien Hoa Air Base, just north of Saigon. Because the Geneva agreement of 1954 prohibited the introduction of bombers in Indochina, the B-26s and SC-47s were redesignated 'reconnaissance-bombers' in an operation code-named 'Farm Gate.' On 16 December 1961, Farm Gate aircraft were authorized to fly combat missions provided a Vietnamese crew member was aboard. The first combat mission was 13 January 1962, when T-28s were flown in support of a South Vietnam outpost under attack by Viet Cong. On 29 January, T-28s and RB-26s flew attack missions from Saigon north to Quang Tri Province, near the 17th Parallel. By the end of the first month USAF planes had flown 229 Farm Gate sorties. Meanwhile, the Viet Cong improved their antiaircraft measures, using mainly 12.7 mm Soviet or Chinese-built heavy machine guns, and scored 89 hits against Farm Gate and other USAF planes during the first four months of 1962.

The first Farm Gate mission casualties occurred 11 February 1962 when nine US and South Vietnam crew members were killed in an SC-47 crash about 70 miles north of Saigon. An earlier USAF loss was the crash of a Fairchild C-123 defoliation plane on an 'Operation Ranch Hand' mission on 2 February 1962, six months after it was first proposed as a 'modern technological area-denial technique' to control roads and trails used by the Viet Cong forces. Nearly six million acres would eventually be treated with herbicides between 1962 and 1971, in addition to about 160,000 acres of Laos. The herbicides or defoliants included Agent Orange which contained a chemical, 2,4,5-T, that was contaminated with a toxic substance, dioxin.

As US aircraft casualties increased, new plans had to be developed for search and rescue missions. When an aircraft was reported overdue, it was reported to Detachment 3 of the Pacific Air Rescue Center at Tan Son Nhut Air Base and a rescue force was marshalled. Because a survivor or body might be located in hostile territory, it was sometimes necessary to transport an entire South Vietnamese army battalion by helicopter to secure the area so the survivor or body could be removed.

Early American entry in the Vietnam fighting was hampered in part by the military's own penchant for secrecy. Until 1962, all returning military advisers were required to sign certificates binding them to secrecy regarding their activities in Vietnam. Information gained from assisting South Vietnamese troops in fighting the Viet Cong could not be published or discussed openly. As a result, when large US troops deployment began in 1965 there was no ready reservoir of information available for field commanders who could have benefited from the experiences of colleagues whose familiarity with Vietnamese terrain and Viet Cong tactics dated back to 1957.

The first American military advisers often were frustrated by disregard for their recommendations by the South Vietnamese political

and military leaders. President Diem, for example, was so fearful of a possible *coupe d'état* by his own armored troops that he limited the amount of fuel available to tanks and armored personnel carriers so they would be unable to travel from their bases outside of Saigon to the presidential palace without literally running out of gas. Unfortunately, this precautionary rule also made it impossible for US military advisers to encourage extended armored sorties against the enemy. (Because tanks, armored cars and armored personnel carriers were used in repeated attempts to overthrow the government of South Vietnam in the 1960s, armored units were sometimes identified as 'coup troops' and tanks were called 'voting machines.')

Despite Diem's efforts to guard against an attack on himself by his own armored units, such vigilance failed on 1 November 1963 when armored units converged on the presidential palace for an assault that ended with the death of Diem. Diem and his brother, Ngo Dinh Nhu, were executed in a US-built M113 armored personnel carrier after they were captured

Above: Guard duty at a Civil Guard outpost in a fortified village. The British had used a system of fortified villages to help defeat Communist insurgents in Malaya in the 1950s but this technique proved less effective in Vietnam.

Left: Australian forces pictured during a SEATO exercise in Thailand in 1963. Australian troops also served in Vietnam.

while trying to flee Saigon. In the next 20 months, there were 10 successive heads of state of South Vietnam, with one general replacing another. Meanwhile, President Kennedy, who reportedly was at least aware of the plot to depose Diem, was himself the victim of assassination three weeks later.

Rolling Thunder and Flaming Dart + Overt US Operations in Vietnam

The war, which had continued at a plodding pace since the Eisenhower administration, failed to show any signs of success for South Vietnam or the US despite the buildup of US military advisers from 685 in 1960 to 16,000 during the Kennedy years. A steady flow of White House advisers, consultants and observers between Washington and Saigon also had failed to provide a viable plan for resolving the conflict without surrendering South Vietnam and its 17 million people to the Communist world.

Events were suddenly moving at a much

faster pace at the end of 1963. Both South Vietnam and the United States had acquired new political leadership in less than a month. And North Vietnam was starting a new campaign to seize South Vietnam by sending regular military units across the border to reinforce the Viet Cong infiltrators. The new American President, Lyndon Johnson, was abruptly jolted out of his own milieu of liberal domestic policies and into the role of avenging angel sent to smite the Communist forces in a dark jungle 9000 miles away.

Turmoil in Asia was not a new experience for Lyndon Johnson. He had served as a naval reserve officer in the World War II battles with Japan; had witnessed, as a former member of the US Congress, his Democratic party's embarrassment in the 'loss' of China to the Communists, and the frustrations of the Korean War; and as a US Senate floor leader in 1954, had led his party in blocking US intervention in the French Indochina War during the last battle for Dien Bien Phu. However, after nearly three years as Kennedy's Vice-President, Johnson actually knew very little about the US role in Vietnam before 22 November 1963, particularly the covert activities directed by the Kennedy White House. As Kennedy had failed to reveal the secret details of the Bay of Pigs invasion to UN Ambassador Adlai Stevenson, Kennedy also failed to brief Johnson about important details concerning America's undeclared war against Communists in Vietnam. The fact that Kennedy's personal advisers on Vietnam offered conflicting recommendations provided little guidance to Johnson, who overnight found himself required to make decisions affecting the lives of millions.

Among President Johnson's first decisions, General William Westmoreland was sent to Saigon to direct American military activities, and General Maxwell Taylor was assigned to Saigon as US Ambassador, replacing Henry Cabot Lodge. Johnson also authorized the use of US Navy and Air Force jets on reconnaissance support missions over Laos and a continued use of South Vietnamese torpedo boats in raids along the North Vietnam coast. During one such raid on 31 July 1964, South Vietnamese PT boats attacked two offshore islands in the North Vietnamese Gulf of Tonkin. Two days later, on 2 August 1964, three North Vietnamese torpedo boats attacked the USS *Maddox*, a destroyer on an intelligence-gathering mission in the Gulf of Tonkin. Johnson ordered a second destroyer, the USS *C Turner Joy*, to join the *Maddox*. On 4 August 1964, a second attack was reported, after South Vietnamese torpedo boats made another midnight raid on North Vietnamese territory.

Although the coded messages of the 4 August

attack were unclear regarding the actual sighting of North Vietnamese ships, the incident was regarded by the White House as an unprovoked attack on the US Navy in international waters. On 5 August 1964, President Johnson appeared on national television to announce that 'hostile actions on the high seas' had required him to order the military forces of the United States to take action in reply.' As Johnson spoke, more than 60 carrier-based planes from the *Constellation* and *Ticonderoga* bombed the port and oil storage facilities at Vinh, North Vietnam, just north of the 17th Parallel.

In a retrospective endorsement of the President's decision to order an overt US military operation against North Vietnam, Congress on 7 August 1964 passed the so-called Gulf of Tonkin Resolution. The resolution, which many members of Congress believed would encourage the North Vietnamese to back down quickly rather than face the military might of the United States, passed the House by a vote of 416–0 and the Senate by 88–2. Senator Wayne Morse of Oregon, who opposed the resolution, said the United States had become 'drunk with military power.' The wording of the resolution would become the subject of a constitutional controversy years later: was the Gulf of Tonkin Resolution the 'functional equivalent' of a declaration of war? The resolution did not, as experts later argued, 'authorize' or 'empower' the President to make war, but it did 'approve' and 'support' such military activity 'as the President determines.'

After 5 August 1964, there was no longer any question of US military involvement in Viet-

Left: Typical terrain in the Hau My area, 50 miles south of Saigon, seen from an H-21 helicopter of the 57th Transport Company on 20 February 1963 while the unit was airlifting men of the 7th Vietnamese Division into the area.

Above: South Vietnamese troops set up a mortar position.

Right: Among the most reliable allies for the US forces were the Montagnard tribesmen. The picture shows a Montagnard village from the gun position of an approaching H-21 helicopter.

nam. With Congressional endorsement and a public announcement by the President of the United States, America no longer needed to hide behind CIA-directed operations of Vietnamese nationals or mercenaries, military aircraft repainted with the insignias of other nations, US military personnel labeled 'advisers,' equipment mislabeled to avoid violations of the 1954 Geneva agreement and other subterfuges. The ground rules had changed.

But North Vietnam was not cowed by threats of US military power. In Hanoi, the response was one of anger, air raid drills and other civil defense measures. It was the South Vietnamese who were 'really nervous,' as described by a Saigon official, about the prospect of being chosen the silent partner in an undeclared war

between the United States and the Moscow and Peking-backed North Vietnamese armies. There were riots, rumors of coups and rapid changes in occupants of the presidential palace. At one point, US Ambassador Taylor reportedly told a meeting of South Vietnamese political and military leaders, 'We Americans are tired of your coups.'

Close to 80 American military personnel had been killed in the Vietnam fighting by the end of 1963. During 1964, attacks on US military personnel increased in frequency and intensity. On the eve of the 1964 US presidential elections, Communist guerrillas staged a mortar attack on a US airbase at Bien Hoa, destroying US B-57 bombers and killing a number of US airmen stationed at the airbase. On 1 January

1965, US combat ground troops were placed on a first phase alert for action in Vietnam. And as 1965 began, the 'Free World' countries were joining in. There had been no particular effort by the US to secure United Nations support for its action in Vietnam, and none had been given. However, the US 'internationalized' its mission in Vietnam by inviting other countries to contribute troops. South Korea, Thailand, and the Philippine Islands responded favorably, as did Australia and New Zealand.

As the Johnson administration took office again in 1965, a series of retaliatory air raids, code-named 'Rolling Thunder,' was immediately planned against the North Vietnamese for the attack on Bien Hoa. Pentagon generals described the operation as 'surgical' missions. They believed that Hanoi would quit the war when USAF bombers began destroying cities and other targets in North Vietnam. Scattered air raids against Viet Cong and North Vietnamese targets had seemed only to harden the resolve of the Communist Vietnamese.

Then, on 7 February 1965, when the Viet Cong mortared a US military compound at Pleiku and left nine Americans dead and 75 wounded, about 50 carrier-based planes of the US 7th fleet attacked the Dong Hoi barracks above the 17th Parallel. Called Operation Flaming Dart, and authorized by Johnson, it began the countdown to the full-scale Rolling Thunder. With this plan activated, the US began evacuating the families of US military personnel from South Vietnam.

As President Johnson's announcement on 2 March 1965 that 'necessities of war have compelled us to bomb North Vietnam,' Phase I of the operation began with air strikes directed against military and transportation targets in North Vietnam below 20 degrees North latitude, and continued until 11 May. Rolling Thunder began as gradual reprisals rather than hard-hitting military campaigns, but gradually escalated into major air strikes as the war continued.

Two battalions of US Marines were also being sent to Vietnam to guard US bases there against retaliation for the bombing raids. Their mission was identified as 'offensive patrolling for defensive purposes,' a euphemism for what later came to be known as 'search and destroy.' Among the last to learn about plans for the landing of the Marines were members of the South Vietnamese cabinet. Although South Vietnam had an army of 500,000, deployed mainly in 'pacification' missions, the Saigon government was embarrassed by the announcement that the US had decided unilaterally to send Marines to protect South Vietnam from North Vietnam. South Vietnamese Chief of Staff Nguyen Van Thieu asked that the introduction of the Marines be 'inconspicuous.'

At 0900 hours on March 8, hundreds of members of the US Marine Corps hit the beaches at Da Nang in full combat gear, rifles ready for attack. Brigadier General Frederick J Karch led the 9th US Marine Expeditionary Brigade ashore in the 65-minute landing operation, complete with M-48 medium tanks, 106-

mm recoilless rifles and 105-mm howitzers. While television cameras taped the scene, a committee of young Vietnamese girls welcomed the Americans with leis of orchids. The event went unnoticed in the United States, where media attention was focused on Selma, Alabama, as 200 state troopers attacked 550 blacks protesting voting rights discrimination.

Although Da Nang had experienced only one reported guerrilla attack before the arrival of the Marines, the presence of US Leathernecks seemed to attract Viet Cong to the airbase. During one of the first nights at Da Nang, I Company Marines fought off three successive attempts by guerrillas to infiltrate their position. The Marines were helped by a newly introduced piece of equipment: radar that detected enemy ground troops.

As the US increased the intensity of its attacks on Viet Cong and North Vietnamese forces, representatives of 19 Communist countries were summoned to Moscow to discuss the situation in Vietnam. But, except for condemning US intervention as 'barbarous,' there was no sign of unified action against the United States by members of the Communist world.

In May 1965, US Air Force and Navy pilots were authorized to fly missions under 'new rules of engagement.' In Phase II of Rolling Thunder, targets north of 20 degrees latitude were cleared for attack, but pilots were not permitted to enter a 30-mile buffer zone along the Chinese border, or within 30 miles of Hanoi and 10 miles of Haiphong. Air strikes were continued in four-ship flights spaced one to three minutes apart. US planes also began using Lazy Dog anti-personnel bombs, which exploded 100 feet above ground and hurled tiny steel darts over a 100-yard square area.

In April 1965, two more battalions of US Marines arrived in Vietnam, and by May General Westmoreland had plans for 'holding

Left: President Diem making a radio broadcast shortly before he was overthrown and assassinated in a coup.

Above: Vietnamese soldiers aboard a transport helicopter. The American crew chief in the background waits to give landing instructions.

Right: Wounded Vietnamese soldiers being evacuated to a field hospital.

Below: A South Vietnamese intelligence officer questions a villager about possible Viet Cong sympathies.

positions' at Chu Lai, Quang Ngai, Qui Nhon, Bien Hoa and Vung Tai, plus a new Naval base at Cam Ranh Bay. The holding positions, or enclaves, required more than 80,000 additional US troops. By June 1965, General Westmoreland had command of more than 115,000 troops including 20,000 from 'Free World' countries. In July, President Johnson increased the US contribution alone to 125,000 men and 'foresaw the possibility' that still more Americans might be needed in Vietnam.

At the same time, President Johnson revealed publicly that rules of engagement for ground troops also had been changed. Since 26 June 1965, US ground forces had been authorized to engage in combat in 'any situation in which the use of such troops is required.'

Airborne US and Australian troops wasted no time in implementing the new rules for ground forces. On June 27, they launched the first major offensive in Zone D, about 30 miles north of Saigon, after flights of B-52 bombers based on Guam had rained 270 tons of bombs on the area, known to the troops on the ground as the 'OK Corral.' It was the first use of B-52 Superfortresses in the Vietnam War and the results were disappointing. A helicopter survey of the jungle wilderness following the air raid failed to detect a single Viet Cong casualty but the 'Victor Charlies' demonstrated that they were alive and well by sniping at the survey teams. The ground forces, consisting mainly of 600 members of the US 173rd Airborne Brigade, were sent into the zone to do the job SAC bombers apparently failed to do.

Within a few days, the US 101st Airborne Division (which had been commanded by then General, now Ambassador Maxwell Taylor during World War II) arrived in Vietnam. The tough paratroopers were quickly aware of the incongruities of the Vietnam War, as were the US Marines who preceded them four months earlier. A member of the 101st Airborne saw a resort area and asked, 'Where's the war?' 'Wait until after dark,' he was told. It was a war unlike any other war experienced by American troops. Taylor was himself amazed at the complexity of conflict, which on any particular day could manifest itself differently in tactics or political maneuvers in each of South Vietnam's 44 provinces.

Nonlinear and Multidirectional Combat

Because of the strategic and political considerations, US tactical operations were directed toward defeating the enemy within a particular Communist-controlled province rather than capturing terrain features or other conventional objectives. Such tactics theoretically would enable the South Vietnamese government to extend its control over the people within an area. The ground strategy was that of a very large mobile defense. The Pentagon described the nature of this kind of warfare as nonlinear and multidirectional.

The American units benefited from experience gained during the Korean War of fighting on a dispersed battlefield. Advances in tactical communications and the development of larger and better helicopters increased the mobility and control of US combat units. General Westmoreland responded to any change in tactics of the Viet Cong and North Vietnamese Army with a 'fire brigade' approach in which offensive missions were generally ordered only against enemy forces that constitute an 'immediate and grave' threat. US offensive operations utilized mainly artillery fire and air power until ground strength would increase in 1966 to an effective fighting level.

In mid-August 1965, members of the 3rd Marine Tank Battalion became involved in the first major battle in Vietnam using US armored troops. Operation Starlite began as a preempt attack to block reported plans by a Viet Cong regiment to raid the Chu Lai airfield southeast of Da Nang. Using helicopters, amphibious tanks, fighter-bombers, and fire from six-inch guns of a US Navy cruiser offshore, the American force under the command of Marine Lieutenant General Lewis Walt battled the Viet Cong above ground and through tunnels and caves for three days. After the Marines had driven the Viet Cong to the sea, the enemy body count was over 700 while Marine casualties included 45 killed in action. In addition to being the first tank battle of the Vietnam War, the Chu Lai fight was the first 'all-American' operation and the first regimental-size battle for US forces since the Korean War.

Operation Starlite also was considered a fair test of the new American approach to fighting by combining firepower with mobility. To emphasize the importance of the approach, the US 1st Cavalry Division was rechristened the Airmobile Division and equipped with 400 Chinook and Iroquois helicopters, six OV-1 Mohawk reconnaissance aircraft with infrared scanners, radar and photographic devices, and a fleet of C-130 and C-133 AF transports capable of moving everything except the largest helicopters.

The Airmobile Division underwent its first test in the Battle of the Ia Drang Valley, which began in October 1965 in the western Pleiku Valley near the Cambodian border. Within hours after debarking at Qui Nhon, the Airmobile Division was en route by helicopter to the Central Highlands, where the 66th Regiment of the North Vietnamese Army had been discovered. The US 9th Cavalry was the first unit to engage the North Vietnamese troops, a concentration of enemy soldiers guarding a regimental hospital. The US unit was joined by reinforcements from the 8th Cavalry. Meanwhile, units of the US 4th Cavalry assigned to secure a highway leading to the American firebase at Lai Khe began to receive mortar fire south of Ap Bau Bang. Viet Cong troops moved to within 50 yards of the US cavalry troops, pouring a hail of small arms and automatic weapons fire into the American defenses. The US troops drove back the Viet Cong with 50-caliber machine gun fire from M113 armored personnel carriers moved to the perimeter of the defensive position. The VC attacked five times in six hours, each assault coming from a different direction, but they finally withdrew after failing to destroy the US armored unit.

The Ia Drang Operations continued for a month and included fighting which General Westmoreland described 'as fierce as any ever experienced' by American units. As in early engagements of US units, air support was given by highflying USAF B-52s whose half-ton bombs could eliminate Viet Cong tunnels and caves that often provided sanctuary for the enemy troops. US combat losses in the October-November battles numbered about 300, compared to an estimated 1800 Viet Cong and North Vietnamese Army casualties.

If the Viet Cong and North Vietnamese strategy and tactics created a war unlike wars fought previously by Americans, the US troops proved they were equally innovative in their new uses of modern technology. The Viet Cong were baffled by the use of M133 armored personnel carriers at first and fled the field when the vehicles approached, although they later found the machines vulnerable to 57-mm recoilless rifle fire. The American use of fleets of helicopters altered traditional concepts and

Right: Apprehensive Viet Cong prisoners taken during a search and destroy operation in 1964.

Below right: US Army Huey helicopters ready to embark South Vietnamese infantry for a mission in October 1964.

Below: ARVN troops cross a makeshift bridge after the concrete permanent structure, built not long before by US Army engineers, had been blown up.

Above: Vietnamese soldiers undergoing training.

Left: US Army advisers to a Vietnamese Special Forces unit inspect a machine gun post near Thoi Minh, November 1964.

tactics of ground fighting. A floating pier the length of a football field was towed to Cam Ranh Bay from Charleston, South Carolina, to ease the pressure on Saigon port facilities. C-47 transports were rigged with six-barrel Gatling-type guns and named 'Puff the Magic Dragon.' UH-1B helicopters were fitted with brilliant landing lights for night searches along canals and rivers. A flying command post was created in a C-130 transport with eight television screens and computer data bases from which battle maps and other information could be projected and studied by officers circling high above the fighting front.

Tactics were designed to fit the developing encounter with the enemy, with no fixed model for search-and-destroy missions. 'Horseshoes' were formed by placing some units in blocking positions while others drove the

enemy to the center of the horseshoe. In a 'hammer and anvil' mission, a blocking position was occupied by some units while others drove the enemy toward it. US troops also employed ambush emplacements. Firebases were created by blasting a 300-foot wide hole in a hilltop and ferrying in 105-mm howitzers by helicopter to control huge jungle areas.

The Pentagon, always mindful of the public relations aspects of a war, objected to General Westmoreland's choice of words for a mission called 'Operation Masher,' just as Washington had protested against General Ridgway's 'Operation Killer' during the Korean War. Washington officials also eliminated the term, 'search-and-destroy,' which was replaced by 'reconnaissance in force' or 'clearing operations,' although the objective was unchanged. The tactics actually employed by US forces were

Right: Prisoners under guard while a patrol continues its search for hidden arms.

determined largely by the enemy's own organization and tactics. There were local or provincial Viet Cong, part-time guerrillas who were civilians by day and fought at night in squad- to battalion-size units. Main-force Viet Cong were organized into battalions or regiments and were capable of large-scale, violent operations. Units of the regular North Vietnamese Army (NVA) operated as battalions, regiments or divisions and were equipped with tanks and heavy artillery. NVA troops did not blend with the local population and usually operated near the border of a neighboring country, which provided sanctuary when chased by US military personnel.

Just beyond the South Vietnamese frontier was the Ho Chi Minh Trail, used by the North Vietnamese Army. When the war started it was little more than a jungle path through rugged mountainous country. The Ho Chi Minh Trail eventually stretched some 3500 miles with all its spurs and side roads, and was being developed by the North Vietnamese into something more like a two-lane highway. Troop reinforcements moved down the trail from North Vietnam at a rate of 7500 per month despite US efforts to disrupt the traffic. Americans bombarded the trail by day and Communist volunteers repaired the damage by night.

Mobility was the key to all Viet Cong and North Vietnamese operations. Their doctrine was: 'withdraw when the enemy advances, harass when he defends, attack when he is tired, pursue when he withdraws.' However, the slogan of the US ground forces was: 'find, fix, fight, and finish.' Despite the semantics approved by the Pentagon, US operations were essentially unchanged and consisted mainly of search-and-destroy, clear-and-secure missions as a period of prolonged offensives began in 1966.

The cost of the war for Americans increased as troop strength and combat operations increased from an average of 25 Americans killed per year from 1961 through 1963; the toll rose to nearly 40 per week during the last half of 1965. The price in dollars also rose from about $1 million per day to nearly $35 million per day by 1966, when US combat deaths would jump to nearly 100 per week.

In March 1966, the biggest search-and-destroy mission of the war to date, with Operation White Wing and Operation Double Eagle, was at a large Viet Cong controlled area at Binh Dinh. Double Eagle was manned by 5000 US Marines with support by 2000 South Vietnamese troops moving southward along the coast, while White Wing involved 12,000 members of the US 1st Cavalry Division plus South Vietnamese troops headed northward for a linkup of the two operations. The combined operation trapped two Communist regiments, one North Vietnamese regulars and one Viet Cong, and ended with 2400 enemy dead and thousands of prisoners. One prisoner, a Viet Cong colonel, led White Wing troops to a VC regimental headquarters which the 1st Cavalry took in hand-to-hand fighting that accounted for 150 of the enemy dead.

While US Marines and infantrymen were

fighting in the Binh Dinh area, President Johnson announced the resumption of Rolling Thunder bombing raids on North Vietnam on 1 April 1966. Navy jets from the US aircraft carrier *Ranger* and USAF F-105s hit targets north of the 17th Parallel to end a 37-day bombing moratorium called by Johnson to give North Vietnam an opportunity to make a peace gesture. Hanoi had used an earlier bombing break to install SAM antiaircraft missile launchers and to send 6000 fresh army regulars into South Vietnam to reinforce units already across the DMZ. Now all of North Vietnam, aside from specific sanctuary areas, was vulnerable to attack by Rolling Thunder. And the US aircraft were equipped with radar homing and warning devices. Thus, the US Air Force had its first real capability to detect an impending SAM launch.

As the war continued through 1966, there was an increasing demand by field commanders for armored support. These were forces whose primary means of combat was to fight mounted, such as in tanks or other mechanized carriers. Because of the nature of enemy tactics, armor was often used to find the enemy. Armor also was used to protect highway links between Saigon and provincial capitals. A series of battles was fought during the summer of 1966 along Route 13 between Saigon and Loc Ninh, also known as the Minh Thanh Road. After five major engagements on the road between June and September 1966, members of Task Force Dragon, composed of 4th Cavalry and 2nd Infantry troops, developed counter-ambush techniques that accounted for 850 casualties among three regiments of the 9th Viet Cong Division. One technique, called 'herringbone,' required all armored vehicles to stop immediately and pivot to face outward, alternate vehicles facing either side of the road with all weapons firing.

During the herringbone maneuver, the 'soft-skin' vehicles hid behind the armored vehicles. The withering fire laid down by the vehicles reduced the ability of the enemy to use antitank weapons while artillery and air strikes focused on the enemy positions. The tactics developed by armored units in Vietnam in 1966 were somewhat contrary to traditions established in previous military operations. Armored units

were found to be effective as a fixing force while airmobile infantry became the encircling element. Also, armored force led by tanks had sufficient combat power to withstand a mass ambush until supporting artillery, air and infantry could be brought in to destroy the enemy. Thus armored elements could be used to create or force a fight while other units provided the encircling action.

During the years of American involvement in the Vietnam War, most of the action had been in northern provinces. Saigon, in the south, had been spared. But below Saigon was the Mekong Delta with its many waterways. By 1966, the US Navy had established Task Force 115 to help patrol coastal areas and Task Force 116 to repel enemy attacks on river outposts. As in much of the rest of South Vietnam, the government claimed control of the Mekong Delta by day but by night it appeared to belong to the Viet Cong.

To help the South Vietnamese government establish more effective control over the region, the US Military Assistance Command, Vietnam (MACV) created a 'riverine' force of floating barracks supported by patrol boats, landing craft and helicopters, a joint Army-Navy effort. The force was based aboard US Navy craft that included self-propelled barracks ships, LSTs, harbor tugs, landing craft, and repair ships. These were staffed by a US Army infantry reinforced brigade. Riverine troops were members of the US Army 9th Infantry Division who received special training by a team from the Naval Amphibious School. The riverine force operated nearly 200 assault-craft and other vessels, inspecting thousands of sampans, conducting landing operations in places not easily accessible to helicopters or land vehicles, and protecting populated areas with river frontage as far inland as the Plain of Reeds.

By the end of 1966, American combat deaths had reached a total of 7000. The mighty US military machine was cannibalizing billions of dollars worth of equipment and supplies from mainland defenses and NATO commitments in order to fill a growing gap of fighting requirements not covered by the already massive funding allocated by the Johnson administration.

Top left: Soldiers of the 1st Air Cavalry Division unload supplies from a C-130 Hercules at An Khe, 25 August 1965.

Above: Vietnamese soldiers and American advisers come under fire while unloading supplies from a US Marine helicopter.

Right: US Army Special Forces sergeant directs the fire of a Vietnamese machine gun team in an operation in the so-called Iron Triangle area in November 1964.

Far right: Viet Cong prisoners are loaded into a UH-1 helicopter to be taken for questioning. The UH-1 Huey was the workhorse of the US forces in Vietnam.

VIETNAM–FROM COMMITMENT TO VIETNAMIZATION

Before 1967, US military policy in Vietnam had been that operations by units smaller than a division or brigade were the key to winning battles and skirmishes. In jungle operations, small-unit tactics were essential because heavy vegetation and broken terrain provided ideal concealment for the enemy. If a commander expected to find the enemy, subordinate units had to be dispersed. However, beginning in 1967, division or multi-division forces began to be employed as spoiling attacks or for reconnaissance in force into enemy-held areas.

The Build-up of Operations and the Tet Offensive

In January 1967, the first deliberately planned large unit mission, Operation Cedar Falls, was launched against an enemy base and logistical center in a thick jungle area known as the Iron Triangle, between Saigon and the Cambodian border. The area was to be sealed off by units of the mechanized 5th and 22nd Infantry, 16th and 34th Armor, 4th and 17th Cavalry and 11th Armored Cavalry. More than 50 bulldozers and some tanks—equipped with plow blades to clear out jungle paths or move burned-out vehicles—accompanied the M113s and M48A3 tanks into the area.

By taking the fight to the enemy, the American units scored the greatest intelligence breakthrough of the war. While clearing nine square miles of jungle, the Cedar Falls force captured a half-million pages of documents which contained the command structure and battle plans of the entire North Vietnamese and Viet Cong armies.

Following completion of Operation Cedar Falls on 25 January 1967, the emphasis shifted to Operation Junction City, the largest US military operation of the war up to that time. The Junction City plan was a horseshoe blocking operation that began 22 February 1967 with a 4th Cavalry task force racing along Provincial Route 4 to reinforcing positions near Katum. Artillery and engineering units of the 2nd Mechanized Infantry followed to establish firebases. Then, units of the 25th Infantry Division and the 11th Cavalry Regiment began sweeping the sides of the horseshoe.

Enemy response to Operation Junction City was scattered and sporadic for the first two weeks of the US offensive. But Viet Cong counterattacks in multibattalion strength began on the night of 10 March 1967. A second counterattack on the night of March 19 was particularly fierce. US defenders fired 2500 artillery rounds at the attacking VC. In close-range fighting, the enemy was blasted with cannister and high explosive rounds set on delayed fuses fired into the ground ahead of the Viet Cong.

On 21 March 1967, the Viet Cong launched an unprecedented daylight attack against the American force in an attempt to take Firebase Gold from the 77th Artillery and 22nd Infantry units near Suoi Tre. Using human wave tactics, the Viet Cong overran the east perimeter of the firebase and captured a quadruple .50 caliber

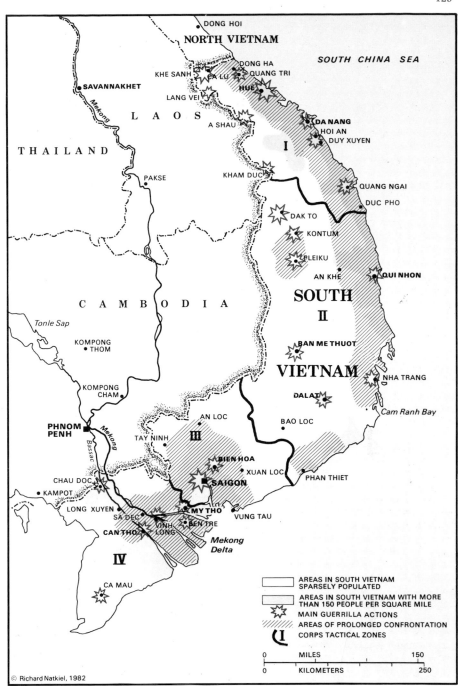

MAP LABELS

NORTH VIETNAM

DONG HOI

SOUTH CHINA SEA

KHE SANH · CA LU · DONG HA · QUANG TRI

SAVANNAKHET

LANG VEI · HUE

LAOS

A SHAU

DA NANG · HOI AN · DUY XUYEN

THAILAND

PAKSE

KHAM DUC · I

QUANG NGAI · DUC PHO

DAK TO

KONTUM

PLEIKU

AN KHE · QUI NHON

CAMBODIA

SOUTH II VIETNAM

Tonle Sap

KOMPONG THOM

BAN ME THUOT

NHA TRANG

DALAT · Cam Ranh Bay

KOMPONG CHAM

AN LOC · BAO LOC

TAY NINH · III

PHNOM PENH

BIEN HOA · XUAN LOC · PHAN THIET

SAIGON

CHAU DOC

KAMPOT

LONG XUYEN · MY THO · VUNG TAU

SA DEC · VINH LONG · BEN TRE

CAN THO · Mekong Delta

IV

CA MAU

AREAS IN SOUTH VIETNAM SPARSELY POPULATED

AREAS IN SOUTH VIETNAM WITH MORE THAN 150 PEOPLE PER SQUARE MILE

MAIN GUERRILLA ACTIONS

AREAS OF PROLONGED CONFRONTATION

CORPS TACTICAL ZONES

0 MILES 150

0 KILOMETERS 250

© Richard Natkiel, 1982

Above: US Army paratroops jump over South Vietnam during Operation Junction City in 1967.

Previous page: Crew chief of a UH-1 stands ready at his M60 machine gun during an operation in the Mekong Delta area in 1967.

Above right: The general situation in Vietnam during the American involvement.

Left: Movie actor Glenn Ford, a reserve naval officer, looks on as a young Marine shares his C Rations with Vietnamese villagers.

Right: Twin 40mm M42 guns of the 60th Artillery during Operation Francis Marian, near the Cambodian border in August 1967.

machine gun which they tried to turn on the American defenders. That weapon was destroyed by artillery fire. As the VC advanced to within hand grenade distance of the command post, US armored and infantry reinforcements arrived with 200 machine guns and 90-mm tank guns firing simultaneously. In the close fighting, Viet Cong troops tried to climb aboard the armored vehicles but were cut down. Some VC were crushed under the vehicle tracks. The enemy finally withdrew, leaving behind 600 dead. This first major American effort to take the fight to the Viet Cong continued into late April when the enemy simply faded away.

During May 1967, much of the fighting between US and Viet Cong forces took place in the Mekong Delta, where units of the US 9th Infantry Division struggled for control of rice paddies and mangrove swamps. One of the hardest fought battles of the campaign centered in the Ap Bac II area, a base for VC operations. On May 2, the US 47th and 60th Infantry Regiments fought through irrigation ditches and dense vegetation for 10 hours just to get within hand grenade distance of enemy bunkers. Enemy resistance consisted primarily of rifle and automatic weapons fire. The 60th Infantry finally charged the VC line of bunkers on foot and in fulltracked armored personnel carriers. A sweep of the area the next morning indicated the VC had lost the equivalent of a reinforced company. The US lost two killed in action.

The riverine force supported much of the US action in the Mekong Delta during the spring of 1967. The force introduced the use of barges for floating helicopter pads and artillery firebases. An artillery barge carrying two M102 howitzers would be towed into position by US Navy LCM-8 assault craft. Floating armored troop carriers moved through the delta water-

ways in convoy battle lines. During June and July 1967, Operation Coronado I was conducted as a mission to secure a US base in the vicinity of Dong Tam. Other Mekong Delta operations during 1967 were fought from Go Cong in July, through Ban Long and Cam Son in September, and Rach Ruong in December. The battle at Rach Ruong involved the US 47th Infantry and ended after two days with a VC body count of 266, and with 98 US Casualties, including nine infantrymen killed.

The Mekong Delta was used by the Viet Cong as an area for testing new tactics, and an upsurge in the number of attacks on US outposts in the area near the end of 1967 suggested that a buildup was underway for a major offensive against US and South Vietnamese forces. The information was confirmed by captured documents, aerial surveillance and boasts by captured Viet Cong soldiers that South Vietnam would be 'liberated by Tet,' the lunar New Year. Tet took place on 31 January 1968. Enemy soldiers were reported infiltrating Saigon, Hue, and other cities, mingling with the holiday crowds. American troops were then shifted from outlying posts to positions closer to populated areas. At the US Marine base near Khe Sanh, just below the 17th Parallel, fighting had started as early as 20 January 1968, but it was not recognized immediately as part of the Tet offensive. The territory had been fought over many times since the Khe Sanh position was first established by a team of Green Berets in August 1962.

The attack on Khe Sanh was directed by North Vietnamese General Vo Nguyen Giap. He had distinguished himself 14 years earlier as the Communist military leader who defeated the French at Dien Bien Phu. His troops at Khe Sanh were two divisions of North Vietnamese regulars and included a Hanoi regi-

Above: A feature of every camp in Vietnam was the provision of ready cover in case of a surprise attack. Here every tent is provided with at least some protection by a barrier of sandbags.

Above right: Crew chief of a helicopter lays down fire on a suspected Viet Cong position. A tracer round from the machine gun can be seen speeding to earth.

Far right: A US Army display of captured Viet Cong equipment.

Right: A wounded man is brought back to a landing zone for evacuation. The US medical services in Vietnam broke all records for the speed with which a wounded soldier could expect to be receiving proper treatment and partly as a consequence a very high proportion of wounded men could be expected to recover.

ment that fought at Dien Bien Phu. The main defense force at Khe Sanh was the US 26th Marine Regiment commanded by Colonel David E Lownds.

The Marines, assisted by South Vietnamese rangers, had M48 tanks with 90-mm guns, 106-mm recoilless rifles with .50 caliber sighting rifles, grenade launchers, 105-mm artillery pieces, .50 caliber machine guns and M-16 rifles. General Giap was equipped with the finest armament the USSR could supply, including 152-mm longtubed cannons, 60-mm and 82-mm mortars, 122-mm rockets and AK-47 rifles. In one test of the M-16 against the AK-47, a US Marine and a North Vietnamese infiltrator came face to face, their rifles pointed at each other. Both pulled the trigger at the same time, but only the M-16 fired; the AK-47 jammed. The Marine later explained, 'I cleaned my weapon last night. The other guy didn't.'

General Giap began his attack on Khe Sanh on 20 January 1968, but the 6000 defenders of the Marine post drove back the North Vietnamese. The Marines were congratulating themselves at 0530 hours the following morning when they began receiving

Left: An infantryman examines a booby trapped 155mm shell found in a sweep near Tay Ninh in 1967. The Viet Cong were most adept at setting booby traps.

Right: Army men disembark from an Air Force C-123 transport during 'Junction City' in 1967.

Far right: Early experience in Vietnam soon led to the M113 armored personnel carrier being fitted with a variety of medium and heavy machine guns. An M113 of the 11th Armored Cavalry is shown, near Ben Cat in January 1967.

Below: Firefighting operations aboard the carrier *Forrestal* following the accidental firing of a missile while the ship was operating in the Gulf of Tonkin in July 1967.

hundreds of rounds of mortar, artillery and rocket fire. The initial bombardment destroyed helicopters, trucks, tent, fuel storage and ammunition stores. An ammunition dump receiving a direct hit burned for 48 hours with shells randomly exploding.

Each day the bombardment continued through February and March, varying mainly in the number of incoming rounds received by the defending Marines. The peak day of shelling was February 23 when 1300 incoming rounds were counted. General Giap used more firepower against Khe Sanh than was expended in the capture of Dien Bien Phu. The American response included a total of over 150,000 artillery rounds plus 100,000 tons of bombs dropped by B-52s and USAF, Navy and Marine fighter-bombers. During Operation Pegasus, the mission to relieve the Marines after 77 days of the siege, there were 45 B-52 strikes plus 1625 tactical sorties by Army, Navy, Air Force and Marine aircraft.

Operation Pegasus was a combined breakout and rescue mission. The besieged Marines were beginning to push back the North Vietnamese troops surrounding Khe Sanh as the US 1st and 3rd Marine Divisions and the US Army Americal Division advanced along old Colonial Route 9 to engage North Vietnam units. One of the bloodiest battles of the operation involved a confrontation between three companies of the US 9th Marines and elements of the 304th North Vietnamese division for control of Hill 471, a key terrain feature overlooking Route 9. For two days in April Marines and North Vietnamese attacked and counterattacked each other until the latter withdrew, leaving 122 dead on the slopes.

The completion of Operation Pegasus was more of a media event than a case of US Marines

being snatched from the jaws of destruction. Marines and US cavalrymen posed for news photographers when the units linked up at Khe Sanh, although both the Marines and the rescuers felt it was just another event in the daily routine of fighting North Vietnamese near the DMZ.

Despite the alerts and preparations for enemy assaults during Tet, not even the top brass of the US military command expected an attack of the magnitude that followed. Initial attacks at some US and allied bases were reported on January 29, nine days after the attack on Khe Sanh had begun, and US troops were ordered on maximum alert. Instead of the usual ambushes and probes, the North Vietnamese Army and tens of thousands of Viet Cong conducted an offensive that was later compared to the German Ardennes campaign of World War II. At least 4000 VC guerrillas had entered Saigon, dressed as farmers, vendors or holiday tourists carrying packages that concealed their weapons. Because of their familiarity with the streets and alleys of the capital city, the Viet Cong were able to operate effectively in the urban battlefield.

In Saigon, the start of the Tet offensive began with an armed attack on the US Embassy during the early hours of January 31. While in a shootout with Viet Cong inside the embassy compound, US Marines were able to escort the new ambassador, Ellsworth Bunker, to the protection of a wine cellar. The incident might have become a forerunner of the seizure of the US Embassy in Teheran by Iranian demonstrators in November 1979, but in the Saigon embassy invasion none of the infiltrators entered the building. The six-hour gun battle on the embassy grounds ended with 19 Viet Cong and seven US Marines killed.

In the city of Hue, near the 17th Parallel, some 5000 infiltrators suddenly changed into the uniforms of North Vietnamese Army troops and were joined by 7000 reinforcements. They quickly gained control of most of the religious and cultural centers. For 26 days, the North Vietnamese held their positions in Hue in one of the most intense and sustained battles of the entire war. The Hue defenders—US air and ground cavalry, and US Marine armored units assisted by South Vietnamese armor—expended remarkably large amounts of ammunition, requiring replenishment of entire vehicle loads every few hours.

From the 17th Parallel to the mouth of the Mekong River, the Tet offensive raged simultaneously through literally hundreds of cities, towns and villages. At Quang Ngai City, the enemy was routed in a mere eight hours, and in Pineapple Forest, near Tam Ky, ground and cavalry units killed 180 Viet Cong with only one casualty, a wounded cavalryman.

But in Pleiku, Viet Cong assaults continued for five days, and a battle in the seacoast city of Phan Thiet lasted eight days. In the provincial capital of Kontum, the Viet Cong were confronted by units of the US 1st Cavalry Division which had rehearsed various strategies for resisting such an attack and already had a scenario to follow. At least 79 separate engagements were fought in the Saigon area. The urban fighting there ranged from a mechanized infantry counterattack on a downtown Saigon racetrack to a hand-to-hand struggle among the tombstones of a cemetery.

General Westmoreland regarded the successful defense of South Vietnam against the Viet Cong and North Vietnamese troops as a victory. But military and political leaders around the world, and Americans at home, viewing the battle scenes on television, were deeply concerned that North Vietnam and its VC cadres were capable of mounting a nationwide offensive, invading Saigon in force and holding Hue against a US military might for 26 days—just as the world was amazed 15 years earlier by the ability of cotton-clad Chinese peasants armed with rifles and grenades to frustrate a powerful military machine in Korea.

The greatest Communist success was at Lang Vei, southwest of Khe Sanh, where North Vietnamese infantry troops—in their first use of a tank-led assault—overran a Green Beret camp, during 6–7 February 1968, killing 10 of the US Special Forces and 225 South Vietnamese and Montagnard irregulars defending the base. Fourteen of the Green Berets and 175 of the allied defenders escaped when US planes staged a mock air raid on the North Vietnamese; while the enemy troops ducked to hide from the aircraft, the defenders ran from the camp. Some of the Green Berets found refuge with the US Marines at nearby Khe Sanh, under siege itself at the time.

Strategies Shift, Nixon gains Office

The North Vietnamese left behind more than 1300 of their dead at Khe Sanh but shallow graves found later indicated the enemy losses probably totaled closer to 15,000 during the 11 weeks of fighting. US casualties included 22 Marines killed in fighting during the Khe Sanh siege, 54 killed in crashes of C-123 and C-130 transports at the Khe Sanh airstrip, and 92 US Army and Marine deaths during Operation Pegasus. The Khe Sanh battle, like the Tet offensive itself, became an issue of controversy between supporters and critics of the Vietnam War back in the United States. The argument reached the boiling point in June 1968 when it was announced that Khe Sanh would be razed

Above left: A US Air Force U-10 utility aircraft drops propaganda leaflets over a Vietnamese village.

Above: Men of the 11th Cavalry load a wounded buddy aboard a casualty evacuation helicopter, following a firefight near Lai Khe during Operation Junction City II, 7 April 1967.

Above right: Mortarmen of the 101st Airborne Division in action in the A Shau valley in August 1968.

Right: Vietnamese Rangers bring in Viet Cong prisoners captured in street fighting in June 1968.

by bulldozers, and the US forces there transferred to the Ca Lu area. Although the US military leaders offered sound reasons for the decision, anti-Vietnam War critics wondered why so much of America's human and physical resources were committed to the defense of an outpost that was to be abandoned a few weeks later.

One reason for the decision to abandon Khe Sanh was a change in the *modus operandi* of the war that coincided with the appointment of deputy commander General Creighton Abrams to succeed General Westmoreland, who had been transferred to Washington as Army Chief of Staff. President Johnson had announced a new policy of shifting more of the burden of fighting to the South Vietnamese army and the end of air strikes against North Vietnamese targets.

Ending the air strikes allowed the North Vietnamese to resume infiltration of South Vietnam with greater impunity and a buildup of forces for a second, 'mini-Tet,' offensive. Internal memos of the North Vietnamese Army command captured by the US laid blame for failure of the Communists to win the January Tet Offensive on excessive secrecy which resulted in poor communications between Viet Cong and North Vietnamese units during the various battles. To avoid a repetition of that problem, less secrecy was imposed by the North Vietnamese military on plans for a spring 1968 offensive, and US intelligence was thus alerted weeks in advance to the new VC and North Vietnamese plans.

Neither side had fully recovered from the Tet offensive when preparations had to begin for a new round of battles. The US as well as the North and South Vietnamese contenders had suffered significant losses of manpower and equipment during the first quarter of 1968. The

US Defense Department announced a call-up of 24,500 Army, Navy, and Air Force reservists which would raise the size of US forces in Vietnam to 549,500. New replacements had to be trained for Vietnam-style fighting. There was also a critical shortage of such vital equipment as M48 tanks for the US units. In South Vietnam, the Tet fighting had resulted in 10,000 civilians killed or wounded and 350,000 made homeless—in addition to the loss of 1733 South Vietnamese soldiers killed in action. In Hue, 80 percent of the buildings were destroyed; in other cities, property destruction ranged from 25 to 50 percent. North Vietnamese battle losses were enormous, particularly considering the nation's population at the start of fighting was only 13 million.

Because of the slow recovery from the January through April battles and the fact that peace talks were scheduled to begin 13 May 1968 in Paris, fighting that began on 5 May at the start of the mini-Tet offensive seemed to be conducted primarily for psychological and political reasons. There were no particular military objectives for the North Vietnamese. But as in the Korean War, there were propaganda reasons for continuing battles during peace talks and a hope that a successful encounter with the enemy might influence the outcome of the peace conference.

Whereas the Tet fighting was concentrated primarily in the populated areas of South Vietnam, the late spring and summer offensives of the North Vietnamese and Viet Cong appeared to be directed against American units and American base camps, despite the failed effort at Khe Sanh. The first attack, on 5 May 1968, involved a North Vietnamese Army battalion that engaged units of the US 4th Cavalry north of Saigon. The firefight lasted two days and ended with 400 North Vietnamese dead and minimal US losses. In a second attack, west of Saigon,

North Vietnamese troops engaged units of the US 47th and 60th Mechanized Infantry. That battle continued for six days in house-to-house fighting and terminated in the withdrawal of the enemy. After failure of the enemy in still another Saigon area battle on 25 May 1968, Viet Cong and North Vietnamese regulars began to come out of hiding places. On a single day in late May a total of 141 enemy soldiers turned themselves in to South Vietnamese troops without further fighting.

The most sustained battle of the 'mini-Tet' campaign began 17 August 1968 when a fire support base north of Tay Ninh manned by units of the US 25th Infantry Division was the target of North Vietnamese troops. That struggle continued for 10 days and ranged over an area of 1500 square kilometers. It peaked on August 21 when an American mechanized infantry company was trapped by two North Vietnamese battalions. The fighting continued for over an hour and ended when the US unit withdrew with only one of its officers still alive.

The last concerted enemy offensive against US troops in Vietnam began 24 August 1968 when three regiments of the North Vietnam Army 2nd Division engaged units of the US 23rd Infantry Division near Tam Ky City, near the Pineapple Forest. During the first day of fighting, enemy dead numbered 200. An additional 250 were killed in the second day of fighting. After fighting subsided on 27 August, a captured North Vietnamese soldier related that more than 400 members of the surviving enemy had fled to the northwest. North Vietnamese troops did not give up their long-range objective of gaining political control of South Vietnam, but after August 1968 they seemed reluctant to do battle with US military units. The seven months of attacks on American units and bases since the start of the Khe Sanh siege had cost the Viet Cong and North Vietnamese

Left: Troops of the 7th Infantry move out to perimeter positions near Cholon, 9 February 1968. They are seen at the Phu Thu race track which adjoined their post.

Right: Patrol operations in the Mekong Delta area. The men are well spread out to avoid a number falling victim to a single shell or burst of fire.

Below: Men of the 9th Infantry Division use an air mattress to help them ferry some of their equipment across an unusually deep canal in the Mekong area.

Bottom: An M113 APC of the 17th Cavalry armed with a 106mm recoilless rifle in addition to the usual heavy machine gun, Binh Chanh district, April 1968.

an estimated 60,000 dead without making any tangible gains on the ground.

The last major US tactical unit to be sent to Vietnam—the US 5th Infantry Division's 1st Brigade—arrived at the end of the 'mini-Tet' series of offensives and it was assigned to protection of the area immediately south of the DMZ, near the 17th Parallel. The South Vietnamese Army was recruiting and deploying more of its own troops in the field and the enemy had discontinued the use of large units, particularly for purposes of challenging US forces in South Vietnam. US strategy then turned to one of utilizing small units to find and engage enemy troops still remaining in South Vietnam.

From late 1968 until well into 1969, much of the US military action in Vietnam was directed toward sealing or at least securing the borders of South Vietnam against enemy incursions from sanctuaries in Laos and Cambodia. The frequency and intensity of the border raids seemed to depend upon the logistics of the Ho Chi Minh Trail. Viet Cong and North Vietnamese troops could conduct hit-and-run raids into South Vietnam, then duck back across the border for replenishment of manpower and supplies.

The US deployed engineering battalions equipped with bulldozers to clear jungle and underbrush along the border. The land-clearing operations included the use of mechanized infantry units whose job was to secure and destroy enemy installations uncovered during the bulldozing. Much of the land along the border was honeycombed with tunnels and underground storage facilities.

In addition to land-clearing, US units were deployed along highways and jungle trails known to be used by Viet Cong and North Vietnamese troops entering South Vietnam from Laos or Cambodia. Because the American

Center right: An M48 tank in close support of an infantry unit in operations near Quang Tri.

Far right: Bombs rain down from a B-52 Stratofortress. Despite their massive bomb-loads and accurate navigation and bomb aiming systems the B-52s were often ineffective because the North Vietnamese or Viet Cong positions had not been exactly located before the attack went in. Nonetheless B-52 attacks are said to have been much feared because the planes operated at such great altitudes that the first audible warning of an approaching attack was the whistle of the falling bombs.

Below: Men of the 47th Infantry, 9th Infantry Division, come under fire from North Vietnamese troops during fighting in Saigon on 11 May 1968.

border patrol consisted of many small mechanized units, rapid reinforcement was necessary when a US unit became involved in a firefight with infiltrators. The rapid reinforcement tactic devised by the US troops was nicknamed 'pile-on.' Although 'pile-on' tactics varied somewhat with the particular situation, the general plan was to engage the enemy, radio for reinforcements, then prevent the enemy from escaping while maximum firepower was brought to bear on the infiltrating units.

The Mekong Delta extends from Saigon south and west to the Gulf of Thailand and the border with Cambodia. Securing the border required frequent deployment of units of the US Mobile Riverine Force, which was engaged in hundreds of encounters with armed motorized sampans, sappers, and arms smugglers during the 1968–1969 effort to isolate South Vietnam from enemy infiltration. In December and January alone, riverine patrols reported 1121 firefights resulting in 2100 Viet Cong or North Vietnamese troops killed and 278 captured, and the confiscation of 267 tons of am-

munition and other contraband moving through the Mekong Delta waterways.

The riverine operation, using the code name Sea Lords, established patrols along two parallel canals east of the Cambodian border to form a double barrier against the flow of supplies and troops into South Vietnam. A second operation, named Giant Slingshot, was established to monitor enemy activities in a triangular-shaped portion of Cambodia that protrudes into South Vietnam and was commonly known as the 'Parrot's Beak.' Giant Slingshot resulted in the capture of extremely large quantities of arms, munitions and supplies being moved from the Parrot's Beak into South Vietnam. It also resulted in frequent, heavy clashes between US riverine patrol boats and enemy forces trying to maintain lines of communication between South Vietnamese and Cambodian storehouses.

During the border patrol missions, the United States forces engaged in their first and only tank-versus-tank clash with North Vietnamese armor. The incident occurred near Ben Het, a Green Beret base in the Central Highlands overlooking a portion of the Ho Chi Minh Trail. On 3 March 1969, units of the US 69th Armor were sent to Ben Het to counter an apparent enemy buildup threatening the base. During a firefight between the American troops and the North Vietnam 202nd Armored Regiment, tank sounds were heard against the background noise of mortar and artillery fire at about 2100 hours. Then muzzle flashes were seen, and rounds from a Soviet PT76 tank began falling near the US position. The US gunners opened fire with 40-mm guns mounted on M42s, using only the enemy muzzle flashes to sight on in the dark. The Americans continued to fight until there was no more return fire. A search of the area the following morning revealed the burned out hulls of two PT76 tanks and a Soviet armored troop carrier. Not until March 1971, when South Vietnamese M41 tanks battled North Vietnam armor in Laos, would tanks clash again in the Vietnam War.

President Johnson ordered a suspension of the Rolling Thunder bombing of North Vietnamese targets as a final peace-making gesture on 31 October 1968. In November, the United States changed administrations again, and Richard Nixon became the fourth successive President after Harry Truman to contend with the continuing war in Indochina and the forces of Ho Chi Minh. In early 1969, after Viet Cong and North Vietnamese troops resumed attacks on South Vietnamese population centers, resulting in an additional 1140 more US troop deaths, President Nixon ordered American bombers into the air again. But in addition to targets in North Vietnam, the Nixon policy included bombing of enemy sanctuaries in Cambodia and Laos.

At the end of March 1969, combat deaths of US soldiers in Vietnam had surpassed the 33,629 total of the Korean War. The toll included nearly 10,000 since the start of the Paris peace talks in May 1968. Just as Americans at home had questioned the reasons for razing the Khe Sanh base after months of

defending it against the North Vietnamese, soldiers in the field began to wonder why they were fighting and dying to take pieces of Vietnam geography that seemed to have little, if any, military value, as in the May 1969 battle for control of Hill 937: After a 10-day fight for capture of the hilltop at the cost of 475 US killed and wounded, the field commander ordered the objective abandoned.

At home, while peace negotiations in Paris dragged on inconclusively, resistance to the US role in Vietnam was measured by the refusal of an estimated 250,000 young men to register for the military draft, and the more than 50,000 who fled to Canada or other neutral countries to avoid military service. In previous wars involving the US-citizen soldier there were at least psychological distinctions between good and evil. But since World War II, American men had been sent into combat in a twilight world where there appeared to be no simple guidelines or rationales for their battle missions.

In June 1969, President Nixon made the announcement long awaited by millions of Americans at home and many thousands on duty in Vietnam: US troops would begin withdrawing from Vietnam, one division at a time. He then flew to Saigon to discuss plans with General Abrams for deployment of the US military back to America. Meanwhile, the buildup of South Vietnamese forces to assume US missions had already begun, and during the rest of 1969 very little action would be taken by US forces.

Above: An M551 Sheridan light armored vehicle moves along a Cambodian jungle during a search and destroy mission in 1970.

Above right: A Communist supply base in Cambodia is destroyed. Destroying Communist bases in the former sanctuary of Cambodia was the main aim of extending the war to that country, although few important successes in that respect were achieved.

Above, far right: Troops of the 173rd Airborne Brigade go into action from their UH-1D transport helicopter, near Bong Son in mid-1969.

Right: Men of the 5th Marines move along a devastated street in Hue in February 1968 at the height of the struggle for the city during the Tet Offensive.

The peak level of US forces—approximately 545,000—had been reached in April 1969. By that time also, 40,000 Americans had died in Vietnam and 260,000 more had been wounded. The withdrawal of 25,000 US troops began in June 1969, and by the end of the year, US forces had been reduced by some 60,000.

Winding Down America's Longest War

However, as the US military presence in Vietnam appeared to be winding down, in neighboring Cambodia events were heating up. In March 1970, Marshal Lon Nol seized control of the Cambodian government, and ordered North Vietnamese and Viet Cong forces to quit using his country as a sanctuary, a demand that predictably fell on deaf ears in Hanoi. His next move was a request to the United States and South Vietnam for military assistance, which was immediately accepted. The South Vietnamese Army, with support within South Vietnam by the US 25th Infantry Division, launched an operation called Toan Thang 41 into the so-called Angel's Wing, another of the projections of Cambodian territory into the western frontier of South Vietnam.

American troops at first were not permitted to accompany the South Vietnamese troops into Cambodia, but on 28 April 1970, two weeks after the start of Toan Thang 41, the restriction was modified so that US helicopters and gunships were allowed to attack Communist installations inside Cambodia. The restriction was modified still further to permit US ground participation by military advisers up to a distance of 30 kilometers inside Cambodia.

At 1000 hours on 1 May 1970, the US 11th Armored Cavalry became the first combat unit to enter Cambodia, after four hours of artillery bombardment across the border to silence enemy fire. Six kilometers inside Cambodia, units of the 11th Armored Cavalry encountered a large and well-entrenched enemy force that attacked from three sides. In the ensuing battle, 52 North Vietnamese troops were killed. Two members of the cavalry unit became the first American soldiers killed in Cambodia.

The US 1st Cavalry Division units were soon joined in Cambodia by US 25th Infantry Division forces in the operation that yielded enormous supplies of North Vietnamese weapons, vehicles, food and other items. One multi-ton cache captured by the US 9th Air Cavalry contained more than 1500 weapons and millions of rounds of ammunition. A South Vietnamese unit operating south of the US 25th Infantry Division captured 1220 individual and crew-served weapons, 140 tons of ammunition and 45 tons of rice after a battle in the Parrot's Beak area in which 400 North Vietnamese troops were killed. Near Memot, US cavalrymen discovered 21 American-made trucks that had been used in Korea, rebuilt in Japan and sold to North Vietnam as surplus; the US troops now used the trucks to haul captured equipment and supplies back into South Vietnam.

As US troops captured the Cambodian town

Above: Wounded North Vietnamese soldiers surrender following a heavy air strike on their positions during fierce fighting near Bien Hoa in February 1969.

Left: A Vietnamese sailor mans a combination heavy machine gun and mortar mounting aboard a patrol boat.

Right: CH-47 transport helicopters come in to land at an Army base in May 1970.

of Snuŏl on 7 May 1970, President Nixon announced that American forces would be withdrawn from Cambodia by 30 June. Meanwhile, US troops continued operations in Cambodia, clearing thousands of acres of border jungle and destroying 1100 enemy buildings and other installations. Sporadic fighting with North Vietnamese Army troops continued into June when US forces began withdrawing back into South Vietnam just as the monsoon rains began. South Vietnamese forces, however, were not covered by the US presidential decree and continued operations in Cambodia after the 30 June deadline, with occasional raids into Cambodia until well into 1971.

In 1970, an additional 139,000 US troops were sent home. And by the end of 1971, US troop strength had dropped to 158,000, the lowest level since 1965. But after more than a decade of direct military involvement in the war, the morale of American troops deteriorated while the disengagement was underway. Reports of desertion, AWOL, defiance of military orders and attacks on officers by enlisted men ('fragging'), suddenly soared to the highest rate in history. A later report in 1972 showed that fully 25 percent of US Army troops had violated one or more of the military regulations. Soldiers with drug-abuse problems outnumbered the combat-injured in military hospitals.

In January 1972, with US military manpower in Vietnam reduced to 139,000, Nixon hoped to be able to achieve a peace accord and com-

Right: Chinese-manufactured ammunition captured and destroyed by a unit of the 5th Cavalry.

Above: An 81mm mortar platoon of the 1st Cavalry Division returns enemy fire during fighting in Cambodia in the early part of 1970.

Below: An A-37 Dragonfly makes an attack on enemy positions in 1969. This type of aircraft was originally the USAF's first jet trainer but was later developed for the counter-insurgency role.

plete the withdrawal of American troops in time for the 1972 presidential elections. An announcement was made that the US force in Vietnam would be cut to 69,000 and complete American withdrawal would follow within six months of a signed peace agreement with Hanoi. However, when only 95,000 US troops remained in South Vietnam in March 1972, Hanoi launched a spring offensive by sending 120,000 of its soldiers behind a wedge of Soviet-made T-54 tanks across the DMZ into South Vietnam. With the US force reduced to a bare-bones minimum and a desire by Nixon to with-

draw from the Vietnam quagmire before the November elections, Hanoi assumed it could complete its task of conquering South Vietnam without serious interference from the United States.

In Washington, the view was that the new North Vietnamese offensive would be a good test of the ability of Saigon to go it alone against the North Vietnamese army. Besides, the US actually had only 7000 combat troops in South Vietnam—plus 1200 Marines aboard ships of the US 7th Fleet in the South China Sea—in its total of 95,000 military personnel that had not yet been withdrawn. To reverse the disengagement policy and send new ground forces into South Vietnam would have been political suicide in an election year. Thus, the White House opted for air strikes, and President Nixon ordered a resumption of massive bombing raids above the 17th Parallel in April 1972.

In the renewed bombing, B-52 targets included Hanoi and the important port city of Haiphong, which was used by Soviet ships delivering weapons and other supplies to aid the North Vietnamese. But during the nearly four years that had elapsed since President Johnson halted bombing raids in the Hanoi area, the North Vietnamese capital had taken precautions against future US attacks. Hanoi had acquired one of the finest air defense systems in the world with radar-integrated antiaircraft guns, Soviet SAM missiles and 200 MiG jet fighters.

In addition to B-52s, the US had carrier-based planes to send against the North Vietnam targets. But the US began to take losses almost immediately. In the opening days of the air attacks against the enemy, the US lost two attack planes and six helicopters. As evidence of the new effectiveness of the improved North Vietnam air defense system, one of the first US planes bagged was an EB-66 electronic-counter-measure plane whose mission was to baffle enemy radar so that fighter-bombers could reach their targets safely. The EB-66 was downed with a Soviet surface-to-air missile. The North Vietnamese also were using more sophisticated methods than in previous air defense operations against US planes, such as firing SAM missiles to force US planes into the field of antiaircraft guns as they sought to avoid the missiles. They further adopted use of optical scanners—which could not be jammed like radar—for tracking US attack planes.

In spring 1972, while the North Vietnamese 304th and 308th Divisions marched south along the South Vietnamese coast toward Quang Tri and Hue, four more divisions advanced along Route 13 from Cambodia, and other North Vietnam forces crossed the border toward the cities of Pleiku and Kontum. There were, as one South Vietnam military spokesman reported, 'beaucoup VC' fighting alongside the North Vietnamese regulars. South Vietnamese defenses crumbled in several places and deserters joined refugees fleeing southward.

With the US lacking combat force in Vietnam to repel the North Vietnamese advances, the White House reviewed all the options for reacting to the increasingly successful invasion of South Vietnam and ruled out two—the use of nuclear weapons and sending ground troops to save Saigon once more. Another option, begun in May, was the mining of North Vietnamese ports, an operation that could be carried out by Navy jets flying at altitudes around 10,000 feet above the water. They were equipped with tiny computers to be detonated only when a combination of factors—such as a ship's magnetic field, noise of its screws and pressure of displacement—identified a real enemy ship rather than a dummy ship that might be used to detect the one-ton underwater weapons.

A decision about a second option was more difficult: the resumption of bombing. The US had already lost 1500 aircraft in operations over Southeast Asia since it became involved in the conflict. Flying some 500 sorties a day against the improved North Vietnamese air defense system was bound to result in more casualties. And while it was recognized in Washington that new bombing raids might only hinder the efforts to reach a peace settlement at a cost of increased losses of aircraft and air crews, Operation Linebacker was ordered.

Thus, in May 1972, the US sent four more squadrons of F-4 Phantom jets to South Vietnam and added the aircraft carrier *Saratoga* to the US 7th Fleet ships in the Gulf of Tonkin. The US had more than 1000 planes based in Southeast Asia and a total of 50,000 men with the 7th Fleet. To reduce the risk of US bombers being tagged by the North Vietnamese anti-aircraft systems, the American military in-

troduced the use of so-called 'smart bombs' in the new raids over cities north of the 17th Parallel. The 'smart bombs' operated either by following a laser beam aimed at the target by the aircraft or by a television guidance system in the nose of the bomb. The 'smart bombs' could be released before the planes carrying them came within range of the North Vietnamese antiaircraft guns and had remarkable accuracy. A Pentagon official claimed in June 1972 that current raids were knocking out as many Communist targets in one day as were hit in a week of heavy bombing five years earlier. Linebacker continued use of them until mid-October.

When once again a deadlock in the peace negotiations came during December, the US ordered Linebacker II during the 1972 Christmas season. Nearly 100 B-52s, flying in cells of three, flew from bases in Guam and Thailand for saturation bombing. Supplemented by carrier-based jets of the US 7th Fleet, F-4

Above: Communist arms captured by the South Vietnamese forces in Laos in 1971, supposedly a token of the success of Vietnamization.

Below: President Nixon, left, Admiral McCain, commander of the Pacific Fleet, and Henry Kissinger pictured at a meeting in 1969.

Phantoms and F-111 swingwing fighters from Thailand were used for pinpoint targets and aerial dogfights with North Vietnam's fleet of MiG-19s and MiG-21s. The B-52s dropped 100,000 bombs on Hanoi and Haiphong while US jet fighters destroyed 50 Soviet-built MiGs, compared to 59 MiG kills for the entire year of 1967, the last full year of previous air raids over North Vietnam. However, during Linebacker II, North Vietnamese antiaircraft batteries fired an estimated 1000 SAM missiles against the highflying raids and, in turn, bagged 12 US aircraft in five days, including eight B-52s. During the previous seven years, only one B-52 had been lost to enemy fire.

After the final air raid of 29 December 1972, the United States and North Vietnam agreed to sign a peace accord. The success of Linebacker II was considered the prime factor in forcing Hanoi back to negotiations. A final agreement was reached and signed on 23 January 1973, to become effective four days later. US involvement in Vietnam, which began during the Truman administration and spanned more than 20 years, ended officially on 29 March 1973 as the last US troops were withdrawn and Hanoi began releasing American POWs it was holding. And as the POWs were leaving, a US military task force was implementing a search (which

would continue for years) for some 2500 men missing in action (MIA) or killed in action (KIA), those whose bodies had not been recovered. The cost of the war in lives was measured at 56,379 US dead, 925,692 North Vietnamese soldiers killed, and losses of 189,314 South Vietnamese and other 'Free World' troops.

With the 1973 agreement, the disengagement of the United States in Vietnam was obtained along with the recovery of the POWs. It also brought peace to North Vietnam, but not to South Vietnam. No clause in the Paris Agreement called for the withdrawal of Communist troops. South Vietnam, with a potential army of one million troops, was considered capable of defending itself. Thus, the North Vietnamese plan for its 'liberation' of South Vietnam started up again as a 'land grabbing and population nibbling' operation. But it quickly evolved into division-size military attacks against strategic positions in the South. During the same period, while the United States was absorbed with events of Watergate and the resignation of President Nixon, South Vietnam found itself unable to support its own forces on the drastically reduced military aid funding voted by the US Congress, and began its final collapse.

In early 1975, North Vietnam decided to gamble on an offensive to 'liberate' South Vietnam. The gamble was against the chance that the United States might try again to support the South Vietnamese military organization. It was a safe gamble because the US did not interfere with the final Communist offensive.

As North Vietnamese troops approached Saigon, the remaining military advisers and other personnel initiated their last official military operation in South Vietnam, 'Operation Frequent Wind.' Frequent Wind was the plan to evacuate all American personnel and as many South Vietnamese as possible from among the thousands who sided with the United States in the fight against the Viet Cong and the North Vietnamese. This included pro-US South Vietnamese officials and their families to be saved from possible execution by the Communist invaders.

Frequent Wind became the largest aerial evacuation in history. It was launched 1 April 1975 as convoys of cars and buses began moving personnel from Saigon and other US bases to airfields where USAF and contract transport planes waited to airlift the refugees to Thailand or to evacuation ships of the US 7th Fleet's Task Force 76. In the final hours, members of the South Vietnamese Army threatened to disrupt the evacuation unless they could be flown out of Saigon, also. But cool heads and US military firmness prevailed, and thus the Americans managed to move a total of 130,000 troops and civilians from Saigon before the North Vietnamese armored columns took the city. On 30 April 1975, as Operation Frequent Wind was being completed, 662 military helicopter sorties were flown to move 7014 persons to evacuation ships in the South China Sea.

The last flight carried US Marines bearing the American flag from the embassy.

The long war in Vietnam ended with the formal surrender of the government of South Vietnam to the North Vietnamese and Viet Cong a few hours after the US airlift was completed. Ho Chi Minh, who had led the original anti-French uprising against the French colonialism in 1946, had died in 1969 and thus never saw the final unification of the Vietnams. A decade of massive US military as well as economic involvement in Vietnam was over. But the toll of America's longest and most controversial war would continue to be felt, as the civil strife and economic set-backs it engendered left Americans badly shaken. An era of big-stick American foreign policy, which had been tragically slow to adapt to an increasingly complex global situation, came to an appropriately bitter and confusing end with the evacuation of Saigon. Politically and militarily, the US had bitten off more than it could chew, and as the country realized at last that it was not invulnerable, much-needed questions about foreign policy began to be asked.

Opposite: Clearing up damage in Hanoi in January 1973 following the Linebacker II air attacks.

Below left: Soldiers of the 25th Infantry move past an M48 tank led by a man equipped with an M79 grenade launcher and a full supply of ammunition, Vietnam, September 1970.

Below: A-7 Corsair II attack planes on the deck of the nuclear carrier *Enterprise* while the carrier was providing cover for the final evacuation of Saigon in April 1975.

FRUSTRATIONS OF POWER:
1964-1980

The United States and Russia learned to live with the threat of nuclear warfare through the 1960s and 1970s, each within its own sphere of influence. While there was occasional missile rattling, it was mainly for political and psychological purposes. The White House generally knew when the Soviets might be willing to back a threat and the Kremlin usually knew the point beyond which the United States would be willing to back its words with weapons.

The US did not take direct action in response to the building of the Berlin Wall by East Germany, even though there was a pause after the first barbed-wire stage when the Western powers could have challenged the USSR on the issue of a divided Berlin. The USSR tended to ignore the role of the United States in the Bay of Pigs invasion, and was the first to back down in the Cuban Missile Crisis. In Southeast Asia, the USSR tolerated a covert American war in Laos and the US tolerated contributions by the Soviet Union and the Peoples Republic of China to America's North Vietnamese adversary, while each of the superpowers carefully avoided situations that would easily lead to direct military engagements between the US and the backers of Ho Chi Minh.

US Interests at Stake: Panama, the Dominican Republic, and the Middle East

During the first few months of his tenure in the White House, President Lyndon Johnson averaged at least two meetings a day on matters of foreign affairs and national security. The President found that there were occasions when, to use his words, 'plans are overtaken by events.' In addition to the issues of fighting in Vietnam and uprisings in Latin America: Soviet fighters shot down an unarmed US jet aircraft that strayed too close to the border of East Germany; US Attorney General Robert Kennedy was dispatched to Southeast Asia to arrange a ceasefire between Indonesia and the Federation of Malaysia; the US offered to send 1200 troops to Cyprus as part of a NATO peacekeeping force to prevent civil war between the Greek and Turkish communities; and civil strife erupted in Kenya, Uganda, Tanganyika, Zanzibar, and the Congo, causing casualties among European and US citizens living there. The Johnson administration also was embarrassed to learn that an archive for US military publications, called 'Combined Allied Forces Information Center,' with a Hong Kong post office box number actually was a mail drop for Chinese Communist intelligence agents who found it a convenient way of monitoring US military activities around the world.

Meanwhile, the US Strategic Air Command took operational control of the last liquid-fueled intercontinental ballistic missiles to be added to the US arsenal, two squadrons of 9000-mile range Titan IIs installed at the Little Rock, Arkansas, Air Force Base. The Defense Department revealed the US had 108 Titan and 129 Atlas missiles on operational status, plus

Left: Men of the 82nd Airborne Division distribute food to local people, Santo Domingo, Dominican Republic, in May 1965.

Previous page: A Soviet An-12 transport plane is shadowed by an F-4 Phantom and an A-7 Corsair from the carrier *Midway* during a flight over the Indian Ocean. One of the most important strategic developments of the past decade has been the increase in Soviet forces deployed to the Indian Ocean area. Although the Soviet aircraft is wearing civil Aeroflot colors this may be misleading as to the purpose of its mission.

Below left: Marine M48 tank in Santo Domingo in May 1965.

Below: Troopers of the 82nd Airborne provide water supplies after the normal supply had been cut off during the fighting, Santo Domingo, May 1965.

350 of a scheduled 950 solid-fueled Minuteman missiles, from Plattsburg, New York, to Spokane, Washington, and southward to the Mexican border. The Navy had 10 Polaris submarines, each equipped with 16 A1 or A2 missiles and 25 additional submarines being readied for Polaris A3 missiles with a range of 2500 miles, 1000 miles greater than the A2s.

An anti-US protest that triggered military intervention in Latin America—a crisis over the Panama Canal—took the immediate attention of the Johnson administration. It began 9 January 1964 at a high school in Balboa, the Canal Zone, where American teenagers raised the Stars and Stripes, a seemingly minor incident which triggered an armed clash with both young and old Panamanians. The chant in Panama, led by Castroites wearing red T-shirts, was 'the only good gringo is a dead gringo.'

At first, only 150 Panamanian high school students protested the flying of the US flag over what they considered to be Panamanian territory. But they were soon joined by older Panamanians, armed with guns and Molotov cocktails, who marched through downtown Panama City setting fire to US business and industrial firms. General Andrew P O'Meara of the US Southern Command sent US Army troops to the border between the Canal Zone and the Republic of Panama. Six of the soldiers were wounded by snipers before US sharpshooters picked off the snipers with return fire. The fighting spread to other border areas, including a US housing project. Before the gunfire subsided, three US soldiers had been killed and 85 wounded. Panama claimed the American troops had killed 20 and wounded 280; the US challenged the figures, noting that 7 of the 13 confirmed Panamanian dead lost their lives while torching the buildings of US concerns outside the Canal Zone.

Hoping to cool tempers on both sides, Canal Zone officials agreed to raise both the US and Panamanian flags over Balboa High School, where the encounter began, but also kept US troops on alert for further anti-American violence. US troops also were issued blank cartridges. But Panamanian President Roberto F Chiari ordered all US Embassy personnel out of the Republic of Panama and recalled personnel from his own country's embassy in Washington, turning over diplomatic affairs of Panama to the Embassy of Costa Rica. US consulates continued to operate in Panama as did Peace Corps and other aid-type missions. But many US officials in the area moved to the sanctuary of the Canal Zone and hundreds of Americans were evacuated from Panama by military airlift planes.

Chiari, whose political party faced a national election on 10 May 1964, then announced that diplomatic relations with the United States would not be restored until the US agreed to renegotiate terms of the 1903 Panama Canal Treaty. But negotiations were made particularly difficult by the resignation in August 1963 of US Ambassador to Panama Joseph Farland, who had not yet been replaced. A month after the riots, the Organization of American States

Above: US Air Force F-111F swing-wing bomber. The F-111F is the most modern version of this aircraft in service. The F-111 design encountered many problems in its early, small-scale deployment during the Vietnam War but these have now been overcome.

Left: US Army men round up suspected rebel leaders in Santo Domingo, 24 May 1965.

Right: An M48 tank comes ashore during a joint US-Australian exercise, Kangaroo II, in 1976.

voted to investigate charges that the US was guilty of aggression, and the US announced that it was willing to begin a 'full review and reconsideration' of the 1903 treaty. It would not be until June 1967 that the US and Panama would resolve their conflict with an agreement that gave the Latin American nation 'effective' sovereignty over the Canal Zone. A set of three new treaties would provide for a possible sea-level canal across Panama, division of responsibilities for operation of the canal, and the defense and neutrality of the Canal Zone.

But in April 1965, while President Johnson was making plans to enlist participation of other 'Free World' military units in the Vietnam War, making the support of South Vietnam more of a multinational effort than a US military operation, White House attention was suddenly refocused on a Caribbean coup. On 24 April 1965, Colonel Francisco Caamano Deno led a revolt of junior officers of the Dominican army with the intention of restoring to power former president Juan Bosch, who was living in exile in Puerto Rico. Bosch, a 'reformist,' had taken the helm of the Dominican government following the 1961 assassination of dictator Rafael Trujillo, who had rigged elections since 1930 to keep himself in power. The revolt of April 1965 was faltering when defectors gave weapons to pro-Bosch rebels.

The pro-Bosch rebels were led by members of the '14th of June Movement,' a leftist organization named for an abortive Castroite invasion of the Dominican Republic that had occurred on 14 June 1959. The 14th of June Movement leaders dressed in Cuban military uniforms and broadcast radio appeals for civilians to go into the streets and kill policemen. The rebel leaders also seized control of a television station and urged viewers to make hostages of the wives and children of Dominican Air Force pilots, the idea being to discourage any attempt by government forces to counterattack. Some rebels, many of them young teenage boys, terrorized many of the 2400 US citizens and other foreign nationals by lining them up against walls and threatening to shoot them.

Leading the defense of the government forces was General Elias Wessin y Wessin, who asked for US intervention. President Johnson wasted little time in ordering US Marines and the US Army 82nd Airborne Division to the Dominican Republic. Stating, 'I will not have another Cuba in the Caribbean,' Johnson acknowledged that American intervention would be in violation of the charter of the Organization of American States (OAS), but he explained that unilateral action was necessary because the OAS had failed to respond to requests for unified action in previous crises in Guatemala and Cuba. US Navy Task Force 124, centered about the aircraft carrier *Boxer*, led an 28 April invasion of the Dominican Republic, landing 1800 members of the 6th US Marines near Santo Domingo. The 82nd Airborne Division boarded C-124 and C-130 transports at Fort Bragg, North Carolina, and were flown to the San Isidro Airbase, where General Wessin was headquartered. Within two weeks, the United States had 31,600 military personnel committed to peacekeeping in the Dominican Republic. The figure is particularly impressive when compared to the number of US troops—69,200—in Vietnam at the same time.

As in the 1958 landing of US Marines in Lebanon and the Bay of Pigs invasion, US military
personnel were sent into a strange hostile area
without proper maps. To span that information
breach, Marines scrounged copies of Standard
Oil Company (ESSO) gasoline station road
maps for distribution to their own and 82nd
Airborne units. An early operation of the
Marines was establishment of an International
Safety Zone of approximately nine square miles
in the western part of Santo Domingo and
about 15 miles from San Isidro Airbase. The
Marines were guarding the evacuation of US
civilians from the Polo Grounds, at the western
end of the International Safety Zone and also
helping maintain a safe corridor to the San
Isidro Airbase. A major obstacle between the
two US-held areas was the Duarte Bridge over
the Ozama River, at the eastern edge of Santo
Domingo. Leftist rebels held the bridge during
the first few days and resisted efforts of General
Wessin's troops to enter the capital city with
tanks.

Reinforcements that continued to arrive in
the Dominican Republic included the US 8th
and 10th Marine Regiments. They brought
M14s, M60 machineguns, 3.5-inch bazookas
and tanks armed with 90-mm guns. Most of the
US casualties occurred during the first week of
fighting. Among the first were seven members
of Howtar (a combination of a mortar mounted on a howitzer carriage) Battery, 10th
Marines, who were ambushed by rebels armed
with automatic weapons after making a wrong
turn in the so-called safe corridor. Three of the
Marines were killed, two wounded, and two
taken prisoner but released after they were
displayed for propaganda purposes. Total US
casualties during the first week were 18 dead
and 86 wounded. By the end of June 1965, the
toll was 24 dead and 140 wounded.

During fighting near the Duarte Bridge, one
of General Wessin's F-51s accidentally strafed
a US Marine position. The Marines returned
the fire and shot down a Dominican fighter.
The following day, members of the 82nd Air-

borne Division were ordered to keep all Dominican Air Force planes grounded at San Isidro Airbase and to 'destroy any F-51s trying to take off.'

During June, an 18,000-man multinational peacekeeping force finally was organized under the Brazilian General Hugo Panasco Alvim. In September, a 'government of reconciliation' was established by Hector Garcia-Godoy, but terrorism with sniping and bombing continued in the Dominican Republic. One target of terrorist bombs was a nightclub frequented by US troops.

Ironically, by November 1965, members of the US 82nd Airborne Division were assigned to protect the lives of Colonel Deno and ex-president Bosch from attack by loyalist forces. One group which threatened the rebel leaders identified itself as 'Democratic Anti-Communist Commando No. 1.' In an effort to help stabilize the new government and to impose some leadership on the Dominican rebels, the United States had flown Bosch home from Puerto Rico. In return for the favor, Bosch announced when he arrived in Santo Domingo that he was filing a lawsuit against the United States in the World Court on charges of intervening in the affairs of the Dominican Republic. Bosch said he would ask for $1 billion in damages.

Although US forces were gradually withdrawn from the Dominican Republic, there were still 6800 American troops on duty there in April 1966. On the first anniversary of the 1965 uprising, 10,000 young Dominicans marched through the streets of Santo Domingo shouting, 'Go home, Yankee.' Rocks were thrown at US troops who responded by firing 14 rounds that wounded six Dominicans. It was the last encounter between American military personnel and Dominicans.

The so-called 'hot line' between Washington and Moscow was used for the first time since it was installed in 1962—to cool a threatened military confrontation between the US and the USSR. The problem arose in the Middle East. During the first five months of 1967, no fewer than 22 clashes occurred between Israel and its Jordanian and Syrian neighbors. In March, Syria and Egypt initiated a mutual defense pact providing that an attack on one Arab nation would involve the other as well. Israel tested the treaty of 7 April 1967 by conducting a large-scale retaliatory attack on Syria.

When Egypt failed to come to the aid of Syria, it became the object of taunts by other Arab nations. On 15 May 1967, Egypt placed its armed forces on alert and ordered the withdrawal of United Nations peacekeeping forces along its border with Israel. On 23 May, Egyptian President Gamal Abdul Nasser announced the closing of the Gulf of Aqaba to Israeli shipping. One week later, Jordan and Iraq joined Egypt in a defense pact and almost simultaneously, Soviet naval units began moving into the Mediterranean. The extreme tension culminated in the outbreak of war between Israel and Egypt, Syria and Jordan on 5 June 1967.

In a bold campaign, Israel achieved total victory over Egypt, Syria, Jordan and Iraq

Right: The USS *Liberty* pictured on 16 June 1967 and showing the damage inflicted by the Israeli attack on 8 June. Thirty-four of the *Liberty*'s crew were killed in the attack.

Below: An Israeli McDonnell Douglas A-4 Skyhawk light attack aircraft in 1973. Arms supplies are one of the clearest ways in which the US can signal support for friendly powers. Demonstrating this support is often as important as the advantage the arms might convey.

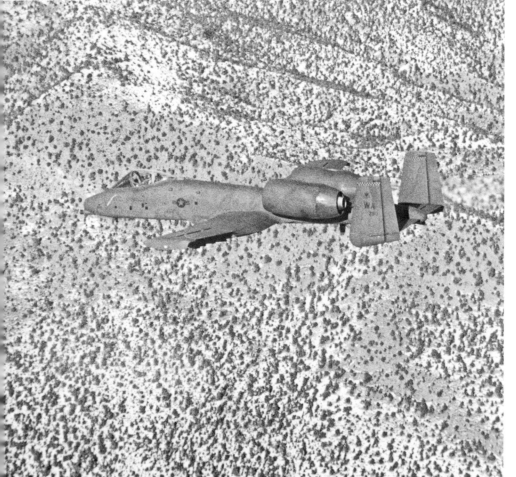

within six days, overrunning all of the Sinai Peninsula, the west bank of the Jordan River, advancing 12 miles into Syria and capturing the old city of Jerusalem. Although there was no direct US involvement in the fighting, the US Navy communications ship *Liberty* became a victim of Israeli attack. The ship, sailing about 14 nautical miles off the Sinai Peninsula on June 8, was flying a 40-square foot US flag at the masthead when Israeli jets slammed rockets into it, then strafed it with rocket and machine gun fire.

The Israeli planes were joined by three of their torpedo boats which sprayed the *Liberty* with machine gun fire and launched two torpedoes, one of which tore a 40-foot hole amidship below the waterline. After putting 821 holes in the hull and superstructure, and leaving 34 US officers and enlisted men dead and 75 wounded, one torpedo boat stopped astern of the *Liberty* and signalled, 'Do you need assistance?' Israel later wired apologies to Washington, but the cause for the attack was blamed on a resemblance between the *Liberty* and the Egyptian supply ship, *El Quseir*—despite the display of the US flag, the identity of the US Navy craft painted in English letters on the stern, and the fact that it was a clear afternoon, and the US ship was in international waters.

On the other hand, the US had failed to advise Israel that it would have a ship in the area.

By the end of the year, relations between the US and the Arab nations had been restored to their pre-war status. And ill feelings between the US and Israel over the *Liberty* attack incident were quickly eased when Israel agreed to share some of the Soviet military equipment it had captured from the Egyptian army.

The US sent transport planes to Israel to pick up three captured MiG-21s. Two were delivered to Edwards Air Force Base in California for flight tests and the third taken to Wright-Patterson Air Force Base in Ohio for laboratory analysis. The USAF would gain knowledge about the MiG-21s that would help its pilots who faced the advanced Soviet jet fighters regularly over Vietnam.

An even more serious loss to the Soviets were a half-dozen SAM missiles complete with computers, guidance systems and fueling equipment, Soviet T55 tanks with infrared gun sights, a Soviet antitank missile with a 1.5-mile long wire umbilical guidance system, and a 130-mm M63 gun that could fire six 70-pound shells per minute over a 17-mile range. The M63 was so new it had not yet been displayed in a Moscow May Day parade although it was believed to be in use against US Marines in South Vietnam. Not long after, the US altered its stated policy of neutrality in the Middle East by selling military aircraft to Israel.

Radio Moscow admitted to the USSR involvement on the Arab side in a 13 June broadcast, stating that 'we had an army of peasants and workers who manned tanks and self-propelled guns, but who had not mastered them completely,' whereas the Israeli army was a 'well-educated force who knew how to handle their modern weapons.'

Simmering Tensions in the Far East and Eastern Europe

In the Far East, meanwhile, one of three ships operated by the US Navy for the National Security Agency became the first US ship to surrender since the USS *Chesapeake* was taken by the British Navy off the coast of Virginia in 1807. The USS *Pueblo* with a crew of 83 was reportedly in international waters, 16.3 miles from the North Korean shore at Wonson on 23 January 1968 when it was approached by a North Korean subchaser which signaled in international flag code, 'Heave to or we will fire.' Within an hour four other North Korean warships appeared to surround the *Pueblo* while two MiG fighters circled overhead.

The 179-foot US ship was loaded with electronic gear for monitoring North Korean military activity and was armed with two .50-caliber machine guns, which normally were covered with tarpaulins. The *Pueblo* captain, Commander Lloyd M Bucher, radioed that his ship was being challenged, followed by a message, 'Send help.' Switching to an emergency wavelength, the *Pueblo* sent an SOS and reported that codes and secret equipment were being destroyed. North Korean sailors boarded the US ship and the *Pueblo* was escorted to Wonsan without a fight. However, Commander Bucher and three of the crew members were wounded, one of the men fatally, as they had gone about destroying the espionage equipment and records.

The *Pueblo* capture occurred around noon in the Korean time zone, which was approximately 2300 hours (EST) in Washington, DC, but the incident was not revealed to the American public for an additional 12 hours. It was the second time within seven months that an

Above: F-4H Phantom fighters shadow a Soviet Tu-16 bomber in the North Pacific. In the background the carrier *Kitty Hawk*. Soviet and US forces make constant efforts to observe any units operating in international waters or air space.

Left: A well-camouflaged A-10 Thunderbolt attack plane, designed specifically for the tank-busting role in the European Theater.

Right: Men of the 1st Battalion, 8th Marines move out into the bush, Santo Domingo, May 1965.

intelligence-gathering ship operated by the US Navy had been attacked in international waters. The *Pueblo* incident was a particularly sticky matter for the Johnson administration because it occurred a day before the Senate Foreign Relations Committee was scheduled to receive a staff report on the 1964 Gulf of Tonkin incident in which at least one US Navy destroyer was reported to be engaged in electronic surveillance of the North Vietnamese coast when it came under attack by North Vietnamese warships.

President Johnson's reaction to the *Pueblo* incident was to dispatch the US aircraft carrier *Enterprise* and a flotilla of 35 other Navy vessels to the waters off the North Korean shore. He also signed orders for the call-up of 15,000 members of the US Navy and Air Force reserves. And he also asked the United Nations to intervene. Because some Washington advisers saw the *Pueblo* incident as part of a 'larger Communist conspiracy,' of which increased North Korean military activity along the 38th Parallel was observed, Johnson also dispatched an additional 80 US jet fighters to American bases in South Korea. The USS *Banner*, another US Navy spy ship, was sent to the Sea of Japan to replace the *Pueblo*.

After the *Pueblo* was captured, it was 11 months to the day before Commander Bucher and his crew were released. The months had been filled with frustrating negotiations for their release and continued restraint of any US military action. The captives were finally freed on 23 December 1968 at Panmunjom, the site of the Korean War armistice talks in 1953. Later, during a formal US Navy hearing on the surrender of the spy ship, Bucher related details of the attack by North Korean gunboats which riddled the *Pueblo* with cannon and machine gun fire when he tried to outrun his captors after the first attempt to board the ship. Bucher said that during their captivity, he and his crew were beaten repeatedly and he had signed a 'confession' when he was convinced the North Koreans would begin shooting one crew member at a time, starting with the youngest.

While the crew of the *Pueblo* faced capture by units of the North Korean Navy, the US Air Force also was experiencing problems thousands of miles from home. In late January 1968, a USAF B-52 on a flight from Plattsburg, New York, Air Force Base, caught fire over Baffin Bay while on a mission above the Arctic Circle. The B-52 was directed by Strategic Air Command Headquarters to Thule Air Base in Greenland but the crew bailed out. The plane, with four hydrogen bombs aboard, crashed into North Star Bay, seven miles southwest of Thule. Each of the bombs was rated at 1.1-million tons of TNT. The plane left a skid mark where it hit the ice and bounced along the surface before exploding. Pieces of B-52 debris and parts of the bombs were recovered by searchers using dog teams but the extent of plutonium contamination was not immediately determined. Eskimos were warned not to eat seal or walrus caught in the area and Denmark demanded 'a discussion with Wash-

ington' about the possible violation of an agreement prohibiting flights of nuclear-armed aircraft over Danish territory.

It was the 14th accident in 10 years involving Strategic Air Command planes carrying nuclear weapons. In a previous mishap at Palomares, Spain, on 17 January 1966, a B-52 on a routine training flight over the Spanish Mediterranean coast was being refueled by a KC-135 flying tanker at an altitude of 32,000 feet. Suddenly, there was an explosion—the cause was never determined—and parts of both giant jet planes rained down over the ocean and the nearby fishing hamlet of Palomares.

Ships of the US Navy's Sixth Fleet joined USAF crews in an 80-day search for one of the four hydrogen bombs that fell into the sea. This ended successfully thanks to a special submarine. The other three were found on the ground in Palomares.

One resident of Palomares, who kicked one of the bombs that had split open after falling to earth, apparently was contaminated by inhaling plutonium dust that leaked from the bomb. He was hospitalized, but survived the experience of being probably the first human to attack a hydrogen bomb. The USAF paid out more than $100,000 in claims, mainly for the loss of vegetables that could not be harvested because of possible plutonium contamination.

Growing concern over nuclear weapons was already a cause of anti-American demonstrations in the capitals of Europe. The Palomares

Right: The American intelligence gathering ship *Pueblo* which was captured by the North Koreans.

Below right: Crew members of the *Mayaguez* relaxing on deck after they had been rescued by the Marines.

Below: North Korean propaganda picture of the captain of the *Pueblo*, Lt Cmdr L M Bucher supposedly writing a confession that the ship was in fact engaged on a spy mission.

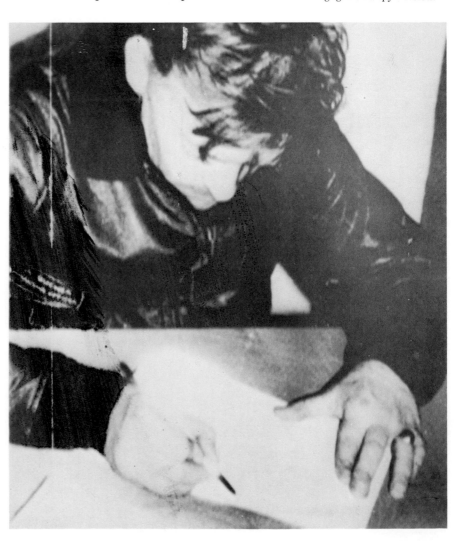

incident added more. Taking advantage of the situation, the USSR protested at a Geneva Disarmament Conference that the Palomares incident constituted an American breach of the nuclear-test-ban treaty. Meanwhile, the USSR was expanding its own sphere of influence in the Mediterranean and by 1968 it could match the size and strength of the US Sixth Fleet. The Soviet Union also began establishing bases at Arab ports, posing a special threat to members of NATO, with warships that had been built in the 1960s. More than half of the NATO ships were of World War II vintage, a period when the USSR lacked a navy.

The Soviet Union also challenged the western powers in August 1968 with a full-scale invasion of Czechoslovakia. The US was shocked by the Russian move because the United States and the Soviet Union were just beginning to establish a condition of *détente*, with cultural exchanges, direct civilian airline connections, a mutual space exploration project, and treaties to limit nuclear proliferation. But in Czechoslovakia, a program of liberalization had started in January 1968 by Alexander Dubcek, who removed Stalinists from key positions in the government and had plans, among others, for a free election with secret ballots. The Kremlin became obviously concerned and warned the Czech leadership against making any radical moves of liberalization.

After a series of attacks on the leaders of Czechoslovakia in the Soviet press, the USSR, claiming that 'party and government leaders' of Czechoslovakia had asked the Soviet Union 'to render the fraternal Czechoslovak people urgent assistance,' began on 20 August 1968 to move in the first of 200,000 tank-led troops. Russian troops were joined by army units from East Germany, Bulgaria, Poland and Hungary —which had experienced a similar halt to the humanizing of Communism 12 years earlier.

President Johnson was one of the first persons in the non-Communist world to learn about the invasion of Czechoslovakia. Soviet Ambassador Anatoly Dobrynin had an appointment with Johnson as the Warsaw Pact troops began moving across the Czech borders. Dobrynin read a two-page handwritten note explaining that Czechoslovakia's security had been threatened and the entire affair was a matter of internal Communist business.

The USSR gambled that the US would not intervene and would not even threaten to intervene. The US President made the expected public statement that he was 'shocked' by the 'tragic news.' An appeal was made to the United Nations Security Council and the USSR cast its expected veto. But once again, the US opted to avoid a confrontation with the Soviet Union. Any American effort to intervene would not be worth the risks. The only significant reaction by the US Congress was a decision to delay action on a proposal to reduce the United States troop commitment to NATO. In addition, the US military already had its hands full with action in Vietnam.

Challenges to the Nixon Doctrine

The possibility of an endorsement of Johnson's Vietnam War policies lost Vice President Hubert Humphrey the 1968 presidential election. The candidate chosen by the Democratic Party to face Republican Richard Nixon, Humphrey failed to win support because voters assumed his association with Johnson might mean continued lack of progress in peace talks. Nixon offered the option of a 'containment' policy in Vietnam with further goals of 'winding down the war' while seeking a negotiated peace.

Encouraged by the support given him, despite continued anti-war demonstrations on college campuses, Nixon began his promised withdrawal of US troops from Vietnam and the program of 'Vietnamization' of the war, assigning South Vietnam responsibility for its own fate.

With a lull in the fighting in Vietnam, for other units not committed to Vietnam, exercises were important events. Although the prisoners taken in the capture of the USS *Pueblo* near North Korea had been released in December, that area continued to be important. In March 1969, one brigade of the US 82nd Airborne Division was flown 8500 miles to South Korea and dropped by parachute in ground maneuvers. The Soviet invasion of Czechoslovakia in August 1968 made significant the US military operation Carbide Ice, from January through March 1969, along the border of Czechoslovakia. Some 12,500 men of the US 24th Infantry Division and the US 3rd

Armored Cavalry were airlifted from the United States to Europe where they joined other US 7th Army troops for the exercise.

In another arena, and on a more subtle level, US-USSR military rivalries continued in advancements in the space race. On 20 July 1969 and again on 19 November 1969, the United States upstaged the USSR in the space race by achieving manned landings on the moon. The events seemed particularly remarkable since only 12 years had elapsed from the 1957 launching of the first artificial satellite, the Russian *sputnik*. Not to be outdone by the American space ventures, the USSR sent an unmanned eight-wheeled remote controlled vehicle, the *Lunokhod I*, to the moon in 1970 and announced establishment of a new endurance record of 17.5 days of manned space flight.

As part of the 'wind down' of the Vietnam War role of the US, the US battleship *New Jersey* was returned to the United States and deactivated, US Navy aircraft forces were reduced, and the vessels provided by the US Navy for the Mekong Delta riverine operations were turned over to the Vietnam government. By 1970, a total of 111 ships and 13 air units were deactivated. The Defense Department also deactivated five interceptor squadrons of the North American Defense Command, the entire SAC force of 86 B-58 supersonic bombers and reduced the number of B-52s based in the Pacific by 30 planes. However, new F-4s and F-111s were deployed to Europe to replace obsolescent aircraft committed to NATO.

In 1970, the Nixon Doctrine of reducing the US military presence overseas continued. Procurement of new aircraft was cut from 945 in 1969 to only 370 in 1970 and aircraft inventory was reduced by nearly 1000. Ground troop strength in Vietnam was cut by 72,000 and USAF manpower in Southeast Asia was reduced by 15,000. Marine Corps troop level was cut by 50,000, including a reduction of 22,000 on duty in Vietnam. The active fleet of the US Navy was reduced from 934 to 704 ships and Navy personnel was trimmed by 50,000. Except for the Vietnam activity still winding down, 1970 operations were minimal. In May 1970, the USS *Guam* with a company of US Marines and a Marine helicopter squadron went to Peru to help in earthquake relief operations. And in September, the strength of the US Sixth Fleet was increased by one aircraft carrier and nine other warships when fighting flared in Jordan, where thousands of demonstrators stormed the US Embassy and burned the US Information Center.

The first ground combat unit deployed to South Vietnam, the 173 Airborne Brigade, returned to the US in 1971 as American army manpower in that country was reduced by an additional 93,000, and the total US Army was reorganized to a 13-1/3-division force from 19-2/3 divisions. The US 35th Tactical Fighter Wing was deactivated and its F-100 fighters returned to the US. The US 17th Special Operations Squadron flew its final air-support mission and turned over its AC-119s to the South Vietnamese Air Force. The last US Marine units were withdrawn from Vietnam

Above: Bolivian troops being trained by US advisers in 1967. US influence in South America, through the Organization of American States, is one of the most important facets of US foreign policy.

Right: Selective Service Director Curtis W Tarr spins the drum containing the birth date numbers for the 1973 draft, the last to date.

to bases in California, Japan and Okinawa. US Navy personnel was reduced by an additional 80,000 and the offshore strength of the US Seventh Fleet was cut from 18,550 to 13,000 in 1971 as part of the Nixon Doctrine wind down in Asia. At the same time, the Navy gained 16 new ships, including the 100th nuclear submarine and the nuclear-powered frigate USS *California*. The submarine-launched multiple-warhead Poseidon missile became operational in March 1971.

By 1972, the phasedown of US military operations in Vietnam was nearly complete. Except for air raids on Viet Cong and North Vietnamese targets, America's role in the fighting was ended. Only 500 US Marines remained in South Vietnam, mainly security troops and air and naval gunfire liaison personnel. The last US Army combat unit completed its final patrol of 11 August 1972 and prepared for withdrawal. The last squadron of USAF combat aircraft was deactivated and the planes turned over to the South Vietnamese Air Force. US Navy strength was cut by 37,000 during 1972 and the active fleet was reduced further to a total of 607 ships.

During 1972, scandals involving the Nixon administration and the US military began to overshadow other events. The US Army investigation of a reported massacre in My Lai, South Vietnam, was completed and a congressional investigation of the reported unauthorized bombing raids by General John Lavelle's US Seventh Air Force began. In June 1972, five men carrying cameras and surveillance equipment were arrested in the Watergate offices of the Democratic National Committee in Washington, DC, but Nixon won reelection to another term as President despite reported links between White House staff members and the burglary.

President Nixon, absorbed in his own defense of the Watergate scandal and facing possible impeachment, had turned over much of the 'war watching' responsibilities to Secretary of State Henry Kissinger during 1973. On 6 October 1973, Egypt initiated the Yom Kippur War by sending 200 attack aircraft, 600 tanks and 70,000 troops across the Suez Canal to attack Israeli positions while the Jewish population was observing the traditional Day of Atonement.

Kissinger had been advised by US intelligence experts only two days before the Egyptian attack that war in the Middle East was unlikely. The attack, which was coordinated with assaults on other fronts by Syria, Jordan, Iraq and other Arab nations, caught the US and even Israel by surprise. The US Navy Sixth Fleet, with 50 ships in the Mediterranean with 20,000 men, was quickly placed on special alert and the US immediately began a covert airlift of missiles, electronic counter measure equipment, and military spare parts to Israel.

The first few days of fighting consumed enormous quantities of arms and equipment, and a proxy 'battle' between the US military and the USSR began. The Soviet Union began airlifting missiles, tanks and other supplies to Egypt and Syria on 11 October, and a few days

later, 14 October, the US announced it was resupplying Israel. The USSR launched six spy satellites to observe the battlefronts, and the US used two satellites and SR-71 high-flying reconnaissance aircraft in matching intelligence service for Israel. The US established an Air Lift Control Element of 50 men at Lod Airport to direct unloading C-5 and C-141 transports delivering M-48 and M-60 tanks, 155-mm howitzers, 175-mm guns, CH-53 helicopters and replacement fuselages for F-4E Phantom jet fighters. The US also diverted 49 F-4s to Israel via the Azores, with a refueling stop aboard the US Navy aircraft carrier *John F Kennedy*, which had been ordered to the Mediterranean to join the Sixth Fleet.

The US military supply pipeline was augmented by C-130 transports that began arriving from Germany with missiles and other supplies from the NATO stockpiles in Europe. American cannibalizing of NATO stockpiles to support the Israeli war nearly led to a breakup of the 24-year old Atlantic Alliance. It was estimated that the US took 90 percent of NATO's TOW (tube-launched, optically-tracked, wire-guided) missiles for Israeli use. Because of the Nixon Doctrine to 'wind down' American military expenditure, production of Phantom jets was limited to three per month, and only one US factory was producing tanks, at a rate of 30 per month. Israel's initial losses of nearly 50 tanks and 20 aircraft a day put an immediate strain on US resources. Many of the US-built Patton tanks delivered to Israel had never been used; when captured by Egyptian forces, they

---

Left: An RH-53 search and rescue variant of the Sea Stallion helicopter on the deck of the nuclear carrier *Nimitz*, 24 April 1980, at the start of the attempt to rescue the Teheran hostages.

Below left: Final checks on an RH-53 in the *Nimitz*'s hangar, evidently not enough to prevent unserviceability problems eventually causing the mission to be aborted.

Below: Happy friends and relatives at Andrews Air Force base to greet the hostages on their return.

showed odometer readings of 175 kilometers—the distance from El Arish on the Mediterranean coast to the Sinai battlefield. On the plus side, the Arab nations were losing Soviet military equipment at an even higher rate.

The US found itself at odds with other NATO members because of its support of Israel. Only the Netherlands, of all European countries, supported the Israelis. Other NATO members not only supported the Arab nations, one NATO member, Turkey, authorized use of its airspace for Soviet transports ferrying military equipment to Egypt and Syria. Great Britain refused permission for US SR-71 spy planes to operate from a base in Cyprus, while Portugal agreed to American use of NATO bases in the Azores only when the US promised to support a Portuguese colonial matter before the United Nations.

Disagreement between the US and USSR over terms of a ceasefire agreement and its enforcement escalated into a confrontation between the two superpowers in mid-October. After an emergency meeting of the Soviet Politburo on 19 October 1973, Moscow sent a request via the 'hotline' to President Nixon requesting that Kissinger fly to Moscow for 'urgent consultations.' On 22 October, the US and USSR jointly issued a call for a ceasefire in the Middle East. An Israeli force, meanwhile, had crossed to the west bank of the Suez Canal and trapped 20,000 men of Egypt's Third Army. The Israelis refused to allow a 'mercy mission' to deliver water, food and medicine to the

Egyptians, who would not surrender. The USSR urged that a joint US-Soviet force be sent to the area and threatened 'unilateral action' if the US refused the offer.

The US did refuse, and its intelligence noted that the Russian fleet in the Mediterranean was being increased from 60 to 85 ships, that 50,000 airborne troops had been placed on alert, two mechanized divisions near the Black Sea had been mobilized, and airlift transports had been ordered home for possible troop movements. The Soviet action was followed by a US 'DefCon 3' alert, or 'Defense Condition 3—all troops report to barracks for possible movement and standby for action.' It was the first worldwide US troop alert since the day President Kennedy was assassinated ten years earlier.

The US Sixth Fleet moved two attack carriers and two amphibious assault carriers, each with 1800 US Marines, toward the war zone, while Guam-based B-52s were ordered back to US bases to receive possible nuclear war assignments. However, the confrontation cooled as Israel and the Arab nations finally agreed to a United Nations-supervised ceasefire and withdrawal of military forces to new defensive positions. A disengagement agreement was signed in Geneva in June 1974.

Off Balance: Power Plays and Acts of Terrorism in the late '70s

The US role in Southeast Asia did not end with the North Vietnam capture of Saigon on 30 April 1975, and the massive US Air Force airlift from the US Embassy compound of South Vietnamese and the remaining Marines and other personnel. On 12 May 1975, the US-registered cargo ship *Mayaguez* was sailing in the Gulf of Siam shipping lanes for the port of Sattahip in Thailand when it was stopped by two gunboats of the Cambodian Khmer Rouge government. The *Mayaguez* sent an emergency radio message that it was being fired upon and boarded by Cambodians. The captain of the *Mayaguez*, Charles T Miller, stalled the Cambodian captors and let the ship ride at anchor to frustrate their efforts to move the ship to the Sihanoukville, Cambodia, harbor. Within hours after the radio message President Gerald Ford was meeting with the National Security Council to discuss the situation while a US Navy P-3 four-engine reconnaissance plane flew to the Gulf of Siam to locate the ship.

President Ford ordered US military personnel still stationed in neighboring Thailand to rescue the 39 crew members of the *Mayaguez* and to take whatever action might be necessary to prevent the Khmer Rouge from taking the US ship to the mainland. On the evening of 13 May, AC-130 gunships orbited around the *Mayaguez*. One Khmer Rouge gunboat fired at the American gunship and was forced aground by return fire. A flight of US A-7 jets sank one Cambodian gunboat, and then observed a wooden fishing boat filled with people heading for the mainland. The A-7s fired on the fishing boat and dropped tear gas around it—not realizing the boat contained the 39 crew members of the *Mayaguez* plus their Cambodian captors and the crew of the Thai fishing boat. The crew members wanted to overpower the Khmer guards, but the tear gas incapacitated all aboard, and the boat continued to Sihanoukville, from where the US prisoners were taken to Kaoh Rong Samloem Island. Flights of A-7s, F-4s and AC-130s continued to fly over the area, sinking several Cambodian patrol boats.

The rescue mission as outlined by the officers in charge would have two phases. One phase called for 60 US Marines aboard the US Navy destroyer *Holt* to board the *Mayaguez*, pirate-style, and recapture the ship. The second, based on misinformation that the crew was being lightly guarded on Koh Tang island, would require landing up to 600 US Marines from USAF helicopters on the island to recover the crew. The first stage of the operation went well; the Marines, armed with tear-gas grenades and M-16 rifles, boarded the *Mayaguez* and found it completely abandoned. Taking Koh Tang island was a different matter. Instead of 20 elderly Cambodians on the island, as the information intelligence had stated, the US Marines encountered a force of 300 well dug-in Khmer Rouge soldiers with automatic weapons.

The first USAF helicopter, carrying Cambodian interpreters for possible negotiations, was shot down when the attack began 15 May. An hour after the rescue effort began, 54 US Marines and US airmen were pinned down on the beaches of Koh Tang, three helicopters had been shot down and two were severely damaged, and 14 Americans were dead or missing.

Unknown to the rescuers at the time, the crew of the *Mayaguez* had been released and were on their way back to their ship aboard a Thai fishing boat. They were spotted by crewmen of the US Navy destroyer *Robert L Wilson*, who sounded battle stations before seeing the white flags rigged by the *Mayaguez* crew from their underwear. Then it became necessary to bring in additional Marines to rescue the 54 Americans stranded on the beaches of Koh Tang. Three transport helicopters prepared to deliver the reinforcements, and two made it on the second try; the third was driven off by small arms fire, machine guns, rockets and mortars. Soon there were 222 Americans on Koh Tang and more helicopters were disabled.

To help the US Marines disengage, a USAF C-130 cargo plane was flown over the center of the island to drop a 15,000-pound bomb which devastated an area 100 yards in diameter. The rescue helicopters then worked through the night, picking up Marines to be airlifted to the US aircraft carrier *Coral Sea*, which had joined the destroyers in the Gulf of Siam. During the action on Koh Tang, 230 US Marines and Air Force personnel had been landed and withdrawn. But total US casualties were 15 killed, 49 wounded and three missing. Of the 15 helicopters used in the rescue mission, 13 were either destroyed or damaged. America's military involvement in Southeast Asia was ended and rescue efforts that had remained in Thailand after the US withdrawal from South Vietnam left Thailand in January 1976.

The election of Jimmy Carter as President in November 1976 was followed by a number of changes in United States defense policies. Among his first acts as President, Carter granted pardons to nearly all Vietnam-era draft evaders, scrapped the B-1 bomber program, vetoed construction of a new nuclear-powered aircraft carrier, deferred production of a neutron bomb, and cancelled SR-71 surveillance flights over Cuba. However, Carter also approved production of a mobile MX missile, created a new Caribbean task force based at Key West Florida, and authorized establishment of a Rapid Deployment Force (RDF) with a potential strength of 200,000 soldiers, sailors, marines and airmen. As a champion of human rights, the Carter administration also began to express its displeasure overtly in dealings with nations with records of political oppression.

Thus when the Shah of Iran tried to buy AWACS planes from the US during the summer of 1977, human rights activists fought the deal from the White House to Capitol Hill where congressional debate on the issue became an attack on the Shah's total regime. At about the same time, groups of young protestors began to appear in Washington with huge portraits of the Ayatollah Khomeini and banners proclaiming the Shah of Iran as a 'puppet of the US.' The Shah also wanted to buy US-made F-16, F-14, and F-4 aircraft, submarines, patrol boats, and missiles launchable from surface vessels, a deal which would have encountered no obstacles under the Nixon Doctrine, which encouraged the arming of friendly nations in order to help protect US interests in those foreign regions. But it was not the Carter Doctrine.

Events to test the Carter foreign policy began to move rapidly in 1978. In the spring of that year, Iran advised the US of plans for a communist coup against the neutralist government of Afghanistan. But Washington dismissed the warning as a concern of the Shah about the encirclement of Iran. On 24 April 1978, as predicted, President Mohammad Daud Khan was killed in a coup by Khalq, the Afghan Communist party. Three days later, Nur Mohammad Taraki, the head of Khalq, was named president. Foreign delegations expressed concern that Taraki held daily meetings with Soviet officials. Then on the home front, in the autumn of 1978, Carter ordered overflights of Cuba by SR-71s resumed when it was discovered that the USSR had moved advanced MiG-23s to that island. Martial law was declared in Iran after 95 people were killed by the Shah's troops in an attempt to put down a demonstration of 100,000 anti-Shah protestors on 7 September 1978.

The Soviet Union, meanwhile, began to gain port facilities in Greece and got Turkey to ban the use of its airspace for U-2 spy flights. In January 1979, General Alexander Haig announced his plans to resign as commander of US forces in Europe because of 'inconsistencies of the Carter administration with respect to NATO policies.' On 14 February 1979, US Ambassador Adolph Dubbs was kidnapped by Moslem terrorists in Kabul, Afghanistan, and

Above: Navy RH-53 helicopters being prepared for the Iranian rescue mission aboard the *Nimitz*, 23 April 1980.

Right: A P-3C Orion antisubmarine plane of the Navy's Patrol Squadron 24. Long-range patrol aircraft play a vital part in the Navy's antisubmarine efforts. Among the items of equipment carried are sonobuoys, radar and a magnetic anomaly detector.

killed in a rescue attempt. Almost simultaneously, a pro-Khomeini mob stormed the US Embassy in Teheran and took US Ambassador William Sullivan hostage. Sullivan was released within hours but the US had counted 20 terrorist attacks on its embassies or embassy personnel around the world within a year.

In September 1979, the Carter administration revealed the presence of a brigade of around 3000 Russian combat troops in Cuba. Carter appeared on TV to assure the US public that 'we consider this a serious matter and this status quo is not acceptable.' However, a review of the agreement reached between President John Kennedy and USSR Premier Nikita Khrushchev in 1962 showed that Russia had promised only to station no 'offensive weapons' in Cuba. There was no agreement about Soviet troops or military activities in Cuba, and so the Russian troops remained in Cuba.

The Shah of Iran, who had abandoned his throne to the supporters of the Ayatollah Khomeini, arrived in New York City on 22 October 1979 for medical treatment. Militant students demanding the return of the Shah of Iran 'to stand trial' stormed the US Embassy in Teheran on 4 November 1979, and took 66 US employees hostage. (There was a security guard

of 13 US Marines at the US Embassy compound that morning but they were ordered not to fire at the attackers.) Washington refused to bow to the student demands and the Ayatollah rejected a US request for the release of the embassy staff. Carter responded by ordering 50,000 Iranian citizens living in the United States to report for deportation proceedings and froze all Iranian assets in the US. On 17 November 1979, the Ayatollah authorized the release of 13 American black and female personnel but announced the others would stand trial as 'spies.' Four days later, a mob stormed the US Embassy in Islamabad, Pakistan. The attempt to seize the embassy failed, but one US Marine and one US Army soldier were killed in the fighting.

As days turned into weeks, the world watched to see what the US would do to free its citizens held hostage in Teheran. If a simple military operation could have been carried out in isolation from all other considerations, the US had the forces to do so. But this was not the case, and though US military planners began to put together some covert method for a rescue operation, the Carter administration had to pursue a series of frustrating negotiations with the Iranians. At the end of November, his patience strained, President Carter ordered a US Navy task force, headed by the aircraft carrier *Kitty Hawk* to the Persian Gulf and threatened military action to rescue the embassy hostages. Carter also authorized B-52 flights from Guam to the Indian Ocean, where Soviet ships now cruised continuously, to demonstrate that the US was able to protect its interests abroad without depending on local friendly governments.

However, the USSR seemed unimpressed and on 25 December 1979 announced in tape-recorded broadcasts claiming to be Radio Afghanistan that Soviet troop units had entered Afghanistan at the request of Prime Minister Hafizullah Amin to 'repel foreign aggression.' Amin had ousted Taraki as the head of the Afghan government three months earlier. Amin, as Carter noted after a 'hotline' dialog with the Kremlin, was assassinated after Soviet troops had arrived to protect him. Carter expressed disappointment that the Soviet President was 'not telling the facts accurately' about the USSR role in Afghanistan.

US intelligence seemed to have erred again; it had advised that Russia probably had 15,000 troops in a position to invade Afghanistan. The fact was later revealed that the Soviets had amassed a force of 50,000 combat troops, transporting them from as far away as the Baltic without US detection. Carter called the Afghan invasion 'more serious than Hungary or Czechoslovakia' and announced the US would retaliate by cutting back grain shipments and high technology sales to Russia, and called for an international boycott of the Olympic Games in Moscow in 1980. A resolution was offered in the UN for withdrawal of Soviet troops but it was not surprisingly vetoed by the USSR.

The Afghan invasion put the Soviets 350

miles closer to the Arabian Sea, within easy range of cutting the flow of oil to the West. Carter now threatened the use of 'military force' to repel any 'attempt by an outside force to gain control over the Persian Gulf region.' Efforts were made to establish new US bases in the area and one, on the Indian Ocean island of Diego Garcia was stocked with enough tanks and other equipment to sustain a division of US Marines for a month.

The US also mounted an effort on 24 April 1980 to free the 53 remaining US Embassy hostages in Teheran, Iran. It was a daring commando raid by an elite team of 180 specially trained members of the Green Berets, US Marines and USAF. But it encountered a chain of bad luck almost from the beginning, which did much to harm the United States' global reputation.

Six C-130 USAF transports left Egypt to rendezvous in Iran with eight RH-53D helicopters which had flown inland from the US Navy aircraft carrier *Nimitz*, one of a fleet of 27 ships in the Arabian Sea. Two of the helicopters experienced electrical problems almost immediately; one had to be returned to the *Nimitz*, another was forced down and its crew had to be rescued. At the rendezvous at Posht-i-Badam, 250 miles southeast of Teheran, a third helicopter broke down. President Carter ordered the mission aborted and in the evacuation one of the remaining helicopters collided with a C-130 transport. Eight members of the team died in the fire and four were badly burned. Back in Teheran, Moslem militants chanted,

Above: Rescue helicopter about to take off from the deck of the *Nimitz*.

Right: President Carter welcomes the hostages on their arrival in Germany after their release. The Hostage Crisis destroyed Carter's hopes of a second term as president.

'The American planes have crashed because God willed it,' when news of the failed mission was revealed.

The surviving members of the rescue team returned to Egypt aboard the remaining C-130s, abandoning the five helicopters. (They were later destroyed by the Iranian military, who feared they had been booby-trapped by the American crews.) The Iranian government also announced that the hostages had been moved to several undisclosed locations to thwart any further rescue attempts. The hostages were finally released 20 January 1981, as Ronald Reagan took the oath of office of President of the US, succeeding Jimmy Carter. In return for their release, the US agreed to return to Iran $8 billion of assets which had been frozen in the United States.

Thus, as the new Reagan administration came to power, it inherited a past with two decades of US diplomatic policies and military operations which had been filled with indecisive and inconsistent reactions. The US had been thrown off balance by the events in Vietnam, and now it seemed that in every confrontation there would be a halfway measure given. The memory of US commitment in World War II remained strong, but now US policy, rather than shaping events, appeared to be reacting to them. The question facing the Reagan administration was one of finding a solution to handling issues without wavering between a hard line and a soft line, between negotiations and a military response.

DEFINING THE LIMITS

When President Reagan assumed control of the administration of the US government in January 1981, neither the American people nor the world at large had a clear idea of his plans for the American military, for although he had signaled something of these, they were clothed in campaign rhetoric. But Reagan wasted little time setting forth his defense budget priorities and related military policies. And once again, the USA and the world at large had to adjust to a relatively sudden and extreme change of direction from that taken in the previous four to eight years, during which—after the disillusionment of the Vietnam War and the promises of detente—the US military had been adjusting to a cutback in its budget role.

Reagan's New Military Program

Now President Reagan moved quickly to 'beef up' the US military by calling for an increase of $4 billion in defense spending within his first budgetary year while trimming non-defense spending and taxes by approximately 10 times that amount. To those who questioned the need for such an increase in the US military, Reagan countered by noting that, while the USA had practiced military austerity since 1970, there had been enormous increases in Soviet military spending since 1970. To this effect, Reagan pointed out, the USSR had acquired 61 new submarines, 6100 military aircraft and 54,000 tanks and other armored vehicles since the end of the Vietnam War, while the US figures for the same types of weapons were 27 submarines, 3050 aircraft, and 11,200 tanks and other armored vehicles.

And Reagan went beyond this, defying critics who questioned this shift in spending priorities and its potential threat to relations with the USSR, but at least answering those who questioned whether this was yet another disconnected lurch in America's military commitment: he called for a long-range defense buildup with a price tag of $1.5 billion. The programs included plans for a 600-ship US Navy to match the Soviets', restoration of B-1 bomber production—reversing the order of Jimmy Carter to cancel the plane designed for the early 1990s—and 7000 new M-1 tanks. The Reagan program also restored the 'big deck' nuclear-powered aircraft carrier plans canceled during the Carter administration and called for a new version of the C-5A military transport plane. The C-5A was the only aircraft capable of carrying an M-1 tank and the USA had an inventory of only 77 C-5As, making it improbable that America could carry out a response to any serious Soviet threat either in Europe or in the Persian Gulf area.

The shift to emphasis on a buildup of conventional warfare weapons also was related to a new US military doctrine. Instead of basing plans on a 30-day nuclear-exchange war, the Reagan administration defense planning was based on a strategy of fighting two or more simultaneous, long-term, conventional wars. The doctrine was a return to a global projection of US military power similar to that of

Left: US Army NCO gives instruction in infantry tactics during Rapid Deployment Force maneuvers.

Right: US Army troops unloading transport ships at San Lorenzo, Honduras, in September 1983.

Previous page: A General Dynamics F-16 fighter in Israeli colors. The F-16 is one of the most important current US aircraft but its sales to foreign powers have been criticized especially after F-16s formed part of the Israeli force which attacked an Iraqi nuclear power station in 1981.

Below: US advisers instructing Honduran soldiers in the operation of the Browning 0.5in heavy machine gun early in 1983.

World War II—before the introduction of the atomic bomb.

Among the Carter innovations adopted was the Rapid Deployment Force. However, the Reagan military advisers felt the original RDF concept would not be adequate for a real test of US strength in an overseas confrontation. Reagan administration planners called for at least three US Army divisions, a 50,000-man force of US Marines, two US Navy carrier battle groups, and four USAF wings with at least 288 planes. It was also calculated that in order to airlift one mechanized division overseas from a US base, all of the planes in the USAF Military Airlift Command would have to operate continuously for two weeks. When Operation Bright Star was launched in November 1981, it was found that 865 paratroopers of the US Army 82nd Airborne Division could be flown from North Carolina to Egypt as an RDF test in 27 hours. However, it required three weeks to deliver the division's M-60 tanks, M-113 armored personnel carriers, and 155-mm howitzers from Savannah, Georgia to Alexandria, Egypt. RDF critics noted that the 'rapid deployment' lasted four days longer than the Yom Kippur War of 1973. However, once organized with their equipment, members of the 82nd Airborne conducted a practice linkup with 4000 Egyptian troops for a successful series of joint maneuvers. An Operation Bright Star exercise conducted a year later was barely able to airlift 1400 US troops to Egypt and the number of planes available for such operations was 258 fewer than the USAF inventory of transports at the end of the Vietnam War.

The TOW (tube-launched, optically-tracked, wire-guided) missile that had proved such a valuable asset to Israel in the 1973 war also came under close scrutiny as the Reagan administration reviewed its arsenal options in 1981. Some

critics observed that a TOW missile might be accurate only when a soldier firing the weapon stood perfectly still for 10 seconds, making himself a target. An alternative antitank weapon, the laser-guided Copperhead, also was considered to be of doubtful value. The US Army had asked for 44,000 Copperhead shells, although some experts argued it would be useless in bad weather or rough terrain, common features of a typical European battlefield.

Jimmy Carter had closed the Minuteman missile assembly line, canceled development of the neutron bomb, and delayed Cruise missile production. Carter had placed his trust instead in a mobile MX missile system in which the ICBMs would be concealed in 4600 above-ground shelters scattered throughout much of Utah and Nevada, but moved to different shelters during the night so the Soviets presumably would never know which of the 4600 shelters contained an MX missile. Now, critics of the Carter plan argued that the USSR could deploy enough warheads to destroy all of the MX shelters and still have enough second-strike ICBMs to destroy other mainland USA targets. Reagan recommended cancelation of the Carter MX scheme and proposed instead putting the MX missiles in old but reinforced Titan and Minuteman silos in Wyoming and Nebraska. Reagan also proposed cutting in half the Carter order for 200 MX missiles.

The wind-down of the US Navy following the end of the Vietnam War had resulted in a badly skeletonized fleet. Nearly 300 US Navy cargo vessels, all of World War II vintage, had been retired. Foreign carriers were hired to transport tanks and guns to Egypt for Operation Bright Star. The US had a total of 171 armed warships, as compared to a total of 319 for the world's largest navy, the USSR. At the start of the Reagan administration, the US Navy's 7th

174

Fleet consisted of a combat core of one aircraft carrier and six surface ships based at Yokosuka, Japan. Facing the 7th Fleet across the Sea of Japan were Soviet naval bases from Vladivostock in Siberia to Cam Ranh Bay in Vietnam. In the four islands north of Hokkaido—the Kurile Islands seized by Russia at the end of World War II—the USSR had stationed Mi-24 antitank helicopter gunships, MiG-23 jet aircraft, *Backfire* bombers, SS-20 mobile missiles with multiple warheads, and 10,000 ground troops. By acquiring the US-built Cam Ranh Bay port facilities, the USSR had a warm-water base halfway between Siberia and the Persian Gulf.

To help balance the naval power of the USSR, the Reagan administration urged the building of 15 carrier task forces, to be based at various strategic locations around the world, as part of the 600-ship US Navy for the late 1980s. However, the US Navy would lose the bulk of the Trident nuclear-powered submarine project. The Tridents were originally authorized in 1974 to replace the aging Polaris and Poseidon subs. Each Trident would carry 24 missiles, each with eight nuclear warheads. Each warhead would be five times more powerful than the Hiroshima atom bomb and the missiles would have a range of 5000 miles. But Trident production was running years behind schedule and the cost per submarine was $250 million over the original budget. Reagan's Defense

Department announced it would curtail Trident production and cancel orders for 19 of the proposed 27 submarines.

The ambitious Reagan plan to return the US to prominence as a world military power was accompanied by a hard-sell campaign for new bases and arms deals in Egypt, Oman, Somalia, Kenya, the Sudan, Tunisia and Turkey. The US offered to sell arms, to lend the money to buy US arms, or aid in building or refurbishing military bases for possible future use by US forces. The Americans also offered funds to train 'security forces' for Caribbean outposts from Barbados to Antigua. An economic benefit to the US in such arms sales, as with France and other competitors, was a reduced per-unit cost for the same items when purchased by the Pentagon. But when the Reagan administration agreed to sell five AWACS planes to Saudi Arabia, it ran into the same sort of flak experienced by the Carter people in an AWACS deal with Iran. More than 50 members of the US Senate signed a petition objecting to the Saudi AWACS deal because of the possibility that the AWACS could be used to track Israeli aircraft in a possible future war with the Arab nations. Objections also were raised to a sale of equipment to improve the range and firepower of 62 F-15s previously ordered by Saudi Arabia, and the Reagan administration rejected outright a request by the Saudis to buy US-made bomb racks and KC-135 aerial refueling tankers,

Above left: Test launch of a Pershing II medium range missile. The introduction of Pershing II and Tomahawk cruise missile into bases in Europe has met with considerable opposition from anti-nuclear protesters but whatever the advisability of deploying them they certainly provide a far-enhanced capability to the NATO forces.

Above: US Army medic treats a young Honduran, September 1983. Aside from obvious humanitarian considerations such programs are vital in any attempt to resist subversion by 'winning hearts and minds' to support government efforts.

Right: A US Air Force reconnaissance picture of Sandino airfield, Nicaragua, taken in 1979 and showing items of Soviet equipment including Mi-8 Hip helicopters. The Reagan administration has sent considerable aid to the anti-government forces in Nicaragua.

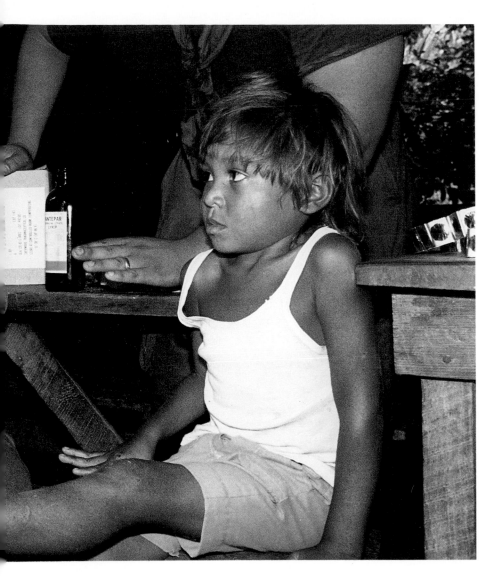

which obviously had offensive rather than defensive military value.

Although Reagan had reversed the Carter decision to scrap the B-1 bomber, Congress looked at the expected cost of $40 billion for 100 B-1s and declared it far too expensive for an aircraft that might not be able to penetrate enemy defenses by the time the bombers would be available, around 1990. The action left the USAF shopping for another type of plane that could replace the B-52s that had been in service since the 1950s. The Air Force also announced a need for an alternative to the C-5 transport, which required a runway longer than would likely be available anywhere the Rapid Deployment Force might be dispatched.

The Reagan dream also was dampened by doubts that US industry could produce the planes, tanks, ships and other equipment required for the five-year rearmament plan. Nearly 2500 subcontractors and suppliers of military hardware had gone out of business since the end of the Vietnam War. There was found to be an even greater shortage of trained defense plant workers. And defense analysts doubted that enough servicemen could be recruited to man the larger forces.

Central America: America's Backyard Quagmire

While the American people were debating these broader issues of their military budget and policies, the Reagan administration found itself confronting the more tangible and immediate realities of an area that has long unsettled the USA—Central America. Whether

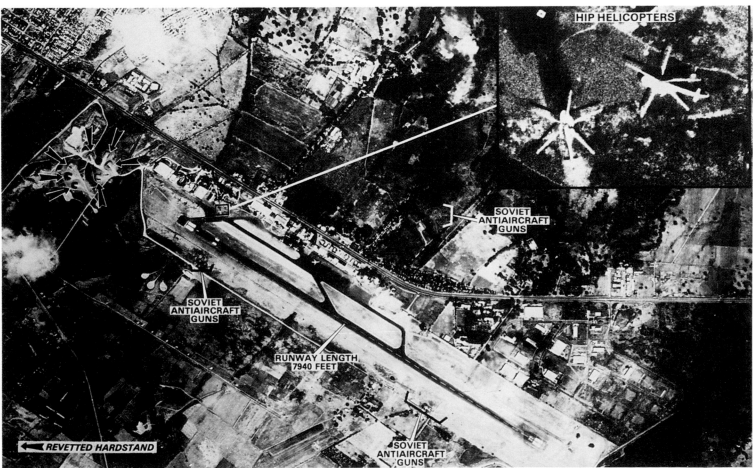

Right: AH-64 Apache helicopter armed with Hellfire antitank missiles. The Apache has a formidable attack capability but each aircraft costs over $10 million and Congress may decline to finance the 450 that the Army wants.

Bottom right: The *Los Angeles* class nuclear-powered hunter-killer submarine *City of Corpus Christi.* The *Los Angeles* class is the most modern class of attack submarine in the US Navy and production is continuing.

Below: US aid to Honduras at its simplest and perhaps most effective level.

it has been the idealism of a President Monroe or a President Wilson or the expediency of a President Theodore Roosevelt or a President Johnson, American Presidents have always considered this region as having a 'special relationship' to the US—and have seldom hesitated to send in the US military when they saw events proceeding in a direction they felt threatening to American geopolitical, economic or military interests. President Carter had tried to effect some reforms in Central America by imposing his program of human rights, but events would not stand still for even a well-intentioned American President. In 1979, Sandinista revolutionaries ousted Anastasio Somaza, the dictator-president of Nicaragua who had long enjoyed at least some support from American governments. El Salvador's problems surfaced on 24 March 1980 when Roman Catholic Archbishop Oscar Arnulfo Romero was assassinated in a chapel in San Salvador, climaxing a series of murders of priests who had opposed the right-wing government and supported the demands for reforms.

President Reagan lost little time indicating that his administration intended to regard events in Central America as so crucial to American interests that the US military would have to become involved. Reagan administration officials, for instance, displayed photographs of caches of weapons reportedly smuggled into El Salvador from Cuba, Nicaragua, and other countries. One photograph showed 100 US-made M-16 rifles, with serial numbers indicating they were captured by Communist forces in Vietnam, smuggled through Honduras

in the false roof of a semitrailer truck. Fighting between Salvadoran government troops and guerrillas was increasing, and the US expressed concern that another Latin American state might become a Soviet base. Reagan increased the number of US military advisers in El Salvador from an original 20 to 54, and gave the Central American nation a $35 million military-aid package.

There were more than a few similarities between the combat situations in El Salvador and Vietnam. As in Vietnam (and Korea and China before that) the rebel guerrillas controlled the countryside while the government forces used towns and cities as garrisons. The guerrillas built elaborate tunnel systems and could disappear into the local population as easily as into the jungle when necessary. Salvadoran government troops scored successes in terms of body counts, although few guerrilla bodies were ever found. With memories of Vietnam still fresh, 55 members of the US Congress introduced a bill to ban all military aid to El Salvador, though it had no chance of passing. A team of 15 Green Berets sent to El Salvador from a Special Forces base in Panama found other similarities with the Vietnam experience —restrictions on their role in combat situations and lack of support from their countrymen in the US.

The US also observed a similarity in the usual war of attrition fought by leftist guerrillas. The rebels destroyed electric power plants, trans-

formers, and lines, bombed bridges and generally interfered with the economic health of the target nation. During the first year of the Reagan effort to neutralize the guerrilla campaigns in El Salvador, there was no evidence of progress. Meanwhile, the Sandinista government of Nicaragua drifted closer to a Marxist-Leninist government. Some US policymakers declared Nicaragua a 'lost cause.' Cuban-guided insurgents also threatened to topple the right-wing government of Guatemala, where human rights issues prevented the use of American military aid. There also were civil disturbances in Costa Rica and Reagan advisers recommended sending military aid to that Central American nation. But Costa Rica declared it had no use for military aid since it lacked a military force, although it could use economic assistance.

In February 1982, and again in June 1982, there were complaints that US military advisers in El Salvador were carrying M-16 rifles and .45-caliber pistols, in violation of a rule that only sidearms could be carried by US military personnel in El Salvador, for personal protection. A request was made for permission for the advisers to carry rifles for self-protection, but the request was denied. One adviser photographed with both a pistol and M-16 rifle was recalled to the US and four others were reprimanded.

On 19 March 1982, the number of US military advisers in El Salvador was increased to 100 and a contingent of Green Berets was sent to Honduras to train Honduran soldiers patrolling that country's border with El Salvador.

As warfare in Central America spread in 1983, the US Defense Department announced it was sending 1600 troops to join 4000 Honduran soldiers in war games near the border of Nicaragua. Nicaragua claimed the US was planning an invasion of that country, using the war games as a cover for the attack. The US troops arrived during the first week of February 1983 and there was no invasion of Nicaragua. But relations with the Sandinista government declined still further in May 1983 when the US announced it was sending an additional 100 advisers to Honduras to train soldiers in anti-guerrilla warfare. The first US combat fatality on Honduras, helicopter pilot Jeffrey Schwab, occurred in January 1984.

On 27 May 1983, Lieutenant Commander Albert A Schaufelberger III, a US Navy SEAL (sea, air and land) expert and military adviser in El Salvador, was assassinated as he sat in his car outside the University of Central America in San Salvador. A rebel radio station credited the leftist Popular Liberation Forces with the killing, America's first casualty of the fighting in El Salvador, as a 'legitimate action of self-defense.' Two days later, the US issued a 'white paper,' illustrated with photos and maps showing USSR and Cuban subversive activities throughout Central America. The white paper noted that the USSR had delivered 25 new T-54 and T-55 tanks to Nicaragua, doubling that country's inventory, and had installed electronic surveillance equipment enabling the

Left: General Robert Kingston, then commander of the Rapid Deployment Force (right), meets an Egyptian general during the 1983 Bright Star exercise.

Right: Marine M60 tank comes ashore at Berbera in Somalia during Bright Star 82 which was in fact conducted in November 1981.

Below left: An Egyptian soldier demonstrates his Russian-made grenade launcher to a GI.

Below: UH-60 helicopters of the 82nd Airborne Division during a mock assault landing as part of the Bright Star maneuvers.

Sandinistas to monitor radio communications and to pinpoint Honduran military communication sites.

Tensions increased further in Central America in late July 1983 when the US Navy aircraft carrier *Ranger* left San Diego with 70 F-14 Tomcat jets and seven support vessels to show the flag off the coast of Nicaragua. Reagan announced that the task force might remain off the coast of Nicaragua for several months for routine 'military exercises.' US Army engineers cleared terrain for roads and airstrips along the Honduran border with Nicaragua. Plans were announced for Operation Big Pine II, involving 4000 US combat troops, in a joint exercise with Honduran military units in August 1983. An earlier Operation Big Pine, in February 1983, involved 1600 noncombat military personnel from the US. After the *Ranger* put to sea, the US announced a second battle group with the US Navy's aircraft carrier *Coral Sea* would patrol the Caribbean coast of Nicaragua. Also joining in the exercise was the US Navy's battleship *New Jersey*, which fired a salvo from its 16-inch guns to announce its presence.

Congress, however, voted to curtail funds for covert military activities by contra-rebel groups fighting the Sandinista army in Nicaragua. An estimated 2000 contras were reported battling Nicaraguan troops from jungle guerrilla bases with US support. The cut-off of funds, however, did not stop reported CIA-directed covert attacks on the Sandinistas. In September 1983, a twin-engine Cessna flew from Costa Rica with a 500-pound bomb which it dropped near the Aeronica national airline

terminal of Managua, Nicaragua, causing minor damage before being shot down by anti-aircraft fire. On 2 February 1984, six warplanes attacked and destroyed a radio command and control center near Casitas Volcano in Nicaragua after a flight from El Salvador. Nicaragua accused the US of ordering the attack, a charge denied by the US, which admitted that the CIA had agents at the Iloppango Air Base in El Salvador where air supply missions to Nicaraguan contras originated. However, the US insisted that the airlifts to Nicaraguan rebels consisted only of medicine, communications equipment and ammunition. But the US public had become sensitive to the complexities of the political situation in Latin America—in El Salvador and Nicaragua in particular—and critical of their government's controversial and seemingly simplistic handling of Latin American affairs. If anything was evident at all, it was that no simple solution would suffice to end the turmoil in the region.

The Dilemmas of Superpowerdom

Although US policy in Central America is influenced by America's self-interest—however controversial—the USA also becomes involved in international episodes less crucial to its own interests, primarily because its status as a world power entails so many alliances and allegiances. As the inevitable price a nation must pay for such status, these commitments can often become quite tricky, and never more so than when the USA finds itself forced to choose sides between two traditional allies or when it ends up backing a former colonial

Above: Trooper of the 82nd Airborne Division stands beside an arms cache of Soviet-designed equipment found on Grenada.

Right: An artillery unit of the 82nd Airborne in action with their M102 105mm howitzer during the invasion of Grenada.

Left: An airborne trooper pictured with a group of relieved American students among those whose rescue from Grenada was a principal motive for the intervention.

Chad's civil war during the Reagan administration. On 18 July 1983, Reagan authorized an airlift of food, clothing, fuel and vehicles to Chad, which had been engaged in a war since 1965 with rebels now supported by Libya. On July 20, Chad accepted an offer of US military equipment. The US Navy aircraft carrier *Coral Sea* was ordered to the Mediterranean coast of Libya because of the fighting in Chad and Libya threatened to destroy another US Navy aircraft carrier, the *Eisenhower*, if it ventured any closer to the Gulf of Sidra, claimed by Libya as part of its territorial waters. On the same day, Chad reported a new round of attacks by Libyan forces and the US sent antiaircraft weapons and three military advisers to Chad. On 6 August, the US sent two AWACS and eight F-15s to Sudan, Chad's eastern border neighbor, in the event further support might be needed. However, on 11 August, Reagan was able to convince France that it should take a more active role in defending the African nation. France agreed to send 450 paratroops to Chad. The US then announced it would discontinue aid to Chad and the USAF planes were withdrawn from Sudan. Although the US military did not become directly involved, it was yet another of those international situations that threaten to entangle the USA.

Grenada: Invasion or Intervention?

Grenada, however, would be another story, a situation in which the USA—whatever its motives, and however necessarily—found itself actively seeking involvement. This tiny

power. Such were the cases of the Falklands War and the War in Chad.

The Falkland Islands off the coast of Argentina had been a British colony for 150 years, during which time the Argentinians—who called the islands the Malvinas—had frequently tried to persuade the British to give up control of the small bits of cold, windswept land. With little warning, 4000 Argentine troops invaded and captured the islands on 2 April 1982. The US had earlier been showing some support for the Argentine government, but the USA's traditional 'special relationship' with Britain claimed precedence. As Britain responded to the invasion by declaring a 200-mile war zone around the Falklands and dispatching a flotilla led by the aircraft carrier *Hermes*, US Secretary of State Alexander Haig shuttled between London and Buenos Aires in an attempt to mediate the dispute, then sided with Great Britain when Argentina failed to compromise on a proposed settlement. The US suspended military exports to Argentina and offered the British use of an Ascension Island airbase for forward operations, aerial tankers for refueling British bombers and tankers en route to the South Atlantic, and USAF C-5A transports to ferry ammunition, spare parts and other supplies from England to the war zone. The fighting ended 14 June 1982, when the last Argentinian units surrendered to the British forces.

The US also became involved briefly in

Grenada was by then in a state of apparent anarchy, and among those whose safety was now arguably threatened were about 800 young Americans attending a medical school on Grenada. (There would be considerable disagreement as to the extent of the danger to the students, but it was a fact that Americans had fallen hostage to the revolutionary anarchy in Iran.)

After consultations with six neighboring Caribbean nations, President Reagan authorized an invasion of Grenada. A US Navy task force of 12 ships, including the aircraft carrier *Independence* and the helicopter carrier, *Guam*, en route to Lebanon, was diverted to waters off Grenada for the rescue effort. The action began at five in the morning on 25 October 1983, led by 1900 US Marines of the I-84 Marine Amphibious Group and US Army Rangers from the 1st and 2nd Battalions of the 75th Rangers. The Marines were ferried from the *Guam* to Pearls Airport at the northern end of the island; within two hours they had it secured. The Rangers were flown in transports from Barbados and parachuted into the Point Salines International Airport area at the southern tip of Grenada. The Rangers were met by unexpectedly heavy antiaircraft fire as well as by machine-gun, mortar, and rifle fire from both Grenadan militiamen and Cubans who were there ostensibly to help build the airport. The Rangers secured the airport within about two hours, and shortly thereafter about 300 soldiers and police officers from Antigua, Barbados, Dominica, Jamaica, St. Lucia, St. Vincent and St.Kitts were put ashore—a token force from the six nations that were supporting the US military intervention.

Many of the Cubans and Grenadian militiamen threw down their weapons and surrendered early in the battles. But an additional 400 Cubans and Grenadians continued to fight with sniper and mortar fire that went on for several days. The Pentagon ordered two battalions of the US Army's 82nd Airborne Division flown from Fort Bragg, North Carolina, to reinforce the Rangers and US Marines, who

Above and right: Scenes as the students evacuated from Grenada arrive home to Charleston Air Force Base.

Top left: Townspeople of Grenville welcome the arrival of US and allied troops to Grenada.

Below: The invasion of Grenada.

Caribbean island-nation just north of the coast of Venezuela, with an area of only 133 square miles, had been a British possession until 1974. In 1979, the fledgling government was overthrown in a Marxist coup led by Maurice Bishop. Within two years Grenada was becoming a virtual satellite of Cuba, with the support of a 300-man contingent of Cuban military personnel. As early as at the time of the Carter administration, there was some talk of a US-led invasion, but the plan was rejected because of concern that other western nations would be upset.

Then in March 1983, President Reagan publicized intelligence reports of Communist military projects on Grenada, including a naval base, air base, barracks, military training areas, and storage facilities for ammunition and supplies. In May 1983, Prime Minister Bishop came to Washington but found no support from the Reagan administration for his evident effort at improving relations. And then on 12 October 1983, Bishop was arrested by still more radical Communists on Grenada, led by General Hudson Austin; a week later, Bishop and 16 of his supporters were killed.

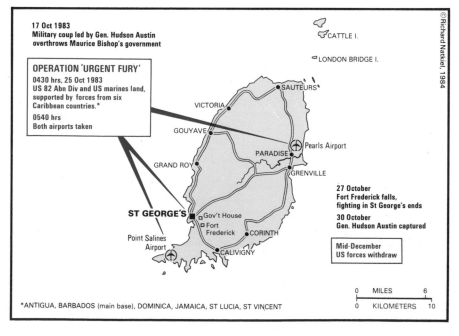

were meeting more resistance than expected. By 28 October, nearly 6000 US Rangers, Marines, and paratroops were on Grenada and fighting was still in progress. Captured documents indicated there had been 1100 Cubans on Grenada when the US invasion started, yet fewer than 640 had been accounted for, suggesting there were still several hundred enemy troops hiding in the hills or within the local population.

Three weeks after the initial assault, some 2300 US troops remained in Grenada, rounding up the last snipers and ferreting out caches of hidden Communist-made weapons. The last of the Cuban prisoners had been returned to their homeland. Official casualty figures showed 18 US troops killed and 116 wounded; there were 25 Cubans and 45 Grenadian soldiers killed. In addition to the Cuban survivors who were evacuated, 126 Russian, Libyan, East German, North Korean, and Bulgarian diplomats who had found sanctuary in the Soviet Embassy were expelled from the island. The US forces found warehouses filled with weapons and ammunition—including Soviet-made personnel carriers—enough, according to the Pentagon, to support 1000 Cuban soldiers for 45 days of fighting. This evidence of a strong Soviet-Cuban presence, both military and economic, did not satisfy all the critics of the US intervention in Grenada, but it did provide a reasonable justification for most. The only American troops left in Grenada by December 1983 were a few hundred logistical and advisory personnel, and most Grenadians did indeed seem grateful for the US action. In a sense, Grenada was a microcosm of the USA's dilemma in the contemporary world: whatever its military did—whether it came ashore or left —it was going to be criticized by some.

The US Presence in Lebanon

And nowhere was this dilemma more sharply— and painfully—posed than by the presence of the US Marines in Lebanon. For the most part, the US had managed to keep its own forces free of direct involvement in the conflict that had been ravaging the Middle East since 1945. (The most notable exception—the landing of troops in Lebanon in 1958—was just that, an incident that did not relate directly to the Arab-Israeli hostilities.) Now this rule would be broken, and it began with what seemed a rather remote incident, the attempted assassination of the Israeli ambassador to Great Britain, Schlomo Argov, in London on 3 June 1982. Three days later Israel invaded Lebanon by land, sea and air with the announced goal of destroying once and for all the strongholds of the Palestine Liberation Organization (PLO), which was blamed for the crime in London but beyond that was firing upon northern Israeli settlements from their safe positions in southern Lebanon. By 10 June Israeli forces had reached Beirut and were exchanging fire with Syrian troops in the Bekaa Valley. After several attempts by President Reagan and the US State Department to establish a firm ceasefire agreement, Reagan announced on 6 July 1982

that the US would contribute a small contingent of troops as part of a multinational peacekeeping force in Beirut. France also agreed to contribute troops four days later. As the fighting continued, the US announced on 16 July that it was holding back on further shipments of clusterbomb artillery shells to Israel pending an investigation of their reported use against civilians in Lebanon. Israel insisted use of the weapons was consistent with an Israeli-American agreement.

The multinational peacekeeping force did not materialize until mid-August 1982 when Israel, Syria, and Lebanon agreed to a US peace plan whereby PLO guerrillas trapped in Beirut by the Israeli army would be evacuated to other Arab countries. On 21 August 1982, President Reagan announced that the first contingent of US Marines would arrive on 25 August. About 300 members of the French Foreign Legion had arrived in Lebanon from Corsica on 21 August as the first peacekeeping troops on the scene. The actions were not without threats from the USSR, which warned that any move to put US troops in the Middle East 'would influence Soviet policy' toward the area. However, the Soviet reaction was not as strong as during the 1973 Yom Kippur War when USSR-US tensions escalated to a worldwide nuclear alert.

The contingent of US Marines was withdrawn from Beirut as promised after the PLO forces were evacuated to other Arab countries. But fighting in Lebanon continued and the US Marines were ordered back into Beirut on 20 September. Events that triggered the second

landing of US Marines were the assassination of newly-elected Lebanese President Bashir Gemayel on 14 September 1982, a drive by Israeli forces into West Beirut the next day and the massacre on 16 September of between 300 and 600 Palestinian men, women and children in an enclave controlled by Israeli troops. Although no Israeli troops were involved in the killings, it was claimed that Israeli soldiers permitted Christian militiamen and Phalangist militia to enter the Palestinian refugee camps in West Beirut. The government of Italy then requested that US and French peacekeeping troops be returned to Beirut.

French and Italian forces landed in Beirut first and US Marines remained on ships offshore until an agreement was reached on a withdrawal of Israeli troops from Beirut International Airport. Reagan announced the US Marines would land on 29 September 1982 and remain on duty there until all Syrian and Israeli troops were withdrawn from Lebanon. The first US casualties were recorded on 30 September when one marine was killed and two wounded by accidental detonation of a cluster bomb. (Two US officers attached to a United Nations observation team were killed a week earlier by a land mine.)

The first US Marine contingent sent into Beirut in 1982 was composed of E and F Companies of the 32nd Marine Amphibious Unit. They had been held offshore since June, when ships of the US Navy's 6th Fleet were ordered to standby off the coast of Lebanon as the Israeli invasion got underway. They were armed only with M-16 rifles and antitank weapons. In

Above: Men and equipment of the 24th Marine Amphibious Unit come ashore to relieve the 32nd MAU with the peacekeeping force in Beirut.

Above right: The situation in Lebanon during the involvement of the peacekeeping force. In retrospect it proved unwise for the US to support a treaty between Israel and Lebanon without also securing the support of Syria.

Right: A patrol of the 24th MAU in downtown Beirut in September 1983.

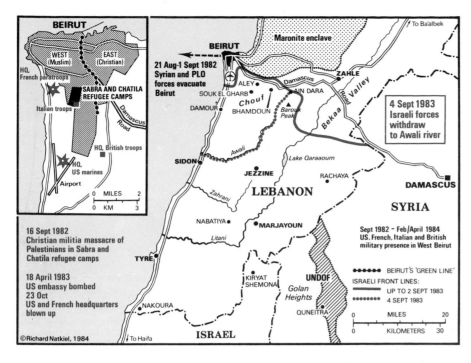

BEIRUT

WEST (Muslim)   EAST (Christian)

HQ. French paratroops

SABRA AND CHATILA REFUGEE CAMPS

Italian troops

HQ. British troops

HQ. US marines

Airport

0 MILES 2
0 KM 3

16 Sept 1982
Christian militia massacre of
Palestinians in Sabra and
Chatila refugee camps

18 April 1983
US embassy bombed
23 Oct
US and French headquarters
blown up

©Richard Natkiel, 1984

To Ba'albek

Maronite enclave

BEIRUT

21 Aug-1 Sept 1982
Syrian and PLO
forces evacuate
Beirut

ALEY   Damascus   ZAHLE
SOUK EL GHARB   AIN DARA
DAMOUR   Chouf   Barouk
BHAMDOUN   Peak

4 Sept 1983
Israeli forces
withdraw
to Awali river

Awali   Bekaa Valley   Road

SIDON   Lake Qaraaoum

JEZZINE   RACHAYA

Zahrani   LEBANON   DAMASCUS

NABATIYA   SYRIA

Litani   MARJAYOUN

TYRE

KIRYAT   UNDOF
SHEMONA
Golan
Heights
NAKOURA   QUNEITRA

ISRAEL   To Haifa

Sept 1982 – Feb/April 1984
US, French, Italian and British
military presence in West Beirut

●●●●● BEIRUT'S 'GREEN LINE'
ISRAELI FRONT LINES:
———— UP TO 2 SEPT 1983
●●●●● 4 SEPT 1983

0 MILES 20
0 KILOMETERS 30

October 1982, the US Marine force was increased to 1200 and, following a meeting in Washington between President Reagan and Lebanon's new president, Amin Gemayel, they began to show a higher profile, patrolling beyond their base at the Beirut International Airport in jeeps displaying the US flag. The Marines also moved in heavy equipment and improved their positions with the expectation of a longer stay in Lebanon as visible evidence of the US support of the Gemayel government. The heavier equipment included M-60 tanks. As 1982 ended, the US announced plans for an $85 million program to rebuild and train a new Lebanese army and the combatant nations began talks intended to result in the withdrawal of all foreign armies from Lebanon.

The USSR, a supporter of Syria, which refused to withdraw its forces from Lebanon, installed nearly 20 new SAM-5 missiles and a number of SAM-11 missiles in Syria and provided Syria with 5000 Soviet technicians. And US Marines were under increasing fire from Jihad Islami, a group espousing an Islamic Holy War. American peacekeepers found themselves identified as 'the American occupation army.' There were even confrontations with Israeli forces. On 28 January and again on 1 February 1983, US Marine and US Army officers were threatened by armed Israeli soldiers. On 18 April 1983, a car bomb exploded outside the US Embassy in Beirut, killing 47 and injuring more than 100. Sixteen of the dead were Americans, including a US Marine manning a bulletproof glass booth in the lobby. The bombing was blamed on an Iranian faction of the Jihad Islami group. Within 45 minutes after the blast, a company of US Marines from the peacekeeping contingent was on the scene to provide security.

A year after the Israeli invasion of Lebanon, there was little to show for the losses of life and property. The PLO had returned to the war zone in full strength. Israel refused to remove its troops entirely from Lebanon until the Syrian and PLO soldiers were withdrawn and Syria said it would not withdraw. The USSR had replaced most of the weapons lost by Syria in the first weeks of the war, including 86 MiG-23s shot down by Israel's US-built F-15s and F-16s and the SAM missiles which had been able to bag only one Israeli jet. The US lifted its embargo on the sale of more F-16s to Israel but refused to reinstate a 'memorandum of understanding' on US collaboration with Israel on military matters; the agreement was suspended after Israel's 1981 annexation of the Golan Heights.

By the autumn of 1983, the US Marines were coming under almost steady shellfire and sniper fire from one or more of the several factions involved in fighting. Although the Marines had gone into Lebanon a year earlier to help rescue PLO members trapped by an Israeli invasion, they now found themselves deeply entangled in a complex Lebanese civil war while the Israeli troops had withdrawn to a relatively safe region in southern Lebanon. The original force of 800 US Marines had nearly doubled and the US had a total of 14,000 servicemen on shore and aboard ships off the coast of Lebanon. The total included 2000 Marine re-inforcements who arrived in September 1983 by which time the US casualty toll was four marines dead and 32 wounded. US Navy ships were firing five-inch guns into the Shouf Mountain positions of Druse moslems, east of Beirut, and the battleship *New Jersey* was en route with 16-inch guns. From the deck of the aircraft carrier *Eisenhower*, F-14s were flying daily reconnaissance missions to locate Druse targets.

The US Marines arrived in Beirut in 1982 with only M-16 rifles. In 1983, they were equip-ped with 105-mm and 155-mm howitzers, M-60 tanks, missile-firing Cobra helicopter gunships and Harrier jump jets. Syria threatened to retaliate for the September naval bombard-ment and the US warned it would respond with the A-6 bombers carried by the carrier *Eisen-hower* in addition to its arsenal of F-14s. Syria announced it was getting Soviet SS-21 mobile missiles, capable of hitting targets in Israel and the Mediterranean Sea, as well as in Lebanon, from positions within Syria.

However, it was not a Soviet missile but a truck loaded with explosives that devastated the US Marine headquarters in Beirut while more than 200 Marines and sailors were sleep-ing in the building early on a Sunday morning, 23 October 1983. In a kamikaze attack, the truck driver gunned his engine as he approach-ed the headquarters at Beirut International Airport. The truck broke through a series of ineffectual barriers and crashed into the lobby of the four-story reinforced concrete building, reducing it to rubble in a deafening explosion. The blast left a crater 30 feet deep and 40 feet across at the precise point of explosion. Only a few shards of truck were found and no trace at all was found of the driver. It was estimated that the truck carried at least 2000 pounds of high explosives.

A few minutes later, the scene was repeated at the Beirut headquarters of the French peace-keeping forces in Lebanon. That blast moved the French nine-story building 30 feet off its foundation and caused 73 casualties, including 58 dead.

For the US Marines, with 241 dead and 71 injured, it was the highest number of casualties on a single day since the start of the Tet offen-sive in Vietnam, 31 January 1968, when 246 American servicemen were killed. But the Vietnam toll represented coordinated attacks throughout an entire country, rather than a single target. Ships of the US Navy's 6th Fleet moved to within one mile of shore to reduce evacuation time for injured servicemen being airlifted from the scene. Some were treated in the operating room of the *Iwo Jima* while others were flown to military hospitals in Italy, West Germany and on Cyprus. Israel offered to treat casualties but US military officials determined that American facilities were adequate.

The French retaliated for the attack on their military headquarters in Beirut, sending 14 Super Etendard fighter-bombers into the Bekaa Valley where they bombed and strafed the

Above: LVTP-7s of the 24th MAU hit the beach during a joint French-US exercise conducted by the troops of the Beirut peacekeeping force.

Left: Marines on patrol on the outskirts of Beirut.

Left: Secretary of State Schultz and Israeli Prime Minister Begin in April 1983 during discussions of the troubles in Lebanon.

any area beyond the Christian sector of East Beirut, President Reagan recommended a redeployment of the Marines to US Navy ships offshore. France simultaneously announced a withdrawal of one-fourth of its commitment to the peacekeeping mission. On 8 January 1984, the 258th member of the US Marine force in Lebanon—Corporal Edward Gargano—was killed in a grenade and rifle attack by a Moslem group on a Marine work detail. In February 1984, the US began evacuating American civilians from Lebanon. In scenes reminiscent of the fall of Saigon nine years earlier, Americans and civilians of other nations, personal possessions in hand, formed long lines at a helicopter pad, waiting their turn to be airlifted to US Navy ships and safe evacuation from the war zone.

Dealing with the Soviets and with the Future

The unnamed factor in these frustrating actions by the US military in Lebanon, the 'missing X,' was, of course, the role that the USSR was playing in the Middle East, both through its immediate support of Syria and through its longstanding attempts to create instability where Israel is concerned. Certainly the conflict between Israel and the Arab world existed independent of any Soviet position and just as certainly the USA has been prepared to intervene where Israel's survival is concerned. But the new US presence, the new activism by the US military, and the new risks involved—these are explained by the Soviet presence.

And the simple fact is that this is what lies behind many of the episodes and operations involving the US military in the years since the end of World War II: the ongoing face-off between the USA and the USSR. President Reagan may have chosen to take a harder, more hawkish line—scrapping the SALT II Treaty and the *détente* policies worked out by his predecessors, speaking out more bluntly against Russia, calling for a buildup of the US military with overt references to the USSR's military—but he could hardly be accused of inventing the Cold War or of originating America's commitment to opposing Soviet expansionism.

Reagan soon found, too, that there would be many instances where all of America's military might would be powerless. Although the unrest in Poland that went on through 1981, Reagan's first year in office, led to the Soviets' stationing 125,000 troops on the border of Poland, the US could only warn the Russians not to invade, but it was doubtful that the USA would have been able to aid Poland militarily had the Russians chosen to do so. Just as with Budapest in 1956 or Prague in 1968, the USA finally had to pull back from outright military confrontation. And as strongly as Americans may have felt about the Solidarity movement and its leader Lech Walesa, when General Jaruzelski imposed martial law in December 1981, suspended the operation of Solidarity and arrested Walesa, such moves, however unwelcome, may have forestalled a Soviet military action.

headquarters and barracks of a group of Shiite Moslem militiamen for 35 minutes, killing a reported 39. The US was expected to make a similar retaliatory strike, but did not. Meanwhile, a third kamikaze attack involving a truckload of explosives was driven into an Israeli military outpost near Tyre, in southern Lebanon. Four Israeli planes carried out a retaliatory raid on Shiite Moslem training camps, antiaircraft positions and an ammunition dump in the Bekaa Valley.

In December 1983, the US abandoned its non-belligerency stance and sent 28 A-6Es and A-7Es against a series of 20 Syrian positions in Lebanon, hitting 14 of them. The Syrians, apparently alerted by Soviet spy ships shadowing the US Navy carriers *Independence* and *Eisenhower*, mounted an ambush of some 40 SAM missiles and thousands of rounds of radar-directed antiaircraft fire at the US Navy planes. Two of the US planes were shot down. One officer, Lieutenant Mark Lange, was killed and another, Lieutenant Robert Goodman, Jr, was captured. Although the Syrians threatened to hold Goodman until the US forces withdrew from Lebanon, Goodman was released 3 January 1984 after negotiations by the Reverend Jesse Jackson, a candidate for the Democratic Party nomination for president, who traveled to Damascus for a personal meeting with Syrian President Hafez Assad.

In 1984, the US Marine force in Beirut had reached a level of 1800, but with increased fighting between Lebanese factions in the West Beirut area and apparent inability of the US-backed Lebanese government forces to control

American economic sanctions were one thing, but the thought of US tanks setting off across Germany to confront the Russians was quite another.

For all his tough talk, then, President Reagan had to go on dealing with the Russians. And when, on 10 November 1982, the Soviet leader Leonid Brezhnev died and was succeeded by former KGB head Yuri Andropov, Reagan had to deal with him. Andropov declared his support of detente with the West and offered to reduce the number of Russia's intermediate range missiles facing Europe, matching the total of England and France. He also offered to reduce the USSR's arsenal of ICBMs by 25 percent if the USA would do likewise. But the USA and its NATO partners argued that the English and French missiles were independent of the NATO stockpile and were in any case far less powerful than the Soviets' intermediate range weapons. The Reagan administration went ahead with its plans to deploy 572 nuclear missiles, including both Cruise and Pershing types, in Europe. Despite efforts by the Russians to persuade West Germany to bar these, and protests by anti-nuclear groups in such countries as Britain and West Germany, the installation began in December 1983. The USSR responded by walking out of the arms negotiation meetings and by deploying their own additional missiles aimed at Europe. Russia also announced it would take 'corresponding measures with regard to United States territory,' a statement generally interpreted to mean the stationing of submarines with nuclear missiles close to the shores of the US.

Increasingly, then, the Cold War has developed into the arms race, as the USA and the USSR seek to outdo each other both in the ingenuity and sheer force of their weapons. In March 1983, for instance, President Reagan outlined a series of weapon systems for the future, including chemical lasers that could destroy incoming enemy missiles, ground-based lasers that would send beams to giant mirrors in space, particle-beam weapons, and nuclear-pumped X-ray lasers. The mirrors in space would deflect the laser beams to attacking missiles while particle-beam weapons would accelerate protons or ions so they could penetrate targets, detonate fuel or explosives, or disrupt electronic circuits. Nuclear-pumped X-rays would destroy attacking missiles with energy from small nuclear explosions. Reagan also reported on the development of *Midgetman* missiles, 30,000-pound versions of the 195,000-pound MX missile, which could be transported by an armored mobile vehicle called an *Armadillo*. In July 1983, Congress approved initial production of 27 MX missiles and the development of binary weapons—shells or bombs with two compartments containing relatively harmless chemicals that would combine on explosion to produce a shower of nerve gas.

Andropov's reaction to the US plans for such 'Star Wars' weapons was expected: the Soviet leader called the Reagan plan 'not just irresponsible but insane,' and said it was 'a bid to disarm the Soviet Union in the face of a US nuclear threat.' But however real some of these

weapons might turn out to be, Andropov did not live to see even the next phase in US-USSR relations; seriously ill evidently almost from his first days in office, Andropov died on 9 February 1984. (Of the five major Russian leaders since the 1917 Revolution, Andropov's tenure of 15 months was the shortest.) Konstantin Chernenko, for 25 years a close associate of Brezhnev, was elected to succeed Andropov on 13 February 1984. Chernenko, a conservative Marxist of the old school of Russian Communism, had been passed over in favor of Andropov after the death of Brezhnev but retained the support of other old comrades of Brezhnev — particularly Foreign Minister Andrei Gromyko and Defense Minister Dimitry Ustinov—who would play key roles in future military maneuvering with the United States. Chernenko, like his predecessors, publicly favored *détente* with the West, but as Kremlin-watchers in the US warned, 'the language of *détente* is not the reality of *détente*.'

But whatever it is called—'*détente*' or 'containment' or 'balance of power' or 'nuclear parity'—something has worked to keep the USA and the USSR from engaging in a direct military confrontation in the years since World War II. The people of the world have been living under the threat of nuclear warfare for nearly 40 years, but the fact is that the awesome weapons have not been used. The USA and the USSR have learned to accommodate disagreement and even conflict without pushing each other to the point of armed hostilities. The USA warns Russia against armed intervention—as, say, in Poland—and the USSR warns the USA against direct military action in, say, Syria, and both sides respect each other's flashpoints. Meanwhile, both the USA and the USSR have taken direct military action when they expect the other power will respect each other's 'spheres of influence': thus the USA can invade the Dominican Republic, as it did in 1965, or Russia can invade Afghanistan, as it did in 1979. But what is at least as important to note is that not only have the USA and the USSR not employed their nuclear arsenal through all these years, they have in fact avoided direct hostilities of any kind. While whole armies of allies and clients are equipped by Russia and America and then proceed to fight each other, the USA and the USSR withhold their own vast military machines. (One of the side results of this type of indirect conflict is that both the USA and the USSR tend to learn much about each other's new weapons from those captured or surrendered to allies.)

Perhaps it is inevitable, then, that the US military has found itself, and must probably continue finding itself, caught in something of a dilemma. Arguably the most powerful military force in the history of the world—with its millions of uniformed personnel, its staggering arsenal of weapons, its planes and ships constantly patrolling the skies and the seas, with new and ingenious weapons constantly on line—this military power must for the most part by 'cabin'd, cribb'd, confined.' What is more, because of the nature of the American

Above: US Army UH-60 Blackhawk helicopters in a transport role. The UH-60 has only recently been introduced as a supplement to the aging fleet of UH-1 Hueys. The Blackhawk has a much-improved performance especially in the 'hot and high' conditions which the US Rapid Deployment Force can expect to encounter if it is committed to the Persian Gulf area.

Right: A Marine jeep patrol in central Beirut, symbolic of the future problems that the US armed forces must face and overcome.

political and social system, the military must be subject to the constant changes and reversals of policy dictated by domestic political situations. But this is the price a democratic, pluralistic society must pay: there will always be at least two sides, and usually far more, to any issue, and the nation's military cannot be placed outside this debate.

But it also must be admitted that those who call for unilateral disarmament or a drastic cutback in the US military budget and a pullback of most American military forces, such people often ignore the facts and responsibilities of America's role. The fact is that numerous lands and millions of people remain grateful to the US military commitment during the 40 years following World War II, just as it is a fact that numerous lands and millions of people would prefer to be free of their Russian and Communist overlords. American tanks and planes may be powerless to change the world's power structures at any given point, but American military strength, preparedness, and vigilance are no less crucial. In 1983, in fact, the US Military Reserve Strength was the highest in 22 years, with the National Guard at 417,200, the Army Reserve at 266,200, the Naval Reserve at 109,100, the Air National Guard at 102,200, the Air Force Reserve at 67,200, and the US Marine Reserve at 42,700. In addition, the newly-created Army Light Infantry Division further bolsters up the USA's conventional military, with a strength of 10,000 composed of 50 percent infantry, three brigades with nine maneuver battalions, and a versatile range of equipment and abilities.

Since the end of World War II, US foreign policy and military doctrine have gone through many changes, reflecting shifting global concerns and trends. From its postwar position of power, the US hesitated to exert its clout in a coercive manner internationally. But as the USA's worldwide military and economic commitments gradually increased from its position of prosperity and power, the US found itself responsible, or at least with concerns at stake, in more and more international situations. However, as the Soviet Union gained nuclear parity and the European community recovered economically, US policy was slow to adapt, resulting in an overcommitment of US abilities. The mid-seventies found questioning minds challenging US military and diplomatic intentions while foreign policy floundered, and the eighties found the US bolstering up its lagging image with an emphasis on military buildup and preparedness. The new US military combined development of the most effective weapons for conventional warfare with the option of nuclear weapons, effecting a compromise that seemed to dull slightly the threat of nuclear warfare brought on by overreliance on nuclear deterrence. At the same time, recent decades have brought the media itself into the spotlight as a factor influencing the US political machinery. The dramatic television coverage of the Vietnam War influenced public opinion just as certainly as the media took on an investigative and sometimes controversial role in censuring government activities and policies of the eighties. Whether the media serves to clarify or cloud the political realities of the future, the US must strive to perceive global situations realistically and to develop policies that respond clearly and effectively to these realities. Diplomacy, negotiations, communication and detente are crucial elements in the realm of foreign affairs, but the realities of any foreseeable future demand a strong and flexible military.

INDEX

Page numbers in italics refer to illustrations

Acknowledgments

The publishers would like to thank David Eldred who designed this book and Ron Watson who compiled the index. The majority of the pictures were supplied by official US Government agencies including the Public Affairs and Audiovisual Services of the Department of Defense, the US Army, US Navy, US Air Force and US Marine Corps and by the National Archives. In addition thanks are also owed to the following for the illustrations on the pages noted.

AP: pp 52 top, 67 bottom, 71 top, 79 right, 118 bottom
Dwight D Eisenhower Library: p 60 top
Gamma/Liaison: pp 172 top, 173 top
General Dynamics: 80 top, 170-171, 177 bottom
Hughes Helicopters: pp 176-177 top
Robert Hunt Library: p. 58 top
Israeli Government Press Office: pp 16-17 top, 154-155 all four, 156-157 bottom, 186 bottom

John F Kennedy Library: p 96
Keystone Press Agency: pp 10-11 both, 12, 18-19 bottom, 20-21, 22-23 top, 24, 25, 27, 28, 29, 64-65, 70-71 main pic, 72-73, 74 top, 74-75 main pic, 76 top, 76-77 main pic, 81 both 83 bottom, 88-89, 91 right, 92 top, 94-95 both, 97 both, 98-99 all three, 100 both, 102-103 bottom center, 150-151 all three, 154 bottom, 160, 161 top, 162-163 both
New York Daily News: p 66
US Army, via Robert Hunt: pp 32-33 bottom
US Marines, via Robert Hunt: pp 50 top
US Navy, via Keystone: 15 bottom, 18-19 top, 157 top
Government of Vietnam: p 146 top
Wide World Photos: pp 26, 51, 68 top, 78, 86-87 both, 90-91 left & center, 161 bottom
Ivan D Yeaton Collection: p 23 bottom

Maps © Richard Natkiel